through a

POSITIVE MENTAL ATTITUDE

NAPOLEON HILL

W. CLEMENT HILL

RUPA

Published by
Rupa Publications India Pvt. Ltd 2024
7/16, Ansari Road, Daryaganj
New Delhi 110002

Sales Centres:
Allahabad Bengaluru Chennai
Hyderabad Jaipur Kathmandu
Kolkata Mumbai

ISBN: 978-93-6156-537-3

First impression 2024

10 9 8 7 6 5 4 3 2 1

Printed in India

CONTENTS

About the Authors 5
Preface 9
Introduction 11

PART I
Where the Road to Achievement Begins

1. Meet the Most Important Living Person 21
2. You Can Change Your World 39
3. Clear the Cobwebs from Your Thinking 59
4. Will You Dare to Explore the Powers of Your Mind? 77
5. ... And Something More 95

PART II
Five Mental Bornbshells for Attacking Success

6. You've Got a Problem? That's Good! 112
7. Learn to See 128
8. The Secret of Getting Things Done 144
9. How to Motivate Yourself 159
10. How to Motivate Others 172

PART III
Your Key to the Citadel of Wealth

11. Is There a Shortcut to Riches? 192
12. Attract—Don't Repel—Wealth 195

13. If You Don't Have Money—Use OPM! 210
14. How to Find Satisfaction in Your Job 231
15. Your Magnificent Obsession 245

PART IV
Get Ready to Succeed!

16. How to Raise Your Energy Level 266
17. You Can Enjoy Good Health and Live Longer 277
18. Can You Attract Happiness? 296
19. Get Rid of That Guilt Feeling 312

PART V
Action Please!

Negligence 329
20. Now It's Time to Test Your Own Success Quotient 330
21. Awaken the Sleeping Giant Within You 342
22. The Amazing Power of a Bibliography 346

ABOUT THE AUTHORS

NAPOLEON HILL

Napoleon Hill was born into poverty in 1883 in a one-room cabin on the Pound River in Wise County, Virginia. When he was 13, he began his writing career as a 'mountain reporter' for small-town newspapers and went on to become one of America's most beloved motivational authors. He dedicated more than 25 years of his life to define the reasons why so many people fail to achieve true financial success and happiness in their life.

His big break came in 1908 when Robert L. Taylor, former Governor of Tennessee and owner of *Bob Taylor's Magazine*, employed Hill to write 'success stories' about famous men. Hill's first assignment was to interview one of the richest men in the world, the steel magnate Andrew Carnegie.

During the interview, Carnegie asked Hill if he wanted the opportunity to organize the World's first philosophy of individual achievement based upon the principles of success that he and other self-made millionaires had used to accumulate their vast fortunes. Carnegie explained that the task would require years of work and that he would only pay Hill's expenses because he wanted to make sure Hill would learn the philosophy and prove it worked through his own success and financial achievements.

Hill accepted the task, so Carnegie commissioned Hill to interview over 500 millionaires, and with Carnegie's help, Hill formulated a philosophy of success (The Law of Success), which was a success formula for the average person. Hill's first publication of *'The Law of Success in 16 Lessons'* was available in 1925 as a multi-volume study course.

It took Hill almost 30 years to produce *'Think and Grow Rich,'* which is still one of the best Personal Development books, and since its introduction in 1937, it has influenced millions of people around the world.

During his life, Napoleon Hill achieved great success as an attorney, a writer, a motivational speaker, and a teacher of the principles of success. He was also an advisor to President Woodrow Wilson and President Franklin D. Roosevelt. *'What the mind of man can conceive and believe, it can achieve'* is one of Hill's hallmark expressions.

Napoleon Hill passed away in November 1970 after a long and successful career. His work stands as a monument to individual achievement and is the cornerstone of modern motivation.

W. CLEMENT STONE

William Clement Stone was born on May 4, 1902, and grew up on Chicago's South Side. His father died when he was 3, leaving the family impoverished because of his gambling losses. At the age of 6, he began hawking newspapers while his mother worked as a dressmaker. At 13, he owned his own newsstand. At the age of 16, he went to Detroit to help his mother in the insurance agency she had opened there. He went from office to office, making cold calls (he called them gold calls) to sell insurance, and he was soon making $100 a week.

Stone turned $100 into millions with a strong desire to succeed, and by putting into practice, the principles in the book *Think and Grow Rich* by Napoleon Hill. He was the living example of the proverbial rags-to-riches story. Eventually, he became an 'angel' to others, lifting some from the gutter to incredible heights. One of his great successes was the famed Og Mandino, an alcoholic at the time whom Stone took under his wing. The relationship brought about a complete change in life for Mandino, who became the publisher of *Success Magazine*.

In 1919, Stone built the Combined Insurance Company of America (a company providing accident and health insurance coverage), and by 1930, he had over a thousand agents selling insurance for him across the United States. By 1979, Stone's insurance company exceeded $1 billion in assets.

In 1960, Stone teamed up with Napoleon Hill to author *Success Through a Positive Mental Attitude*. Norman Vincent Peale said that Stone and Hill 'have the rare gift of inspiring and helping people...In fact, I owe them both a personal debt of gratitude for the helpful guidance I have received from their writings.' In 1962, Stone wrote the Success System That Never Fails, in which he suggested How to become successful and have a healthy, productive lifestyle. In 1964, he and Norma Lee Browning collaborated on writing *The Other Side of the Mind*.

Stone was a supporter of The Napoleon Hill Foundation, which he directed for forty years, and to which his estate contributes funding. He celebrated his 100th birthday with a gift of $100,000 to the University of Illinois at Chicago, and he gave over $275 million to charity, including civic groups, mental health, and Christian organizations.

William Clement Stone was 100 years old when he passed away on September 3, 2002. He was a self-made millionaire, a successful author, and a generous philanthropist.

PREFACE

The great Danish philosopher and religious thinker Soren Kierkegaard once wrote, 'It is the sign of a good book when the book reads you.'

You hold in your hands such a book—one that has not only become a classic in the self-help field but also has that rare ability to relate to your problems, sympathize with them, and then advise you on their solutions as a wise old friend would.

Still, I must warn you.

Success Through a Positive Mental Attitude will do nothing for you. If you truly wish to change your life for the better and are willing to pay a price in time and thinking and effort to reach your goals—and if you're not kidding yourself— then you hold in your hands a diamond plucked from a beach of pebbles, a road map to a better future, a valuable blueprint that will enable you to completely restructure your future.

I speak from experience. Many years ago, through my own stupidities and faults, I lost everything that was precious to me—my family, my home, and my job. Nearly penniless and with no guidance, I began to wander the country, searching for myself and for some answers that would make my life bearable.

I spent much time in public libraries because they were free—and warm. I read everything from Plato to Peale, seeking that one message that would explain to me where I had gone wrong—and what I could do to salvage the remainder of my life.

I finally found my answer in W. Clement Stone's and Napoleon Hill's *Success Through a Positive Mental Attitude*. I have employed the simple techniques and methods found in this classic for more than fifteen years, and they have provided me with riches and happiness far beyond anything I deserve. From a penniless vagrant without a single root, I eventually became the president of two corporations and the executive editor of the finest magazine of its kind in the world, *Success Unlimited*. I also wrote six books, and one of them, *The Greatest Salesman in the World*, has now become the best-selling book for salespeople of all time; it has been translated into fourteen languages and has sold more than three million copies.

None of these things would have been accomplished without the daily application of the principles of success and living that I found in Stone's and Hill's classic. If I could accomplish what I did starting from ground zero, just think what you can do with all you have going for you already.

We live in a strange and fast-moving world; each day, a new false prophet arises preaching his own brand of happiness and success attainment. Like hula hoops and pet rocks, they will all disappear as quickly as they appeared, and when the fog lifts, the truth of Stone's and Hill's book will still be changing the lives of thousands yet unborn.

Do you really want to change your life for the better?

If you do, *Success Through a Positive Mental Attitude* can be the luckiest thing that has ever happened to you. Read it. Study it. Read it again. Then get into action. It's all very simple, really, if you make up your mind to work at it.

And wonderful things will begin happening to you.

I should know.

—OG MANDINO

INTRODUCTION

Every inspirational, self-help action book, including this one, should be evaluated by what happens to you, the reader, as a result of the book's power to motivate you to motivate yourself to desirable action. By this standard, *Success Through a Positive Mental Attitude* is reputed to be one of the outstandingly successful inspirational, self-help action books of this century. It has inspired countless thousands of men, women, and teenagers to acquire good physical, mental and moral health; seek happiness; pursue wealth and reach for high goals or other objectives that do not violate the laws of God or the rights of their fellow men.

Something wonderful is going to happen to you—if you are ready. To prepare yourself to be ready, understand clearly Andrew Carnegie's observation *that all achievement, all earned riches, have their beginning in an idea!*

Before proceeding further, I'd like to give you a background of my co-author Dr. Napoleon Hill.

Think and Grow Rich, the book by Napoleon Hill, has motivated more persons throughout the world to acquire wealth and succeed in their careers than any book written in the twentieth century. Its author was born in poverty in a log cabin in Wise County, Virginia, on October 1883, and he passed away in Greenville, South Carolina, on November 8, 1970.

As a boy, young Hill was blessed, inspired, and motivated to high achievement by his calm, patient stepmother, who loved him dearly. It was she who motivated 'a problem child' to develop character and motivate himself to work hard to become educated and an achiever.

In 1908, while working for a magazine and attending college, young Hill was assigned to interview Andrew Carnegie, the great steelmaker, philosopher, and philanthropist.

Andrew Carnegie was so impressed with his interviewer that he invited him to his home as a guest. Hour after hour each day during the three-day visit, the two men discussed philosophy. The elder romanced the lives of philosophers and the impact their philosophy had had on world civilization to the younger, who listened with rapture.

In his discussions, Carnegie made it a point to express in simple, clear language the principles involved and the concepts of each of the philosophers he romanced. And he told *something more: how to apply* those principles in everyday living as they pertain to an individual, his family, his career, or any human activity.

A challenge. Andrew Carnegie knew human nature. One way to motivate an aggressive extrovert with a high energy level who has drive and stick-to-itiveness and whose reason and emotions are in balance is to challenge him. The young guest was just such a person. And he was challenged.

'What is there in the climate of this great nation whereby I, a foreigner, can build a business and acquire wealth—or anyone can achieve success?' asked Carnegie. And before Hill could answer, he continued, 'I challenge you to devote 20 years of your life to the study of the philosophy of American achievement and come up with an answer. Will you accept?'

'Yes!' was the quick response.

Andrew Carnegie had an obsession: *Anything in life-worth having was worth working for.* He was willing to give the young author his personal time to consult with him and letters of introduction to the outstanding Americans of his day, and to reimburse him for any necessary out-of-pocket expense, such as traveling to interview people. But it was clearly understood that Napoleon Hill would have to earn his own livelihood.

In the following 20 years, Hill interviewed over 500 successful men. Among them were Henry Ford, William Wrigley, Jr., John Wanamaker, George Eastman, John D. Rockefeller, Thomas A. Edison, Theodore Roosevelt, Albert Hubbard, J. Ogden Armour, Luther Burbank, Dr. Alexander Graham Bell, and Julius Rosenwald.

And Hill did earn his own livelihood—by applying many of the principles he learned from Carnegie and the men he interviewed. And in 1928, he completed the eight volumes of *The Law of Success*—books that motivated thousands to acquire wealth or to become outstanding achievers.

On the recommendation of Senator Jennings Randolph of West Virginia, Napoleon Hill became an adviser to two Presidents of the United States: Woodrow Wilson and Franklin D. Roosevelt. He influenced certain decisions they made that affected the course of American history.

When, exactly twenty years after the interview with Andrew Carnegie, *The Law of Success* was published, it had a worldwide impact. Seven years later, while he was an adviser to Franklin D. Roosevelt, he began writing the manuscript for Think and Crow Rich. It was published in 1937. More than ten million people have read the book.

A profitable discovery. In 1937, *Think and Grow Rich* was given to me by Morris Pickus, a well-known sales executive, sales counselor, and lecturer. The philosophy in so many respects coincided with my own that I sent the book to every one of my sales representatives throughout the United States. (At that time, I owned and operated Combined Registry Company, a national sales organization that specialized exclusively in the sale of accident insurance.)

Bingo! I hit the jackpot, for I made a profitable discovery. I found a working tool that would motivate sales representatives to motivate themselves to increase their sales and profits—and *something more*: to acquire wealth through responding to an inspirational, self-help action book.

'Now, what has relating the story about Carnegie, *The Law of Success* and *Think and Grow Rich* to do with *Success Through a Positive Mental Attitude*?' you ask. My answer: 'If it were not for each of them, the manuscript for this book would not have been written. But it was written, and it was first published in 1960 by Prentice-Hall, Inc.

Think and Grow Rich contains the basic principles of Andrew Carnegie's philosophy—those contained in *The Law of Success*—and Napoleon Hill's philosophy and experiences, as well as stories about many people who acquired wealth and success after reading the eight volumes of *The Law of Success*. *Success Through a Positive Mental Attitude* combines all these in essence and has *something more*. It tells specifically how you can use the greatest machine that was ever conceived—a machine so awesome that only God Himself could create it. This machine is a human-computer; it is your brain and your nervous system from which the mechanical computer was designed.

Success Through a Positive Mental Attitude instructs you on what to do and how to do it when it comes to tapping and using the powers of your subconscious mind. Where have you been taught to constructively use, neutralize, control, or harmonize with your passions, emotions, instincts, tendencies, feelings, moods, and habits of thought and action? Have you been taught how to aim high and achieve your goals regardless of the obstacles? If your answer is 'No,' you will be taught these things if you read and then apply the principles in *Success*

Through a Positive Mental Attitude.

Results are what count. Over the last 16 years, more than 420,000 hardbound copies of *Success Through a Positive Mental Attitude* have been printed. Our readers have had such phenomenal results in changing their lives for the better, meeting life's problems courageously and bringing their desires into reality that I was delighted when arrangements were made for Pocket Books to publish the paperback edition for the books published by Pocket Books reach hundreds of thousands. And my chief goal, and Napoleon Hill's, was to motivate multitudes of people to free themselves from the slavery of their undesirable thoughts, habits and actions and to help them seek and acquire the true riches of life by fulfilling desires that don't violate the laws of God or the rights of their fellow men.

Freedom from the bonds that enslaved them. In the preface by Og Mandino to this edition *of Success Through a Positive Mental Attitude*, you read:

> I speak from experience. Many years ago, through my own stupidities and faults, I lost everything that was precious to me—my family, my home and my job. Nearly penniless and with no guidance, I began to wander the country, searching for myself and for some answers that would make life bearable...
>
> I finally found my answer in W. Clement Stone's and Napoleon Hill's Success Through a Positive Mental Attitude.

Og Mandino is now famous as a lecturer and author of *The Greatest Salesman in the World* and other self-help books. And Norman Vincent Peale and other well-known authors have told me many times how they have inspired others to high personal achievement by quoting illustrations and principles from *Success*

Through a Positive Mental Attitude.

I was recently invited to dinner at one of Washington's famous restaurants by a friend. Jimmy, the waiter, rendered the most pleasant and effective service I have ever gotten at any fine restaurant in any part of the world. After dinner, as my party was leaving the restaurant, Jimmy asked me aside and said, 'May I take half a minute of your time?'

'Certainly.' I responded.

'I just wanted to tell you that *Success Through a Positive Mental Attitude saved my life*,' he said.

Another man, Ted G., told me: 'When I was on the Lee Phillips Show, you said you were going to change my life. Well, you did, and here's a list of the changes that took place in five years: I went into business, and I am doing very well: two of my daughters graduated from college, and one is still attending a private college (previously I had no funds for college education for them); I purchased a condominium with a swimming pool, golf course, etc.: I've had beautiful vacations: and much more! Many thanks again for *Success Through a Positive Mental Attitude*. It is always on my night table, and I consider it one of my valued possessions.'

A doctor who practices in Milwaukee, Wisconsin, on two occasions when I met him said, 'I thought you would be interested in knowing that one of my most effective prescriptions to certain patients with psychosomatic illnesses is a special one. I prescribe a book: *Success Through a Positive Mental Attitude*.'

While there are several thousands of experiences that could be related, the greatest testimonial can be your experience when you learn and apply the principles in this book.

Special instructions. When you read this book, read it as if the authors were your personal friends and were writing to you—and you alone. Underscore sentences, quotations, and words that are meaningful to you. Memorize self-motivators. Keep in mind that this is a book to motivate you to desirable action.

Abraham Lincoln developed the habit of trying to learn from the books he read, the people he met, and casual events. These gave him ideas for reflection. And thus, he was able to relate, assimilate and use ideas as his own.

You, too can convert your creative thinking, artistic talent, knowledge, personality, and physical energy into success, wealth, health, and happiness. This book more than tells you how: it motivates you to try.

Look for the message that is applicable to you. When you recognize it. Pay attention! Get into action! To direct your mind into desired channels, try to answer each question at the end of each chapter during your thinking and planning time.

—W. CLEMENT STONE

PART I

WHERE THE ROAD TO ACHIEVEMENT BEGINS

1

MEET THE MOST IMPORTANT LIVING PERSON

Meet the most important living person!

Somewhere in this book, you will meet him—suddenly, surprisingly, and with a shock of recognition that will change your whole life. When you do meet him, you will discover his secret. You will discover that he carries with him an invisible talisman with the initials PMA emblazoned on one side and NMA on the other.

This invisible talisman has two amazing powers: it has the power to attract wealth, success, happiness, and health, and it has the power to repel these things—to rob you of all that makes life worth living. It is the first of these powers, PMA that enables some men to climb to the top and stay there. It is the second that keeps other men at the bottom all their lives. It is NMA that pulls other men down from the top when they have reached it.

Perhaps the story of S. B. Fuller will illustrate how it works.

'We are poor—not because of God.' S. B. Fuller was one of seven children of a Negro tenant farmer in Louisiana. He started to work at the age of five. By the time he was nine, he was driving mules. There was nothing unusual in this: the children of most of the tenant farmers went to work early. These families accepted poverty as their lot and asked for no better.

Young Fuller was different from his friends in one way: he had a remarkable mother. His mother refused to accept this hand-to-mouth existence for her children, though it was all she had ever known. She knew there was something wrong with the fact that her family was barely getting along in a world of joy and plenty. She used to talk to her son about her dreams.

'We shouldn't be poor, S. B.,' she used to say. 'And don't ever let me hear you say that it is God's Will that we are poor. We are poor—not because of God. We are poor because father has never developed a desire to become rich. No one in our family has ever developed a desire to be anything else.'

No one had developed a *desire* to be wealthy. This idea became so deeply ingrained in Fuller's mind that it changed his whole life. He began to *want* to be rich. He kept his mind on the things he did want and off the things, he didn't want. Thus, he developed a burning desire to become rich. The quickest way to make money, he decided, was to sell something. He chose soap. For twelve years he sold it, door to door. Then he learned that the company which supplied him was going to be sold at auction. The firm price was $150,000. In twelve years of selling and setting aside every penny, he had saved $25,000. It was agreed that he would deposit his $25,000 and obtain the balance of $125,000 within a ten-day period. Written into the contract was the condition that if he did not raise the money, he would lose his deposit.

During his twelve years as a soap salesman, S. B. Fuller had gained the respect and admiration of many businessmen. He went to them now. He obtained money from personal friends, too, and from loan companies and investment groups. On the eve of the tenth day, he had raised $115,000 He was $10,000 short.

Search for the light. 'I had exhausted every source of credit

I knew,' he recalls. 'It was late at night. In the darkness of my room, I knelt down and prayed. I asked God to lead me to a person who would let me have the $10,000 in time. I said to myself that I would drive down 61st Street until I saw the first light in a business establishment. I asked God to make the light a sign indicating His answer.'

It was eleven o'clock at night when S. B. Fuller drove down Chicago's 61st Street. At last, after several blocks he saw a light in a contractor's office.

He walked in. There, seated at his desk, tired from working late at night, sat a man whom Fuller knew slightly. Fuller realized that he would have to be bold,

'Do you want to make $1,000?' asked Fuller straight out. The contractor was taken aback at the question. 'Yes,' he said. 'Of course.'

'Then make out a check for $10,000 and when I bring back the money, I'll bring back another $1,000 profit,' Fuller recalls telling this man. He gave the contractor the names of the other people who had lent him money, and explained in detail exactly what the business venture was.

Let's explore his secret of success. Before he left that night, S. B. Fuller had a check for $10,000 in his pocket. Subsequently, he obtained controlling interest not only in that company, but in seven others, including four cosmetic companies, a hosiery company, a label company, and a newspaper. When we asked him recently to explore with us the secret of his success, he answered in terms of his mother's statement so many years before:

'We are poor—not because of God. We are poor because father has never developed a desire to become rich. No one in our family has ever developed a desire to be anything else.'

'You see,' he told us, 'I knew what I wanted, but I didn't

know how to get it. So I read *The Bible* and inspirational books for a purpose. I prayed for the knowledge to achieve my objectives. Three books played an important part in transmuting my burning desire into reality. They were: (1) *The Bible*, (2) *Think and Grow Rich*, and (3) *The Secret of the Ages*. My greatest inspiration comes from reading *The Bible*.

'If you know what you want, you are more apt to recognize it when you see it. When you read a book, for example, you will recognize opportunities to help you get what you want.'

S. B. Fuller carried with him the invisible talisman with the initials PMA imprinted on one side and NMA on the other. He turned the PMA side up and things happened. He was able to bring into reality ideas that were formerly mere daydreams.

Now the important thing to notice here is that S. B. Fuller started life with fewer advantages than most of us have. But he chose a big goal and headed for it of course, the choice of goal was individual. In these times and in this country, you still have your personal right to say; 'This is what I choose. This is what I want most to accomplish.' And unless your goal is against the laws of God or society, you can achieve it. *You have everything to gain and nothing to lose by trying. Success is achieved and maintained by those who keep trying with PMA.*

What you try for is up to you. Not everyone would care to be an S. B. Fuller, responsible for large manufacturing concerns. Not everyone would choose to pay the costly price of being a great artist. To many, the riches of life are quite different. A skill in day-to-day living which adds up to a happy, love-filled life is success. You can have this and other riches too. The choice is yours.

But whether success to you means becoming rich as it did to S. B. Fuller, or the discovery of a new element in chemistry, or the creation of a piece of music, or the growing of a rose, or the nurturing of a child—no matter what success means to you—the invisible talisman with the initials PMA emblazoned on one side and NMA on the other can help you achieve it You attract the good and desirable with PMA. You repel them with NMA.

Every adversity has the seed of an equivalent or greater benefit. 'But what if I have a physical handicap? How can a change of attitude help me?' you may ask. Perhaps the story of Tom Dempsey, a boy who was disabled at birth, will give you your answer.

Tom was born without half a right foot and only a stub of a right arm. As a boy, he wanted to engage in sports as the other boys did. He had a burning desire to play football. Because of this desire, his parents had an artificial foot made for him. It was made of wood. The wooden foot was encased in a special stubby football shoe. Hour after hour, day after day, Tom would practice kicking the football with his wooden foot. He would try and keep on trying to make field goals at greater and greater distances. He became so proficient that he was hired by the New Orleans Saints.

The screams of 66,910 football fans could be heard throughout the entire United States when, within the last two seconds of the game, Tom Dempsey—with his crippled leg—kicked a record-breaking 63-yard field goal. It was the longest field goal ever kicked in a professional football game. It gave the Saints a winning score of 19-17 over the Detroit Lions.

'We were beaten by a miracle,' said Detroit coach Joseph Schmidt. And to many, it was a miracle—an answer to a prayer.

'Tom Dempsey didn't kick that field goal, God kicked it,' said Lion linebacker Wayne Walker.

'Interesting. But what does the Tom Dempsey story mean to me?' you may ask.

Our response would be: 'Very little—unless you develop the habit of recognizing, relating, assimilating and using universal principles and adopt them as your very own. Then follow through with desirable action.'

And what are the principles you could apply from the Tom Dempsey story, whether or not you are physically disabled? They can be learned and applied by children and adults:

- Greatness comes to those who develop a burning desire to achieve high goals.
- Success is achieved and maintained by those who try and keep on trying with PMA.
- To become an expert achiever in any human activity, it takes practice ... practice ... practice.
- Effort and work can become fun when you establish specific desirable goals.
- With every adversity there is a seed of an equivalent or greater benefit for those who are motivated with PMA to become achievers.
- Man's greatest power lies in the power of prayer.

To learn and apply these principles, turn up your invisible talisman to the PMA side.

When Henley wrote the poetic lines, 'I am the master of my fate, I am the captain of my soul,' he could have informed us that we are the masters of our fate *because* we are masters, first, of our *attitudes*. Our attitudes shape our future. This is a universal law. The poet could have told us with great emphasis that this law works whether the attitudes are destructive or constructive. The law states that we translate into physical reality the thoughts and attitudes which we hold in our minds, no matter what they are. We translate into reality thoughts of poverty just as quickly as we do thoughts of riches. But when our attitude towards ourselves is big, and our attitude towards others is generous and merciful, we attract big and generous portions of success.

A truly great man. Consider the example of Henry J. Kaiser, a truly successful person because his attitude towards himself is big. Companies identified with the name Henry J. Kaiser hold assets of more than one billion dollars. Because he is generous and merciful to others, the speechless have been made to talk, the crippled have been restored to useful lives, and hundreds of thousands of persons have received hospital care at a very low cost All this grew from seeds of thought planted within him by his mother.

Mary Kaiser gave her son Henry the *priceless gift*. She also taught him to apply *the greatest value in life.*

1. *The priceless gift:* After her day's work, Mary Kaiser would spend hours as a volunteer nurse, helping the unfortunate. Often, she said to her son, 'Henry, nothing is ever accomplished without work. If I leave you nothing else but the will to work, I will have left you the priceless gift: the joy of work.'
2. *The greatest value in life:* 'It was my mother,' said Mr. Kaiser, 'who first taught me some of the greatest values in life. Among these were the love of people and the importance of serving others. Loving people and serving them, she used to say, is the greatest value in life.'

Henry J. Kaiser knows the power of PMA. He knows what it can do in his life and for his country. He also knows the force of NMA. During World War II he built over 1500 ships with such rapidity that he startled the world. When he said, 'We can construct a Liberty Ship every ten days,' the experts said,

'It can't be done—it's impossible!' Yet Kaiser did it. Those who believe they *can't* repel the positive; they use the negative side of their talisman. Those who believe they can repel the negative; they use the positive side.

That is why we must be cautions when we use this talisman. Its PMA side can get for you all the rich blessings of life. It can help you to overcome your difficulties and to discover your strengths. It can help you step out ahead of your competitors, and, as with Kaiser, it can turn what others say is impossible into reality.

But the NMA side is just as powerful. Instead of happiness and success, it can attract despair and defeat. Like all power, the talisman is dangerous if we do not use it properly.

How the force of NMA repels. There is a very interesting story, which illustrates how the force of NMA repels. It comes out of one of the southern states. There, where wood-burning fireplaces are still used to heat homes, lived a woodcutter who also was an unsuccessful person. For more than two years, he had supplied a certain home owner with firewood. The woodcutter knew that the logs could not be larger than seven inches in diameter if they were to fit this particular fireplace.

On one occasion this old customer ordered a cord of wood, but was away when it was delivered. On arriving home he discovered that most of the wood was larger than the specified size. He called the woodcutter and asked him to have the oversized logs exchanged or split.

'I can't do that!' said the wood dealer. 'It would cost more than the whole load is worth.' With that he hung up.

So the home owner was left with the job of splitting the logs himself. He rolled up his sleeves and set to work. About halfway through the job he noticed that one particular log had a very large knothole which someone had plugged up. The homeowner lifted the log. It seemed unusually light and appeared to be hollow. With a hefty swing of the axe he split the log.

A blackened roll of tin foil fell out. The homeowner stooped down, picked up the roll and unwrapped it. To his amazement it contained very old $50 and $100 bills. Slowly he counted them. They amounted to exactly $2,250. The bills had evidently been in the tree for many years, as the paper was very brittle. The homeowner had PMA. His only thought was to get the money back to its rightful owner. He picked up the telephone, called the wood dealer again, and asked him where he had cut this load. Again the woodcutter's NMA asserted its repelling power. That's nobody's business but mine,' he said. 'If you give away your secrets, people will cheat you every time.' Despite many efforts, the homeowner never learned where the logs came from or who had sealed the money inside.

Now, the point of this story does not lie in irony. It is true that the man with PMA found the money while the man with NMA had not. But it is also true that good breaks do occur in everyone's life. However, the man who lives with NMA will prevent life's lucky breaks from benefiting him. And the man with PMA will so arrange his attitudes that he will turn even the bad breaks into advantages.

On the sales staff of the Combined Insurance Company of America there was a salesman named Al Allen. Al wanted to be the company's star salesman. He tried to apply the PMA principles found in the inspirational books and magazines he read. He read an editorial in *Success Unlimited* magazine entitled 'Develop Inspirational Dissatisfaction'. It wasn't long after that he had an opportunity to put into practice what he had read. He had a bad break. This gave him the opportunity to arrange his attitudes so that he could use the PMA side of his talisman effectively.

He developed inspirational dissatisfaction. One icy winter day Al 'cold-canvassed' every store in a city block in Wisconsin; he walked in unannounced, and tried to sell insurance. On that day, Al did not make a single sale. Of course, he was dissatisfied. But Al's PMA turned this dissatisfaction into *'inspirational dissatisfaction.'*

Why?

He remembered the editorial he had read. He applied the principle. The next day before setting out from the local office, he told his fellow salesmen about his failures the day before. He said, 'Wait and see. Today I'm going back to call on those same prospects and I'll sell more insurance than all the rest of you combined!'

And the remarkable thing is that Al did it. He went back to that same city block and again called on every person he had talked to the day before. He sold 66 new accident contracts!

Now, this was an unusual achievement. And it happened because of the 'bad breaks' when Al trudged through the sleet and wind for eight hours without selling a single policy. Al Allen was able to rearrange his attitudes. He was able to convert the negative kind of dissatisfaction that most of us would feel in similar circumstances of failure on one day into inspirational dissatisfaction, which resulted in success the next day. Al did become the company's best salesman and was promoted to a sales manager. This ability to turn the invisible talisman over and use the side which has the force of PMA rather than the side which has the force of NMA is characteristic of so many of our really successful people. Most of us are inclined to look upon success as coming in some mysterious way through advantage that we do not have. Perhaps because we do have them, we don't see them. The obvious is often unseen. Every man's PMA is his advantage, and there is nothing mysterious about it.

Henry Ford, after he had achieved success, was the subject of much envy. People felt that because of good fortune, or influential friends, or genius, or whatever they thought was Ford's 'Secret'—because of these things Ford was successful. And no doubt some of these elements played a part. But there was *something more.* Perhaps one person in every hundred thousand knew the real reason for Ford's success, and those few were usually ashamed to speak of it because of its simplicity. A single glimpse of Ford in action will illustrate the 'secret' perfectly.

Years ago, Henry Ford decided to develop the now famous motor known as V-8. He wanted to build an engine with the entire eight cylinders cast in one block. He instructed his engineers to produce a design for such an engine. To a man, the engineers agreed that it was simply impossible to cast an eight-cylinder gasoline engine block in one piece.

Ford said, 'Produce it anyway.'

'But,' they replied, 'it's impossible.'

'Go to work,' Ford commanded, 'and stay on the job until you succeed no matter how much time is required.'

The engineers went to work. There was nothing else for them to do if they were to remain on the Ford staff. Six months went by and they had not succeeded. Another six months passed, and still no success. The more the engineers tried, the more the thing seemed 'impossible'.

At the end of the year, Ford checked with his engineers. Once again they informed him that they had found no way to carry out his orders. 'Keep working,' said Ford. 'I want it and I'll have it.'

And what happened?

Well, of course, the engine wasn't impossible at all. The Ford V-8 became the most spectacularly successful car on the road, pulling Henry Ford and his company so far out in front of his nearest competitor that it took years for them to catch up. He was using PMA. And the same power is available to you. If you use it, if you turn your talisman to the right side as Henry Ford did, you too can achieve success in bringing into reality the possibility of the improbable. If you know what you want, you can find a way to get it.

A man of 25 has before him some 100,000 working hours should he retire at 65. How many of your working hours will be alive with the magnificent force of PMA? And how many of them will have the life knocked out of them with the stunning blows of NMA?

But how do you go about putting PMA to work in your life rather than NMA? Some people seem to use this power instinctively. When it came to developing the Ford car, Henry Ford was one of these. Others have to learn. Al Allen learned by relating and assimilating what he read in inspirational magazines and books. *Success Through a Positive Mental Attitude* is such a book.

You, too, can learn to develop PMA.

Some people use PMA for a while but when they receive a setback, they lose faith in it. They start out right, but some 'bad breaks' cause them to flip the talisman wrong-si de-up. They fail to realize that success is *maintained* by those who *keep trying with PMA*. They are like the famous old racehorse 'John P. Grier'. John P. Grier was a thoroughbred of great promise, such promise in fact that he was groomed, trained and billed as the only horse that stood a chance of beating the greatest racehorse of all time: Man o' War.

Don't let your mental attitude make you a has-been. In the Dwyer Stakes at Aqueduct in July of 1920, the two horses finally met. It was a magnificent day. All eyes were riveted on the starting post. The two horses got away evenly. Down the track they went side by side. It was clear that John P. Grier was giving Man o' War the race of his life. At the quarter mark they were even. The half mark. The three-quarter mark and still they were even. At the eighth pole—neck and neck. Then in the stretch John P. Grier brought the crowd to its feet. Slowly he edged ahead.

It was a moment of crisis for Man o' War's Jockey. He made up his mind. For the first time in the great horse's career the jockey nicked him solidly on the rump with his whip. Man o' War reacted as though the jockey had set fire to his tail. He shot out ahead and pulled away from John P. Grier as if the other horse were standing still. At the end of the race Man o' War was seven lengths ahead.

But the significant thing from our point of view was the effect of defeat on the other horse. John P. Grier had been a horse of great spirit; victory was in his attitude. But he was so broken by this experience that he never really recovered. All of his races afterwards were weak, half-hearted attempts and he never won again.

People are not race horses, but this story is reminiscent of far too many men who, in the boom years of the 1920's, started off with a wonderful attitude of success. They achieved financial success, and then, when the Depression struck in 1930, they experienced defeat. They were crushed. Their attitude changed from positive to negative. Their talisman flipped to the side that read NMA. They stopped trying. They, like John P. Grier, became 'has-beens'.

Some people seem to use PMA pretty much all the time. Others start and then quit. But others—the vast majority of us—have never really begun to use the tremendous powers available to us.

What about us? Can we *learn* to use PMA, as we've learned

other skills?

The answer, based on our years of experience, is a definite yes.

This is the subject of this book. In the chapters that follow we will show you how it can be done. The effort to learn will be worth it because PMA is the essential ingredient in all success.

Meet the most important living person. The day you recognize PMA for yourself is the day that you will meet the most important living person! Who is he? Why, the most important living person is *you*, as far as you and your life are concerned Take a look at yourself. Isn't it true that you carry with you an invisible talisman with the initials PMA emblazoned on one side and NMA on the other? What exactly is this talisman, this force? The talisman is your mind PMA is a Positive Mental Attitude.

A Positive Mental Attitude is the right mental attitude. What is the *right mental attitude?* It is most often comprised of the 'plus' characteristics symbolized by such words as faith, integrity, hope, optimism, courage, initiative, generosity, tolerance, tact, kindliness and good common sense. A person with positive mental attitude aims for high goals and constantly strives to achieve them.

NMA is a negative mental attitude. It has opposite characteristics to PMA.

After years spent studying successful men, the authors *of Success Through a Positive Mental Attitude* have come to the conclusion that a positive mental attitude is the one simple secret shared by them all.

It was PMA that helped S. B. Fuller overcome the disadvantages of poverty. It was PMA that motivated Tom Dempsey, despite his crippled leg, to kick the longest field goal ever kicked in a professional football game. And it was certainly a positive mental attitude that enabled Henry J. Kaiser to build a Liberty Ship every ten days. It was Al Allen's ability to turn his talisman right-side-up that motivated him to return to his prospects—the very ones who had refused him the day before—and set a new sales record.

Do you know how to make your invisible talisman work for you? Perhaps you do: perhaps you don't. Perhaps you have developed and strengthened your PMA until life is bringing you every worthwhile wish. But if you haven't, you can and will learn the techniques whereby you can release your power of PMA through its magic in your life as you continue to read this book.

A positive mental attitude, what it is, and how it may be developed and applied, is described throughout this book. It is the one *essential* principle of this book's Seventeen Principles for achieving worthwhile success. Achievement is attained through some combination of PMA with one or more of the other sixteen success principles Master them. Begin applying each of them as you recognize them while reading *Success Through a Positive Mental Attitude*. When you make each principle a part of your life, yours will be a positive mental attitude in its most powerful form. And the payoff will be success, health, happiness, wealth, or whatever definite aims you may have in life. These will be yours—provided you don't violate the laws of Infinite Intelligence and the rights of your fellow men. Such violations are the most repellent forms of NMA.

In Chapter Two you will find the formula by which you may keep your mind positive. Master that formula; apply it in all that you do and you will be on your way to the attainment of your every desire.

PILOT NO. 1
Thoughts to Steer By

1. Meet the most important living person! That person is you. Your success, health, happiness, wealth depend on how you use your invisible talisman. How will you use it? The choice is yours.
2. Your mind is your invisible talisman. The letters PMA (positive mental attitude) are emblazoned on one side, and NMA (negative mental attitude) on the other. These are powerful forces. *PMA is the right mental attitude for each specific occasion.* It has the power to attract the good and the beautiful. NMA repels them. It is a negative mental attitude that robs you of all that makes life worth living.
   Self-question: 'How can I develop the right mental attitude?' Be specific.
3. Don't blame God for your lack of success. Like S. B. Fuller, you can develop a burning desire to succeed. How? *Keep your mind on the things you want and off the things you don't want.* How?
4. Like S. B. Fuller, read *The Bible* and inspirational books for a purpose. Ask for divine guidance. *Search for the light.*
   Self-question: Do you believe it's proper to ask for Divine Guidance?
5. *Every adversity has the seed of an equivalent or greater benefit for those who have PAM.* Sometimes the things that seem to be adversities turn out to be *opportunities* in disguise. Tom Dempsey discovered this as a cripple.
   Self-question: Will you engage in thinking time to determine how you can turn adversities into seeds of equivalent or greater benefits?
6. Accept the priceless gift—*the joy of work.* Apply the greatest

value in life: *love people and serve them.* Like Henry J. Kaiser, you will attract big and generous portions of success. You can if you develop PMA.

Self-question: Will you search to find out how you can develop PMA as you continue to read this book?

7. Never underestimate the repellent power of a negative mental attitude. It can prevent life's lucky breaks from benefiting you.

   Self-question: PMA attracts good. How can I develop the habit of PMA?

8. You can profit by disappointment—if it is turned into inspirational dissatisfaction with PMA. Like Al Allen, develop *inspirational dissatisfaction.* Rearrange your attitudes and convert a failure of one day into success on another. How do you think you can develop inspirational dissatisfaction?

9. Bring into reality the possibility of the improbable by acquiring PMA. Say to yourself, as Henry Ford said to his engineers, *'Keep Working'.*

   Self-question: Have you the courage to aim high and strive daily to keep your goal before you?

10. Don't let your mental attitude make you a 'has-been.' When you become successful and a depression or any other unfavorable circumstance arises which causes you a loss or defeat, act on the self-motivator: *Success is achieved by those who try and maintained by those who keep tying with PMA. This is the way to avoid being crushed.*

UNIVERSAL PRINCIPLES IN SELF-MOTIVATOR FORM

- Every adversity has the seed of an equivalent or greater benefit.

- Greatness comes to those who develop a burning desire to achieve high goals.
- Success is achieved and maintained by those who try and keep on trying with PMA.
- To become an expert achiever in any human activity, it takes practice...practice...practice.
- Man's greatest power lies in the power of prayer.

2

YOU CAN CHANGE YOUR WORLD

We now know that PMA is a positive mental attitude. And we also know that a Positive Mental Attitude is one of the 17 success principles. When you begin to apply a combination of these principles with PMA in your chosen occupation or to a solution of your personal problems, you are on the road to success. Then you are on the right track and headed in the right direction towards getting what you want.

To achieve anything worthwhile in life, it is imperative that you apply PMA, regardless of what other success principles you employ. PMA is the catalyst which makes any combination of success principles work to attain a worthwhile end. It is NMA, combined with some of the same principles, that is the catalyst which results in crime or evil. And grief, disaster, tragedy—sin, disease, death—are some of its rewards.

17 success principles. The authors have for many years given lectures, instructed classes, and conducted a correspondence course on the 17 success principles. The title of the course: *PMA, The Science of Success.* These 17 principles are:

1. A Positive Mental Attitude
2. Definiteness of purpose
3. Going the extra mile
4. Accurate thinking
5. Self-discipline

6. The master mind
7. Applied faith
8. A pleasing personality
9. Personal initiative
10. Enthusiasm
11. Controlled attention
12. Teamwork
13. Learning from defeat
14. Creative vision
15. Budgeting time and money
16. Maintaining sound physical and mental health
17. Using cosmic habit force (universal law)

These 17 success principles are no creation of the authors. They were extracted from the lifetime experiences of hundreds of the most successful persons our nation has known during the past century.

As long as you live, from this day forward, you can analyze your every success and every failure—that is, if you imprint these 17 principles indelibly in your memory.

You may develop and maintain a permanent Positive Mental Attitude by making it your responsibility to adopt and apply these 17 principles in your daily living.

There is no other known method by which you may keep your mind positive.

Analyze yourself courageously, now, and learn which of these 17 principles you have been using and which of them you have been neglecting.

In the future analyze both your successes and your allures, using the 17 principles as a measuring device, and very soon you will be able to lay your finger on what has been holding you back.

If you have PMA and don't succeed, then what? If you use PMA and don't succeed, it may be because you are not using each of the principles that are necessary in the combination for success to attain your specific goal.

You may wish to check the stories of S. B. Fuller, Tom Dempsey, Henry J. Kaiser, the woodcutter, Al Allen, and Henry Ford, to recognize which of the 17 success principles each person applied or neglected to apply. You might analyze someone you know who is a has-been in real life. As you read the case histories in the chapters which follow, do the same thing. Ask yourself: Which of the 17 success principles are used? Which are omitted? At first it may be difficult to understand and apply the principles. But as you continue to read *Success Through a Positive Mental Attitude*, each of these principles will become more clear to you. You will then be able to use them. When you get to Chapter 20, you will be able to check yourself accurately by the 17 success principles. There you will find a self-analysis chart under the heading 'Success Quotient Analysis'.

Has the world given you a raw deal? The students who have enrolled in the PMA Science of Success course have often been people who considered themselves failures in some area of their lives. The very first question such a person might be asked when he enters the class is: Why? Why are you taking this course? Why haven't you had the success you would like to have? And the reasons which *they give* tell us a tragic story about the causes of failure.

'I never really had a chance to get ahead. My father was an alcoholic, you know.'

'I was raised in the slums and that's something you can never get out of your system.'

'I only had a grammar school education.'

These people are all saying, in essence, that the world has given them a raw deal. They are blaming the world and circumstances outside themselves for their failures. They blame their heredity or their environment. They start out with a negative mental attitude. And, of course, with that attitude, they are handicapped. But it is NMA that is holding them down, not the external handicap which they give as the cause of their failure.

A lesson learned from a child. There is a wonderful little story about a minister who, one Saturday morning, was trying to prepare his sermon under difficult conditions. His wife was out shopping. It was a rainy day and his young son was restless and bored, with nothing to do. Finally, in desperation, the minister picked up an old magazine and thumbed through it until he came to a large brightly colored picture. It showed a map of the world. He tore the page from the magazine, ripped it into little bits and threw the scraps all over the living room floor with the words:

'Johnny, if you can put this all together, I'll give you a quarter'.

The preacher thought this would take Johnny most of the morning. But within ten minutes there was a knock on his study door. It was his son with the completed puzzle. The minister was amazed to see Johnny finished so soon, with the pieces of paper neatly arranged and the map of the world back in order. 'Son, how did you get that done so fast?' the preacher asked.

'Oh,' said Johnny, 'it was easy. On the other side, there was a picture of a man. I just put a piece of paper on the bottom, put the picture of the man together, put a piece of paper on top, and then turned it over. I figured that if got the man right, the world would be right.'

The minister smiled, and handed his son a quarter. 'And you've given me my sermon for tomorrow, too,' he said. *'If a man is right, his world will be right.'*

There's a great lesson in this idea. If you are unhappy with your world and want to change it, the place to start is with yourself. If you are right, your world will be right. This is what PMA is all about. When you have a Positive Mental Attitude, the problems of your world tend to bow before you.

You were born a champion. Have you ever thought about the battles you won before you were born? 'Stop and think about yourself,' says Amram Scheinfeld, an expert on genetics. 'In all the history of the world there was never anyone else exactly like you, and in all the infinity of time to come, there will never be another.'

You are a very special person. And many struggles took place that had to be successfully concluded in order to produce you. Just think: tens of millions of sperm cells participated in a great battle, yet only one of them won—the one that made you! It was a great race to reach a single object: a precious egg containing a tiny nucleus. This goal for which the sperms were competing was smaller in size than the point of a needle. And each sperm was so small that it would have to be magnified thousands of times before it could be seen by the human eye. Yet it is on this microscopic level that your life's most decisive battle was fought.

The head of each of the millions of sperms contained a precious cargo of 24 chromosomes, just as there were 24 in the tiny nucleus of the egg. Each chromosome was composed of jelly-like beads closely strung together. Each bead contained hundreds of genes to which scientists attribute all the factors of your heredity.

The chromosomes in the sperm comprised aft the hereditary

material and tendencies contributed by your father and his ancestors; those in the egg-nucleus the inheritable traits of your mother and her ancestors. Your mother and father themselves represented the culmination of over two billion years of victory in the battle to survive. And then one particular sperm —the fastest, the healthiest, the winner— united with the waiting egg to form one, tiny living cell.

The life of the most important living person had begun. You had become a champion over the most staggering odds you will ever have to face. For all practical purpose you had inherited from the vast reservoir of the past all the potential abilities and powers you need to achieve your objectives.

You were born to be a champion, and no matter what obstacles and difficulties lie in your way, they are not one tenth so great as the ones that have already been overcome at the moment of your conception. Victory is built in to every living person. Take the case of Irving Ben Cooper who was one of America's most respected judges. But this was very far from the way young Ben Cooper thought of himself as a young boy.

How a frightened boy developed PMA. Ben grew up in a nearslum neighborhood in St. Joseph, Missouri. His father was an immigrant tailor who earned little money. Many days there simply wasn't enough to eat. To heal their small home, Ben used to take a coal scuttle, and walk down to the railroad tracks that ran nearby. There he would pick up pieces of coal. It embarrassed Ben to have to do it. He'd often try to sneak through the bad streets so children from school wouldn't see him.

But they often did. There was one gang of boys in particular who found great sport in ambushing Ben on his way home from the tracks and beating him up. They would scatter his coal all over the street and send him home with tears streaming from his eyes. Thus it was that Ben lived in a more or less permanent state of fear and self-despising.

Something happened, as it always must when we break the pattern of defeat. The victory within us does not assert itself until we are ready. Ben was inspired to positive action because he read a book. It was *Robert Coverdale's Struggle* by Horatio Alger.

In it, Ben read the adventures of a youngster like himself who was faced with great odds, but who overcame these odds with the courage and moral strength which Ben wished to possess.

The boy read every one of the Horatio Alger books he could borrow. As he read, he lived the part of the hero. All winter he sat in the cold kitchen reading stories of courage and success, unconsciously absorbing a Positive Mental Attitude.

Some months after he had read his first Horatio Alger book, Ben Cooper was again making a trip down to the railroad tracks. Off in the distance he saw three figures dart behind a building. His first thought was to turn and run. Then he remembered the courage that he had admired in his book heroes, and, instead of turning, his hand gripped the coal scuttle more tightly and he marched straight ahead, *as if he were one of the Alger heroes.*

It was a brutal fight. The three boys jumped at Ben all at the same time. His bucket dropped, and he started flailing his arms with a determination that caught the bullies by surprise. Ben's right hand smashed into the lips and nose of one of the boys—his left hand into his stomach. To Ben's surprise, the boy stopped fighting and turned and ran. Meanwhile the other two boys were hitting and kicking him. Ben managed to push one boy away and knock the other down. He jumped on the second boy with his knees, while he plowed punch after punch into his stomach and jaw—as if he were mad. Now there was just one boy left. This was the leader. He had jumped on top of Ben. Ben managed to pull him aside and get on his feet. For a second the two boys stood and looked each other squarely in the eyes.

And then, bit by bit, the leader stepped backwards. He, too, ran away. Perhaps it was righteous indignation, but Ben picked up a chunk of coal and threw it at the retreater.

It wasn't until then that Ben realized that his nose was bleeding and that he had black and blue marks on his body from the punches and kicks he had received. It was worth it! It was a great day in Ben's life. In that moment he overcame fear.

Ben Cooper wasn't much stronger than he had been a year earlier. His attackers were no less tough. The difference came in Ben's own mental attitude. He had faced danger in spite of fear. He decided that no longer was he going to be pushed around by bullies. From now on, he himself was going to change his world. And, of course, this is exactly what he did.

Identify yourself with a successful image. The boy gave himself an identity. When he fought the three bullies on the street that day, he was not lighting as frightened, undernourished Ben Cooper. He was fighting as Robert Coverdale or any other of the plucky and daring heroes of Horatio Alger's books.

Identifying one's self with a successful image can help break the habits of self-doubt and defeat which years of NMA set up within a personality. Another and equally important successful technique for changing your world is to identify yourself with an image that will inspire you to make the right decisions. It can be a slogan, a picture, or any other symbol that is meaningful to you.

What will your picture say to you? The president of a midwest concern operating internationally was visiting his San Francisco office. He noticed a large photograph of himself on the wall of the office of Dorothy Jones, a private secretary. 'Dotti, that's a rather large picture for this size room, isn't it?' he asked.

Dorothy responded, 'When I have a problem, do you know what I do?' Without waiting for an answer, she demonstrated by placing her elbows on her desk, propping her head on the fingers of her folded hands, and looking up at the picture. 'Boss, how the heck would you solve this problem?' she asked.

Dotti's remarks seem rather humorous. Yet the essence of her idea is startling. Perhaps you have a picture in your office, your home, or in your wallet, that could give you the right answer to an important question in your life. Yours may be a picture of your mother, father, wife, husband—of Benjamin Franklin or Abraham Lincoln. It may be that of a saint.

What will your picture say to you? There is one way to find out. When you are faced with a serious problem or decision, ask your picture a question. Listen, for the answer.

Another essential ingredient for changing your world is to have *definiteness of purpose*, one of the 17 principles of success.

Definiteness of purpose is the starting point of all achievement. Definiteness of purpose, *combined with PMA*, is the starting point of all worthwhile achievement. Remember—your world will change whether or not you choose to change it. But you have the power to choose its direction. You can select your own targets. When you determine your definite major aims with PMA, there is a natural tendency for you to use seven of the success principles:

(a) Personal initiative
(b) Self-discipline
(c) Creative vision
(d) Organized thinking

(e) Controlled attention (concentration of effort)
(f) Budgeting of time and money
(g) Enthusiasm

Robert Christopher had definiteness of purpose with PMA.

Now, let's see how the natural tendencies for these additional principles manifested themselves in this success story. For, like many boys, Bob's imagination was stimulated while he read Jules Verne's thrilling, imaginative story *Around the World in 80 Days.* Bob told us:

'I used to daydream a great deal but when I grew older, I read two books on motivation: *Think and Grow Rich* and *The Magic of Believing.*

'Around the world in 80 days. Now, why couldn't I go around the world on $80.00? I believed that any given aim could be accomplished if I had faith and confidence that it could be. That is: if I started from where I was to get to where I wanted to be.

'I thought: 'Others had worked on freighters to earn their transatlantic passages and hitchhiked all over the world, so why couldn't I?"

And then Bob took his fountain pen from his pocket and wrote on a piece of note paper a list of the problems with which he would be faced. Also, he made notes of what he thought were workable answers to each.

Now Bob Christopher was an expert photographer and he did have a camera. It was a good one at that. When he reached his decision, he went into action:

(a) Entered a contract with Charles Pfizer Company, a large pharmaceutical company, to collect soil samples from the various countries he intended to visit.
(b) Obtained an international driver's license and a set of

maps in return for a promised report on Middle East road conditions.

(c) Picked up seamen's papers.

(d) Obtained a letter from the New York City Police Department to prove that he had no criminal record.

(e) Arranged for a Youth Hostel Membership.

(f) Contacted a freight airline which agreed to transport him by plane over the Atlantic on his promise to obtain photographs which the company intended to use for publicity.

And when his plans were completed, this young man of 26 left New York City by plane with $80.00 in his pocket *Around the world on $80.00* was his definite major aim. And here are a few of his experiences:

- Had breakfast at Gander, Newfoundland. How did he pay for it? He photographed the cooks in the kitchen. And they were pleased.
- Bought four cartons of American cigarettes at Shannon, Ireland that cost him $4.80. At that time cigarettes were as good as money as a medium of exchange in many countries.
- Arrived at Vienna from Paris. The fee—one carton of cigarettes to the driver.
- Gave the conductor four packs of cigarettes to take him from Vienna to Switzerland on a tram through the Alps.
- Rode a bus to Damascus. A policeman In Syria was so proud of the picture that Bob had taken of him that he ordered the bus driver to take him.
- Took a photograph of the president and staff of the Iraq Express Transportation Company. This earned him

a ride from Baghdad to Teheran.

- In Bangkok, the owner of a very fine restaurant fed him like a king. For Bob gave him the information he wanted—a detailed description of a specific area and a set of maps.
- Was brought from Japan to San Francisco as a crew member of *S.S. The Flying Spray.*

Around the world in 80 days? No—Robert Christopher went around the world in 84 days. But he did accomplish his objective. He went around the world on $80.00

And because he had definiteness of purpose with PMA, he was automatically motivated to use an additional 13 of the 17 success principles to achieve his specific goal.

The starting point of all achievement. Let us repeat: The starting point of all achievement is definiteness of purpose with PMA. Remember this statement and ask yourself, what is my goal? What do I really want?

Based on the people we see in our PMA Science of Success course, we estimate that 98 out of every 100 persons who are dissatisfied with their world do not have a clear picture in their minds of the world they would like for themselves.

Think of it! Think of the people who drift aimlessly through life, dissatisfied, struggling against a great many things, but without a clear-cut goal. Can you state, right now, what it is that you want out of life? Fixing your goals may not be easy. It may even involve some painful self-examination. But it will be worth whatever effort it costs, because as soon as you can name your goal, you can expect to enjoy many advantages. These advantages come almost automatically.

1. The first great advantage is that your subconscious mind begins to work under a universal law: 'What

the mind of man can *conceive* and *believe*—the mind of man can *achieve* with PMA.' Because you visualize your intended destination, your subconscious mind is affected by this self-suggestion. It goes to work to help you get there.

2. Because you know what you want, there is a tendency for you to try to get on the right track and head in the right direction. You get into action.
3. Work now becomes fun. You are motivated to pay the price. You budget your time and money. You study, think, and plan. The more you think about your goals, the more enthusiastic you become. And with enthusiasm your desire turns into a burning desire.
4. You become alerted to opportunities that will help you achieve your objectives as they present themselves in your everyday experiences. Because you know what you want, you are more likely to recognize these opportunities.

These four advantages are illustrated by an early experience of the man who was later to become editor of the *Ladies Home Journal*. Edward Bok came from Holland as a boy with his parents. He was imbued with the idea that some day he was going to run a magazine. With this specific goal before him, he was able to seize upon an incident so trivial that with most of us it would have passed unnoticed.

He saw a man open a package of cigarettes, take a slip of paper from it, and drop the paper on the floor. Bok stooped and picked up the scrap of paper. On it was a picture of a famous actress. Below the picture was a statement that this was one of a series. The cigarette buyer was urged to collect the complete set of pictures. Bok turned the piece of paper over and noticed that the back side was perfectly blank.

Bok's mind, filled as it was with a purpose, sensed an opportunity here. He reasoned that the value of the picture enclosed in the package of cigarettes would be greatly enhanced if the blank side were devoted to a brief biography of the person pictured. He went to the lithograph firm, which printed the enclosure and explained his idea to the manager. The manager promptly said:

'I'll give you ten dollars each if you will write me a 100-word biography of 100 famous Americans. Send me a list, and group them—you know: presidents, famous soldiers, actors, authors, and so on.'

This is the way Edward Bok got his first literary assignment. The demand for his short biographies became so great that he needed help, so he offered his brother five dollars each if he would help him. Before long, Bok had five journalists busy turning out biographies for the lithograph presses. Bok—he was the editor!

You have success born in you. Notice that none of the men we have been talking about had success handed to him on a platter. At first the world was not particularly kind to Edward Bok or Judge Cooper. And yet each carved from the raw material around him a career of great satisfaction. And each one did it by developing the many talents he found within himself.

Everyone has many talents for surmounting his special problems. It is interesting to note that life never leaves us stranded. If life hands us a problem, it hands us also the abilities with which to meet the problem. Our abilities vary, of course, as we are motivated to use them. And even though you are in ill health, you can nonetheless lead a useful and happy life.

You may fear ill health is too great a handicap to overcome.

If this is true, take courage from the experience of Milo C. Jones. Milo had not tried to acquire wealth when he had good health. And then he became sick. When he became sick, the odds were stacked heavily against him.

Here's the story of his experience.

When Milo C. Jones had been in good health he had worked very hard. He was a farmer and he operated a small farm near Fort Atkinson, Wisconsin. But somehow he seemed unable to make his farm yield much more than the bare necessities for himself and his family. This kind of existence went on year after year. Then suddenly something happened!

Jones was stricken with extensive paralysis and confined to his bed. Here was a man who late in life became completely incapacitated. He was barely able to move his body. His relatives were certain he would be permanently unhappy as a hopeless invalid. And he would have been had not *something more* happened to him. And he made it happen. It brought the kind of happiness to him that comes with achievement and financial success.

What was it Jones used to bring about this change? He used his mind. Yes, his body was paralyzed. But his mind was unaffected. He could think and he did think and plan. One day while engaged in thinking and planning, he recognized the most important living person with the magic talisman with PMA on one side and NMA on the other. He saw clearly that he was a *mind with a body*. He made his own decision right then and there!

PMA attracts wealth. Milo C. Jones chose to develop a positive mental attitude. He chose to be hopeful, optimistic, happy and to convert creative thinking into reality by starting right from where he was. He wanted to be useful. And be wanted to support his family, instead of being a burden to them. But how could he turn his disadvantage into advantage? He didn't let this vital problem stop him. He found the answer.

First, Jones counted his blessings. He discovered that he had so very much for which to be thankful. This thankfulness led him to search for additional blessings which he might enjoy in the future. And because he was searching for, among other things, a way to be useful, he found and recognized that for which he was looking. It was a plan and it required action.

So Jones went into mental action.

He revealed the plan to members of his family.

'I am no longer able to work with my hands,' he began, 'so I have decided to work with my mind. Every one of you can, if you will, take the place of my hands, feet, and physical body. Let's plant every tillable acre of our farm in com. Then let's raise pigs and feed them the com. Let's slaughter the pigs while they are young and tender and convert them into sausages. And then we can package and sell them under a *brand name.* We'll sell them in retail stores all over the country.' And then he chuckled as he said:

'They'll sell like hot cakes!'

And they did sell like hot cakes! In a few years the *brand* name 'Jones' Little Pig Sausages' became a household byword. And these four words became a symbol that tantalized the appetites of men, women, and children throughout the nation.

And Milo C. Jones lived to see himself a millionaire. He had achieved something even more through a positive mental attitude. For he bad flipped his talisman to PMA. And thus, although he was physically handicapped, he became a happy man.

He was happy because he was useful.

A formula to help you change your world. Fortunately, not every life is faced with such great difficulties. Yet everyone has problems. And everyone reacts to motivating symbols through suggestion or self-suggestion. A most effective form is a self-motivator deliberately memorized for the purpose of flashing from the subconscious to the conscious in time of need.

What, then, is a formula that can help you change your world? *Memorize*, *understand*, and *repeat* frequently throughout the day: What the mind of man can *conceive* and *believe*, the mind of man can achieve with PMA. It is a form of self-suggestion. It is a self-motivator to success. When it becomes a part of you, *you dare to aim higher*.

Bill was a sickly farm boy in the southeastern Missouri country. A dedicated grammar school teacher motivated young William Danforth to change his world. The teacher did this with a challenge: *I Dare You!* 'I dare you to become the healthiest boy in school!' *I Dare You!* became William Danforth's selfmotivator throughout life.

He became the healthiest boy in his school. Before he died at the age of 85, he helped thousands of other youths develop good health—and *something more*: to aspire nobly, to adventure daringly, and to serve humbly. During his long career be never lost a day at work because of illness.

I Dare You! motivated him to build one of America's largest corporations. The Ralston Purina Company. *I Dare You!* motivated him to engage in creative thinking and turn liabilities into assets. *I Dare You!* motivated him to organize The American Youth Foundation: its purpose is to train young men and women in Christian ideals and to prepare them for the responsibilities of life.

I Dare You! motivated William Danforth to write a book entitled *I Dare You!* Today this book is inspiring boys and girls, men and women, to have the courage to make this world a better world to live in.

What a remarkable testimony to the power of a self-motivator to develop a positive mental attitude!

Are you, yourself, ever tempted to blame the world for your failures? If so, *pause* and *reconsider*. Does the problem lie with the world, or with you? Dare to learn the 17 success principles! Dare to memorize self-motivators! Dare to apply them with the full assurance that they will work for you just as effectively as they are working every day for hundreds of others.

Perhaps you don't know how. Perhaps you need to learn to think mere accurately. Be guided by Pilot No. 2.

Then turn to Chapter Three. Its purpose is to help you—clear the cobwebs from your thinking.

PILOT NO. 2
Thoughts to Steer By

1. You can change your world! To achieve anything worthwhile in life it is necessary to set high goals for yourself and want to achieve them. Have you thought about the high goals you would like to achieve?
2. Imprint the 17 success principles indelibly in your memory. Have you memorized them?
3. Do you tend to 'blame the world'? If you do, memorize the self-motivator: *If the man is right, his world will be right.* Is your immediate world right?
4. You were born to be a champion. For all practical purposes, you have inherited from the vast reservoir of the past all the potential abilities and powers you need to achieve your objectives. Are you willing to pay the price to develop your abilities and use the powers within you?
5. Identify yourself with a successful image, as Irving Ben Cooper did. Who will you select?
6. Ask yourself an important question: What will your picture say to you? Listen for the answer.
7. Definiteness of purpose with PMA is the starting point of all worthwhile achievement. Have you selected some definite, specific, desirable goal? Will you keep it in mind daily?
8. When you determine your definite aims, there is a tendency for several additional success principles to begin to operate automatically to help you achieve them.
9. Everyone has many talents for surmounting his special problems. What special talents do you think you have that you can develop?
10. Here is a formula that has helped many to change their

world: What the mind of man can *conceive* and *believe* the mind of man can *achieve* with PMA. Have you memorized this formula?

A POSITIVE MENTAL ATTITUDE AND DEFINITENESS OF PURPOSE IS THE STARTING POINT TOWARD ALL WORTHWHILE ACHIEVEMENT!

3

CLEAR THE COBWEBS FROM YOUR THINKING

You are what you think. But what do you think? How orderly are your thought processes? How straight is your thinking?

And how clean are your thoughts?

There are certain mental cobwebs that clutter up the thinking of almost everyone, even the most brilliant minds. *Negative:* feelings, emotions, passions—habits, beliefs and prejudices. Our thoughts become entangled in these webs.

Sometimes we have undesirable habits and we want to correct them. And there are times when we are strongly tempted to do wrong. Then, like an insect caught in a spider's web, we struggle to get free. Our conscious will is in conflict with our imagination and the *will* of our subconscious mind. The more we struggle, the more we become entrapped.

Some persons give up and experience the mental conflicts of a living hell. Others learn how to tap and use the powers of the subconscious through the conscious mind. They are victorious. And *Success Through a Positive Mental Attitude* teaches you how to tap and use these powers.

An insect may not be able to avoid being caught in the spider's web. And when once trapped, it is unable to free itself. There is one thing, however, over which each person has absolute, inherent control, and that is his mental attitude.

We can avoid mental cobwebs. We can clear them. And we can sweep them away as they begin to develop. We can free ourselves when once enmeshed. And we can *remain* free.

You do this by accurate thinking with PMA. Accurate thinking is one of the 17 success principles revealed in *Success Through a Positive Mental Attitude*.

To think accurately you must use reason. The science of reasoning or accurate thinking is called logic. One can learn it from books written specifically on this subject, such as: *The Art of Clear Thinking*, by Rudolf Flesch; *Your Most Enchanted Listener*, by Wendell Johnson; *Introduction to Logic*, by Irving Copi; and *The Art of Straight Thinking*, by Edwin Leavitt Clarke. These books can be of immense practical help.

But we don't act from reason alone. And action based on common sense is the result of more than just reason. It depends upon habits of thought and action, intuitions, experiences and other influences such as tendencies and environment.

One of the cobwebs of our thinking is to assume that we act from reason alone when in reality every conscious act is the result of doing what we want to do. We make decisions. There is a tendency, when reasoning, to draw conclusions favorable to the strong *inner urges* of our subconscious mind. And this tendency exists in everyone—even the great thinkers and philosophers.

In 31 B.C. a Greek philosopher who lived in a city on the Aegean Sea wanted to go to Carthage. He was a teacher of logic; therefore be contemplated reasons in favor of making the voyage and reasons against it. For every reason as to why he should go he found that there were many more reasons why he shouldn't. Of course he would be seasick. The boat was so small that a storm might jeopardize his life. Pirates with swift sailing vessels were lying in wait off Tripoli to prey upon merchant vessels. If his ship were captured by them, they would take his worldly goods and sell him into slavery. Discretion indicated that he should not make the trip.

But he did. Why? *Because he wanted to.*

It so happens that emotion and reason should be in balance in everyone's life. Neither should always hold the controlling hand. So *sometimes* it is good to do what you want to do instead of what reason *fears*. As to this philosopher—he had a most pleasant journey and arrived back home safely.

Then there was Socrates, the great Athenian philosopher who lived from 470 B.C. to 399 B.C. He has gone down in history as one of the outstanding thinkers of all time. Wise as Socrates was, there were cobwebs in his thinking too.

As a young man Socrates fell in love with Xanthippe. She was very beautiful. He wasn't good looking, but he was persuasive. Persuasive individuals seem to have the ability to get what they want. Socrates was successful in persuading Xanthippe to marry him.

Are you seeing only the mote in the other fellow's eye? After the honeymoon was over, things didn't go along so well at his house. His wife began to see his faults. And he saw hers. He was motivated by egoism. He was selfish. She was always nagging him. Socrates reportedly said, 'My aim in life is to get on well with people. I chose Xanthippe because I knew if I could get on well with her, I could get along with anyone.'

This is what he said. But his actions disproved his words. It is questionable that he tried to get on well with more than a few. When you always try to prove to persons whom you meet that they are wrong, you repel rather than attract as Socrates did.

Yet he said that he endured Xanthippe's nagging for his own personal self-discipline. But he would have developed real self-discipline had he tried to understand his wife and to influence her through the same considerate attentions and expressions of love that he used in persuading her to marry him. He didn't see the beam in his own eye, but he saw the mote in Xanthippe's eye.

Of course, Xanthippe wasn't blameless either. Socrates and she were just like many husbands and wives living today.

After their marriage they neglect to continue to communicate their true feelings of affection, understanding, and love to each other. They neglect to continue to employ the same pleasing personalities and mental attitudes that made their courtship such a happy experience. Negligence is a cobweb too.

Now Socrates didn't read *Success Through a Positive Mental Attitude.* Neither did Xanthippe. Had she done so, she would have known how to motivate her husband so that their home life would have been a happier one. She would have seen the beam in her eye, rather than the mote in Socrates'. She would have controlled her own reactions and been sensitive to the reactions of her husband. In fact, she might have even proved the fallacy of his logic after she read Chapter Five entitled '*... And Something More.*'

And because the story of Socrates proves he saw only mote in Xanthippe's eye we shall tell you about another young man—he learned to see the beam in his own eye. But before we do, let's see how the habit of nagging develops.

You see, when you know the cause of a problem, you can often avoid it or you can find your own solution to that problem if you already have it.

S.I. Hayakawa in *Language in Thought and Action* wrote:

> In order to cure (what she believes to be) her husband's faults, a wife may nag him. His faults get worse, so she nags him some more. Naturally his faults get worse still, and she nags him even more. Governed by a fixated reaction to the problem of her husband's faults, she can meet it only one way. The longer she continues, the worse

it gets, until they are both nervous wrecks; their marriage is destroyed, and their lives are shattered.

Now what about the young man? It was the first evening of a PMA Science of Success class when he was asked, 'Why are you taking this course?'

'Because of my wife!' he responded. Many of the students laughed—but not the instructor. He knew from experience that there are many unhappy homes when husband or wife sees the other's faults but not his or her own.

He restored happiness to his home. It was four weeks later in a private conference that the instructor asked the student, 'How are you coming along with your problem?'

'It's solved!'

'That's wonderful! But how did you solve it?'

'I learned: *when I am faced with a problem that involves misunderstandings with other persons, J must first start with myself.* When I examined my own mental attitude, I discovered that it was negative. My problem was really not with my wife after all—it was with me! In solving my problem, I found that I no longer had one with her.'

Now, what if Socrates had said to himself: 'When I am faced with a problem that involves a misunderstanding with Xanthippe, I must first start with myself?' And what would happen if you would say to yourself: 'When I am faced with a problem that involves a misunderstanding with another person, I must first start with myself?' Would you life be a happier one?

But there are many other cobwebs that interfere with happiness. Oddly enough, the one that is the greatest hindrance is the very tool of thought itself: *words.* Words are symbols, as S. I. Hayakawa tells us in his book. And you, will find that a one-word symbol can mean to you the sum total of a combination of innumerable ideas, concept, and experiences. And you will also see as you continue to read *Success Through a Positive Mental Attitude* that the subconscious instantaneously communicates to the conscious mind through symbols.

Through one word you can motivate others to act. When you say to another person 'You can!' this is *suggestion*. When you say to yourself 'I can!' you motivate yourself by *self-suggestion*. But more about these universal truths in the next chapter. First let's recognize that a whole science has grown up around the important discoveries made about words and the communicating of ideas through words: the science of semantics.

And Hayakawa is an expert in this field. He tells us that to find out what a word really means on the lips of another person, or even on your own lips, is essential in the process of accurate thinking.

But how does one do this?

Just be *specific*. Start with a meeting of the minds and many needless misunderstandings will be avoided.

One word can cause an argument. The uncle of a nine-year-old boy was visiting in the home of the boy's parents. One evening when the father came home, the following dialogue developed:

'What do you think of a boy that lies?'

'I don't think very much of him, and I know one thing certain: my son tells the truth,'

'He told a lie today.'

'Son, did you tell your uncle a lie?'

'No, father.'

'Let's clear this thing up. Your uncle says you lied. You say you didn't. Just exactly what did happen?' he asked, turning to the uncle.

'Well, I told him to take his toys down to the basement.

He didn't do it, and he told me that he did.'

'Son, did you take your toys to the basement?'

'Yes, father.'

'Son, how do you explain this? Your uncle says that you didn't take your toys to the basement and you say that you did.'

'There are several steps leading from the first floor down to the basement... About four steps down is a window... I put my toys on the window sill... The basement is the distance between the floor and the ceiling... My toys *are* in the basement!'

The argument between the uncle and his nephew was due to the definition of one word: basement. The boy probably knew what his uncle meant, but he was lazy and hadn't wanted to run all the way downstairs. When he was faced with punishment, the boy tried to save himself by using logic to prove his point.

Now this may be intriguing. But more motivating will be the story of a young man who didn't know what the most important word symbol in any language means. And what is the most important word in any language? That word is *God.*

Not so long ago a student from Columbia University called on the Rev. Harry Emerson Fosdick, Minister Emeritus of The Riverside Church of New York City. The student had hardly gotten through the door before he said:

'I am an atheist!' When he sat down, he repeated defiantly, 'I don't believe in God.'

Let's start with a meeting of the minds. Now, fortunately, Dr. Fosdick was also an expert in the field of semantics. He knew from long experience that he could never really communicate with another person unless he understood exactly what that other person meant by the words he used. He also knew that it was necessary for the other person to comprehend his meaning. So instead of taking offense at the student's brash remark, Dr. Fosdick expressed a genuinely friendly interest in him and then asked, 'Please describe to me the God you do not believe in'.

The young man had to think, as everyone has to thick when he is asked a question that doesn't cause a reflex 'yes' or 'no' answer. Dr. Fosdick knew that the right question could sweep strong cobwebs of negative thinking out of the youth's mind.

After a little while the student began to try to describe the God he didn't believe in. In so doing he gave the minister a very clear picture of the God he rejected.

'Well,' said Dr. Fosdick when the student had finished, 'if that is the God you don't believe in, I don't believe in him either. So we are both atheists. Nevertheless,' he continued, 'we still have the universe on our hands. What do you make of it—its formation, its meaning?'

Before the young man left Dr. Fosdick, he discovered that he was not an atheist at all, but a very good theist. He did believe in God. Now Dr. Fosdick had not been thrown by the undefined use of a word. In this instance he helped sweep away the cobwebs of the young man's thinking by asking him questions. The simple, clear response as to what the young man didn't believe in was enough to allow a meeting of the minds. The second question directed the youth's thoughts into the proper channels. And it gave Dr. Fosdick an opportunity to explain his meaning of the universal God.

Frog legs taught him logic. As we have seen, the student reached two entirely different conclusions. Each was based on a different premise. Cobwebs will interfere with accurate thinking and cause you to reach a wrong conclusion when you start with a false premise. W. Clement Stone had an amusing experience with this which he describes as follows:

> As a boy I enjoyed eating frog legs. One day at a restaurant I was served jumbo frog legs and didn't like

them. Then and there I decided that I didn't like large frog legs.

Some years later I was at a quality restaurant in Louisville, Kentucky and saw frog legs on the menu.

My conversation with the waiter was as follows:

'Are these small frog legs?'

'Yes sir!'

'Are you sure? I don't like the large ones.'

'Yes sir!'

'If they're the small ones, that'll be fine for me.'

'Yes sir!'

When the waiter brought the entree, I saw that they were jumbo frog legs. I was irritated and said: 'These aren't the small frog legs!'

'These are the smallest we could find, sir,' the waiter responded.

Rather than be unpleasant I ate the frog legs. And I enjoyed them, so much that I wished they had been larger.

I learned a lesson in logic.

In analyzing the matter I realized that my conclusions about the merits of large and small frog legs had been based on the wrong premise. It wasn't the size of the frog legs that made them distasteful.

It was the fact that the jumbo frog legs I had eaten the first time hadn't been fresh. I had associated my distaste for jumbo frog legs with size rather than with spoilage.

Now we see that cobwebs prevent accurate thinking when we start with the wrong premise. So many persons think inaccurately when they allow all-embracing word symbols to clutter up their minds with false premises. Such words or expressions as: always—only—never—nothing—every—

everyone—no one—can't—impossible—either... or— are most frequently false premises. Consequently, when they are so used their logical conclusions are false.

Necessity plus PMA can motivate you to succeed. Now there is one word which, when used with PMA, motivates a person to honorable achievement. When used with NMA, it becomes the excuse for lies, deception, and fraud. *Necessity* is the word. Necessity is the mother of invention and the father of crime.

Inviolable standards of integrity are fundamental to all worthwhile achievement and are an integral part of PMA.

You will read many success stories throughout this book in which persons are motivated by *necessity*. And in each case, you'll find that such persons achieved success without transgressing an inviolable standard of integrity. Lee Braxton is such a man.

Lee Braxton, of Whiteville, North Carolina, was the son of a struggling blacksmith. He was the tenth child in a family of twelve. '... so you might say,' says Mr. Braxton, 'that I became acquainted with poverty early in life. By hard work I managed to get through the sixth grade in school. I shined shoes, delivered groceries, sold news-papers, worked in a hosiery mill, washed automobiles, and served as a mechanic's helper.'

When he became a mechanic, it appeared to Lee that he had risen as far as he could go. Perhaps he had not yet developed inspirational dissatisfaction. In due course he married. And together he and his wife scrimped along. He was used to poverty. And it now seemed to him that it was impossible for him to break the ties which held him down, although he was poorly paid and just barely supporting his family. The Braxtons were already having a terrible time making ends meet when, to complete the picture of defeat, he lost his job. His home was about to be taken from him because he was unable to meet the mortgage payments. It seemed a hopeless situation.

But Lee was a man of character. He was also a religions man. And he believed that God is always a good God. So he prayed for guidance. As if in answer to his prayer, he received the book *Think and Grow Rich* from a friend. This friend had lost his job and his home in the Depression. And he had been motivated to recoup his fortune after reading *Think and Grow Rich.*

Now Lee was ready.

He read the book again and again. He was searching for financial success. He said to himself: 'It seems to me there is something I have to do. I have to add something. No book will do it for me. The first thing I must do is develop a Positive Mental Attitude regarding my abilities and my opportunities. I must certainly choose a definite goal. When I do, I must aim higher than I have in the past. But I must get started. Ill begin with the first job I can find.'

And he looked for a job and found one. It didn't pay much to start.

But it wasn't many years after he had read *Think and Grow Rich* that Lee Braxton organized and became president of the First National Bank of Whiteville, was elected mayor of his city, and engaged in many successful business enterprises. You see: Lee had aimed high—in fact, very high. He had taken as his major purpose the goal of being rich enough to retire at the age of 50. He achieved this goal six years ahead of time—retiring from active business with substantial wealth and a fine independent income at the age of 44. Today Lee Braxton is leading a useful life. He is devoting his entire efforts to helping Oral Roberts, the evangelist, in his ministry.

Now, the jobs that he took and the investments he made in climbing from failure to success are not important here. What is important is that *necessity motivates a man with PMA to action without transgressing recognized inviolable standards.* An honest man won't deceive, cheat, or steal because of necessity. *Honesty is inherent in PMA.*

Necessity, NMA and crime. Now, contrast such a man with the many thousands of persons with NMA who are imprisoned because of stealing, embezzling, or other crimes. When you ask them why they stole in the first place, their answer invariably is: 'I had to'. And that's how they landed in prison! They allowed themselves to become dishonest because cobwebs in their thinking caused them to believe that necessity forces one to become dishonest.

Some years ago, Napoleon Hill, while doing personal counseling in the prison library in the federal penitentiary at Atlanta, had several confidential talks with Al Capone. In one of these talks, the author inquired: 'How did you get started in a life of crime?'

Capone answered with one word: 'Necessity'.

Then tears came into his eyes and he choked up. He began to tell of some of the good things he had done which the newspapers had never mentioned. Of course, these seem insignificant compared to the evil that is attributed to his name.

That unfortunate man wasted his life, destroyed his peace of mind, undermined his physical body with deadly disease, and spread fear and disaster in the path he followed—all because he never learned to clear the cobwebs of his thinking regarding necessity.

And when Capone told of his good deeds, which he implied offset to some great degree the wrongs he had done, he clearly indicated another cobweb which was preventing him from thinking accurately. While a man can neutralize the evil he has done by true repentance followed by a life of good deeds, Capone was not such a man.

But there was such a man. He was a teen-age problem child. Yet his mother never lost hope even though many of her specific prayers for him seemed unanswered. And she never lost faith, regardless of her son's escapades or wrongdoing.

He was a teen-age problem child. This young man became an educated, intellectual, passionate, and sensual teen-age problem child. He took pride in being first, even in evil. It is said that he disobeyed his parents and teachers, lied and deceived, committed petty thefts, cheated in gambling, indulged in alcoholic and sexual excesses.

Yet because of his mother's constant and earnest pleas to him to mend his ways, he *struggled to find himself* even before he reached the lowest point in his moral life. Sometimes he was filled with shame by the knowledge that men with less education were able to resist temptations which he thought he was powerless to resist. And because he was educated, and because he was searching, he studied *The Bible* and other inspirational books of his day.

Even so, he lost many battles with himself. And then one day be won the battle that turned the tide to personal victory. This is what happens when a person *keeps trying.* It was during a period of remorse when he was overcome with self-condemnation that he overheard a conversation in which one voice said, *'Take up and read!'*

He reached for the nearest book, opened it, and read: 'Let us walk honestly, as in the day; not in rioting and drunkenness, not in chambering and wantonness, not in strife and envying. But put ye on the Lord Jesus Christ, and make not provision for the flesh, to fulfill the lusts thereof.'

It often happens. After a person suffers a serious defeat in a personal battle with himself, he may at that point be ready. His remorse can be so emotional and sincere that he is motivated to take immediate action and through perseverance make the change that keeps him on the road to a complete victory.

Now this young man was ready!

And once he made his irrevocable decision, he had peace of mind. He *believed* that Divine Power would help him overcome the sins which he had previously fought in vain and he developed a deep spirituality. His subsequent life proved this by results. The young man devoted himself to God and the service of his fellowmen.

It is because of what he had been and what he became that he is considered a man who has had a most powerful influence in giving hope even to the hopeless. Augustine was his name. And he was made a saint.

It is well known that the power of *The Bible* has been instrumental in changing even the attitudes of human derelicts from negative to positive. And because of the special power in this Written Word they were inspired to clear the cobwebs from their thinking. Thus, they became clean in thought and habit. Many, like St. Augustine, have been moved to deep repentance and, like him, they have been motivated to devote their lives to the service of God and mankind. And many great evangelists climbed from these ranks.

Now, there are some good people of strong religious faith who also read their *Bible*s but say to us, 'Don't try to interfere with God,' when we recommend other inspirational books. Cobwebs prevent them from trying to extract the good wherever it can be found.

You don't try to interfere with God. Now these good people fear that it is sacrilegious to dare to explore the powers of the mind God has given them: to choose, to plan, and to control their future. Many books of inspiration are written to motivate the reader to direct his thoughts, control his emotions, and ordain his destiny. And they often help the reader to comprehend the truths of *The Bible*.

This is true, for example, in such a non-fiction best seller as *The Power of Positive Thinking*. In his book Norman Vincent Peale endeavors to motivate the reader to better himself. To do so, he quotes directly from the Good Book in which such people do believe. Some of the quotations Dr. Peale uses (and which it would be wise to memorize) are:

As he thinketh in his heart, so is he.

If thou canst believe, all things are possible to him that believeth.

Lord, I believe; help Thou mine unbelief!

According to your faith be it unto you. Faith without works is dead.

What things so ever ye desire, when ye pray, believe that ye receive them, and ye shall have them.

If God be for us, who can be against us?

Ask and it shall be given to you; seek and ye shall find; knock, and it shall be opened unto you.

You have just seen several mental cobwebs as we have pointed them out to you. Some of these are:

1. Negative: (a) feelings, (b) emotions, (c) passions, (d) habits, (e) beliefs and (f) prejudices.
2. Seeing only the mote in the other fellow's eye.
3. Arguments and misunderstandings due to semantic difficulties.
4. False conclusions resulting from false premises.
5. All-inclusive, restrictive words or expressions as basic or minor premises.
6. The idea that necessity forces dishonesty.
7. Unclean thoughts and habits.

8. Fear that it is sacrilegious to use the powers of your mind.

And so you see there are many varieties of cobwebs- some small, some large, some weak, some strong. Yet if you make an additional listing of your own, and then examine the strands of each cobweb closely, you will find that they are all spun by NMA.

And when you think about it for a while, you will see that the strongest cobweb spun by NMA is the cobweb of inertia. Inertia causes you to do nothing; or, if you are moving in the wrong direction, keeps you from resisting or stopping. You go on and on.

Ignorance is the result of Inertia. That which seems logical to the person who is ignorant of the facts or know-how may be illogical to the man who does know. When you make decisions because you refuse to keep an open mind and learn the truth—that is *ignorance*. And NMA keeps alive and grows fat on ignorance. Eliminate it! *Success Through a Positive Mental Attitude* indicates clearly *how* you can eliminate it.

The man with PMA may not know the facts or have the know-how. He may not understand. Yet he recognizes the basic premise that truth is truth and is not false regardless of his lack of knowledge or understanding. He therefore endeavors to keep an open mind and to learn. He must base his conclusions on what he does know, yet be prepared to change them when he becomes more enlightened.

Will you dare to clear the cobwebs from your thinking? If your answer is 'yes,' then let Pilot No. 3 guide you as you move forward into Chapter Four. You will be ready to see with an open mind. You will be ready to explore the powers of your mind. And when you do—your exploration will lead you to a great discovery. But only you can make it for yourself.

PILOT NO. 3
Thoughts to Steer By

1. You are what you think. Your thoughts are evaluated by whether your attitude is positive or negative. Take a look at yourself. Are you 1) a good person?... 2) evil?... 3) healthy?... 4) psychosomatically ill?... 5) wealthy?... 6) poor? If you are, then 1) you have good thoughts...your thoughts are evil... 3) your thoughts are of good health... 4) your thinking makes you so... 5) your thoughts are of riches... 6) your thoughts are of poverty.
2. Negative: feelings, emotions, passions—prejudices, beliefs, habits: you clear these mental cobwebs by turning your talisman from NMA to PMA.
3. You can clear the mental cobwebs of negative passions, emotions, feelings, tendencies, prejudices, beliefs and habits by flipping your invisible talisman from NMA to PMA. You will learn how as you respond to what you read in *Success Through a Positive Mental Attitude.*
4. When you are faced with a problem that involves a misunderstanding with other persons, you must first start with yourself.
5. One word can cause an argument, develop misunderstanding, generate unhappiness and end in misery. One word with PMA, when compared to the same word with NMA, brings opposite effects. One word can bring peace or war, yes or no, love or hate, integrity or dishonesty.
6. Let's start with a meeting of the minds. When Dr. Fosdick brought about a meeting of the minds, the young man himself concluded that he was not an atheist, he did believe in God.
7. Frog legs taught him logic. When you reason by inference,

be certain that your major and minor premises are correct.

8. Such all-inclusive, restrictive words as: always—only never—nothing—every—everyone—no one—can't—impossible should be eliminated as premises in reasoning until you are certain that they are correct.
9. *Necessity* is the word. Does *necessity* motivate you to high achievement through your personal honesty and integrity, or does necessity motivate you to try to get results through deception or dishonesty?
10. A teenage problem child: you may know one. But don't give up hope. He may not become a saint. But someday be may make his world and your world a better world to live in.
11. *Direct* your thoughts; *control* your emotions; and *ordain* your destiny! Memorize and repeat frequently the self-motivators quoted from *The Bible.*
12. Learn to separate 'facts' from fiction. Then learn the difference between important facts and un-important facts.

DIRECT YOUR THOUGHTS WITH
PMA TO CONTROL YOUR EMOTIONS
AND TO ORDAIN YOUR DESTINY

4

WILL YOU DARE TO EXPLORE THE POWERS OF YOUR MIND?

'You are a mind with a body!'

Because you are a mind, *you* possess mystical powers—powers known and unknown. Dare to explore the power of your mind! Why explore them?

When you make the discoveries that are awaiting you, they can bring you: (1) physical, mental and moral health, happiness, and wealth; (2) success in your chosen field of endeavor; and even (3) a means to affect, use, control, and harmonize with powers known and unknown.

And dare to investigate all non-physical forces lying outside the realm of known physical processes—forces which you can use when you learn how to apply them. And this will not be so difficult for you—no more difficult than turning on a television set for the first time.

For a little child can tune into his favorite television program. Now, when he does, he neither knows the construction of the broadcasting station or his receiving set nor the technology involved. But that's all right. For all the child needs to know is how to turn the right knob or push the right button.

You will see in this chapter how you can turn the right knob or push the right button to get what you want from the most effective electrical machine ever conceived. Although this particular machine is the sublime handiwork of Divine Power—you own it. How is it made? Well, among other things, it is comprised of over 80 trillion electrical cells. Naturally, it has many component parts. And each part is in itself an electrical mechanism.

And one part is an electrical marvel. Yet it weighs only fifty ounces. Its mechanism consists of over 10 billion cells, which generate, receive, record, and transmit energy.

What is this wonderful machine that you own? Your body. You are and will be the same *you* even though you lose an arm, an eye, or other parts of your body.

And the electrical marvel? *Your brain and your nervous system.* It is the mechanism through which your body is controlled *and through which your mind functions.*

And your mind: it, too, has parts. One is known as the conscious, and the other the subconscious. They synchronize. They work together. Scientists have learned a great deal about the conscious mind. Yet it has been less than a hundred years since we began to explore the vast unknown territory of the subconscious—even though primitive man has deliberately used the mystical powers of the subconscious from the beginning of man's history, and even today the Aborigines of Australia and other primitive peoples do so to a very great extent.

Let's start exploring now!

Day by day in every way, I'm getting richer and richer! Let's begin by accompanying Bill McCall of Sydney, Australia on a journey from failure and defeat to success and achievement.

It was at the age of 19 that Bill started a business of his own—hides and skins. He failed. At the age of 21, he ran for Federal Congress. And again, he failed. Now it seems that instead of crushing him, these and other defeats motivated this young Australian to develop inspirational dissatisfaction.

So he began searching for rules of success.

You see, Bill McCall wanted to become rich, and he thought he could find rules for acquiring wealth in inspirational books. Therefore, while checking the inspirational book section of the library, Bill became intrigued by the title *Think and Grow Rich*. He borrowed the book and began to read. He read it once, and then he read it again. And even though he read it the third time, Bill McCall was unable to understand exactly how he could apply the principles whereby some of the richest men in the world acquired their wealth. He told us:

'I was reading *Think and Grow Rich* for the fourth time while walking leisurely along a business street in Sydney. And then it happened! It happened suddenly. I stopped in front of a meat market window and glanced up. And in that very fraction of a second I had a flash of inspiration.' He smiled as he continued:

'I exclaimed aloud, 'That's it! I've got it!' I was startled at my emotional outburst. So was a lady who was passing by. She stopped and looked at me in amazement. I hurried home with my new discovery.' He continued seriously:

'You see, I was reading Chapter Four entitled *Autosuggestion*. The subheading was *The Medium for Influencing the Subconscious Mind.*

'Now I remember that when I was a boy my father read aloud from Emile Coués little book *Self-Mastery Through Conscious Autosuggestion*'. He then looked al Napoleon Hill and said:

'It was you who pointed out in your book that if Émile Coué was successful in helping individuals avoid sickness and in bringing the sick back to good health, through conscious autosuggestion, autosuggestion could also be used to acquire riches or anything else one might desire "Get rich through autosuggestion": that was my great discovery. It was a new concept to me.' McCall then described the principles. It almost seemed as if he had memorized them from the book itself.

'You know: conscious autosuggestion is the agency of control through which an individual may voluntarily feed his subconscious mind on thoughts of a creative nature, or, by neglect, permit thoughts of a destructive nature to find their way into the rich garden of his mind

'When you read aloud twice daily the written statement of your desire for money with emotion and concentrated attention, and you see and feel yourself already in possession of the money, you communicate the object of your desire directly to your subconscious mind. Through repetition of this procedure, you voluntarily create thought habits, which are favorable to your efforts to transmute desire into its monetary equivalent.

'Let me say again: It is most important that when you read aloud the statement of your desire through which you are endeavoring to develop a money consciousness, you read with emotion and strong feeling.

'Your ability to use the principles of autosuggestion will depend very largely upon your capacity to concentrate upon a given desire until that desire becomes a burning desire.

'When I arrived home, out of breath for running, I immediately sat down at the dining room table and wrote: "My definite major aim is to be a millionaire by 1960"'. Still looking at Napoleon Hill, be continued, 'You mentioned that a person should be specific as to the amount of money he wants and set a date. I did.'

Now, the man to whom we were talking was not the young Bill McCall who failed at the age of 19. He became known as the Honorable William V. McCall, the youngest man ever to become a member of the Australian Parliament; as the former chairman of the board of directors of the Coca-Cola subsidiary in Sydney; and as the director of 22 family-owned corporations. And as to riches—he became a millionaire, and quite as rich as some of the men he had read about in the book from which he got the inspiration to explore the power of his subconscious mind with self-suggestion, (Incidentally, he became a millionaire four years ahead of schedule!)

Day by day in every way, I am getting better and better! *You will note we use the word 'self-suggestion' as being synonymous with the term 'conscious autosuggestion' used by Emile Coue.*

McCall remembered that when he was a boy his father had benefited from a great discovery found in a book of his day—a discovery that every man, woman and child can effectively employ when he finds it for himself. Like Bill McCall and his father, you too can properly employ the power of conscious autosuggestion.

Now conscious autosuggestion was revealed to Emile Coue because he dared to explore the powers of his own mind and the minds of others. Before he made his great discovery, he used hypnosis to cure the physical illnesses of his patients. But after making his great discovery, which was in reality based on a simple natural law, he abandoned the use of hypnosis.

And how did he find and recognize this natural law?

Emile Coues great discovery was made when he found the answer to some questions he asked himself. They were:

> Question No. 1: Is it the suggestion of the doctor, or is it the suggestion in the mind of the patient, that effects a cure?
>
> Answer: Coue proved conclusively that it was the mind of the patient that subconsciously or consciously made the suggestion to which his own mind and body reacted.

> Without either (unconscious) autosuggestion or conscious autosuggestion, external suggestions are not effective.
>
> Question No. 2: If the suggestion of the doctor stimulates internal suggestion of the patient, why can't the patient use healthful, positive suggestions on himself? And why can't he refrain from harmful negative suggestions?

The answer to his second question came quickly: Anyone, even a child, can be taught to develop a positive mental attitude. The method is to repeat positive affirmations such as: *Day by day, in every way, through the grace of God, I am getting better and better.*

Throughout *Success Through a Positive Mental Attitude* you will see many self-motivators which you can use for your own self-suggestion. And if by now you don't know how to use self-suggestion, you will be after you complete this book.

When death's door is about to open. There are over 450,000 children born out of wedlock in the United States each year, and over a million and a half teenagers enter penal institutions for car thefts and other crimes. These personal tragedies could in many instances be avoided if: (a) the parents learned how to employ suggestion properly, and (b) if their sons and daughters were taught how effectively to use spiritual self-suggestion. Through the proper use of suggestion, these young people could be motivated to develop inviolable moral standards through their own conscious autosuggestion. And they would know how to neutralize or repel the undesirable suggestions of their associates in an intelligent manner.

Of course, every individual responds to *(unconscious)* autosuggestion throughout his life more often than he does to *conscious autosuggestion*. In such instances he responds to habit and the inner urge of the subconscious. When a man with PMA is faced with a serious personal problem, selfmotivators flash from the subconscious to the conscious to aid him. This is especially true in times of emergency—especially when death's door is about to be opened. Such was the case with Ralph Weppner of Toowoomba, Queensland, Australia, one of our PMA Science of Success course students.

It was 1:30 in the morning. In a small hospital bedroom two nursing sisters were keeping vigil beside Ralph's body. At 4:30 the afternoon before an emergency call had been made to his family to rush to the hospital. When they arrived at his bedside, Ralph was in a state of coma as the result of a severe heart attack. The family was now out in the corridor, each one worrying or praying in his own special way.

In the dimly lit bedroom two nursing sisters worked anxiously—one on each wrist—trying to feel a pulse beat. Because Ralph had not come out of the coma during this entire six hour period and the doctor had done all that he felt he could, the doctor had left the room. He had gone to visit one of his other hospital patients who was also in a critical condition.

Ralph couldn't move, talk, or feel anything. Yet he could hear the voices of the sisters. He could think quite clearly during portions of this period. He heard one sister excitedly state:

'He's not breathing! Can you pick up a beat?'

The answer was, 'No'.

Again and again he heard the question and answer: 'Can you now pick up a beat?' 'No'.

'I'm all right,' he thought, 'but I must tell them. Somehow I must tell them.'

At the same time he was amused at the sisters for being fooled like that. He kept thinking, 'I'm quite all right. I'm not going to die. But how—how—can I tell them?'

And then he remembered the self-motivator he had learned: *You can do it if you believe you can!*

He tried to open his eyes, but it seemed the more he tried, the more he failed. His eyelids wouldn't respond to the command of his will. He tried to move his arm, his leg, his head—but he couldn't feel any reaction at all. In fact, he didn't feel a thing. Again and again he tried to open his eyes, until at last he heard the words: 'I saw one eyelid flicker—he's still there.'

'I felt no fear,' Ralph says, 'and still thought how amusing it was. Periodically one sister called to me, "Are you there, Mr. Weppner? Are you there?" To which I would try to respond by moving my eyelid to tell them that I was all right —I was still there.'

This went on for a considerable time until through constant effort Ralph was at last able to open one, then both, eyes. It was then that his doctor returned. With wonderful skill and persistence the doctor and nurses brought him back to life.

Hidden persuaders. But it was the autosuggestion: *You can do it if you believe you can*—that he had memorized from the PMA Science of Success course—that helped to rescue him when he was at death's door.

Now the books we read and the thoughts we think affect our subconscious minds. But there are also unseen forces that likewise have powerful effects even though they are subliminal—below the realm of consciousness.

These unseen forces can be from known physical causes or from unknown sources. Before discussing the unknown, let's illustrate with an example that is now common knowledge since the publishing of *Hidden Persuaders* by Vance Packard. The story first appeared in American newspapers and later was picked up in magazines. Let's consider a report that appeared in a leading national magazine on the subject of subliminal advertising. The report tells of an experiment conducted in a New Jersey movie theater, in which advertising messages were flashed on the screen so fast that the viewers were not consciously aware of them.

During a period of six weeks, more than forty thousand persons unknowingly became subjects of this test, while attending the theater. Flashed on the screen by a special process that made them invisible to the naked eye were two advertising messages concerning products that were available in the theater lobby. At the end of the six weeks, results were tabulated: sales of one of the products had soared over 50 per cent, while sales of the other product rose almost 20 per cent.

The inventor of the process explained that, although the messages were invisible, they still had taken effect on many in the audience because of the ability of the subconscious mind to absorb impressions that are too fleeting to be registered consciously.

When this story appeared in the press, the public was horrified 'by this attempt to channel our thinking habits, our purchasing decisions, and our thought processes' by the use of subliminal suggestion. People were afraid. They feared brainwashing in its most subtle form. Yet it is amazing to us that someone didn't take the PMA approach. Subliminal suggestion can be employed for desirable objectives, too. Everyone knows that power can be used for evil or for good, depending upon how it is directed.

Now that the experiment has proved its purpose, it doesn't take much imagination to see what the beneficial results to the viewers would, be should the following selfmotivators be flashed on a movie screen:

> God is always a good God!
>
> Day by day, in every way, through the grace of God, you are getting better and better!

Have the courage to face the truth!

What the mind of man can conceive and believe, the mind of man can achieve with PMA!

Every adversity has the seed of an equivalent or greater benefit for those who have positive mental attitude!

You can do it if you believe you can!

This would be a PMA approach, provided, of course, the consent of the audience was obtained in advance.

Another illustration of a known physical force affecting the subconscious mind can be shown by the effect of radar on navigators.

Why did the SS *Andrea Doria* and the SS *Valchem* sink? When the *Andrea Doria*, captained by Pierre Clamai, and the *Stockholm*, under Captain H. G. Nordenson, collided approximately 50 miles off Nantucket Island, 50 persons died. The *Andrea Doria* was sighted by the radar operator of the Stockholm when they were 10 miles apart.

The Grace Line luxury liner, the *Santa Rosa* under Captain Frank S. Siwik, collided with the tanker *Valchem* on March 26, 1959, 22 miles off the New Jersey coast. Four crewmen were killed. Second Mate Walter Wells, the radar operator on the *Santa Rosa*, claimed he had made two plottings of the tanker *Valchem*'s course.

No satisfactory explanation of the true cause of these collisions has resulted from the investigations in either of these instances. Could the waves from the radar instruments have been the real cause? Perhaps Sidney A. Schneider has the answer.

As a young teenager, Sidney A. Schneider of Skokie, Illinois, became interested in hypnotism when he observed his older brother, a university student, successfully place his first subject under hypnosis. Sidney became an expert hypnotist. During his business career he became a radio operator and an engineer in electronics.

In the Second World War Sidney Schneider was a vital part of the system known as 'I. F. F.' —Information, Friend or Foe. His job was to see to it that every ship leaving our country was equipped with radar. He noticed that radar operators sometimes went into a trance. *They weren't aware that they had been in a trance when they came out of it.*

Because of his knowledge of hypnosis and electronics, Schneider concluded that the fixed attention of the naval employees took place when the waves from the radar machine were synchronized with the brain waves of the operator. On this theory he changed the waves on the radar instrument and eliminated the recurrence of the trances.

Sidney Schneider told us that he converted his conclusions regarding the principle that placed the seamen operating radar in a trance into the Brain Wave Synchronizer, a machine which he invented after the war.

What is the Brain Wave Synchronizer?

It is an electronic instrument designed to induce various levels of hypnosis by subliminal and photic (light) stimulation of the brain waves. The instrument can be used alone or combined with a tape recording of the therapist's verbal suggestions. No physical connections or attachments are placed on the patient. Results are obtained at any distance in which the light in the machine is visible. The apparatus induces light to deep hypnotic levels in over 90 per cent of the subjects in an average time of three minutes.

In an experiment with the Brain Wave Synchronizer, none of the persons involved was informed about the machine or what it could do. Neither were they told that they were subjects of an experiment. Yet 30 per cent of them were hypnotized to various degrees, ranging from light to deep states.

'Why and how does the Brain Wave Synchronizer work?' we asked.

'It is like a television transmitter,' Schneider said. 'The human brain produces pulses (waves) of electricity in several frequency ranges. This knowledge has been applied in the field of medicine since 1929 and the invention of the electroencephalograph commonly known as the EEG machine, an apparatus for recording brain waves.'

'My machine operates much like a television system,' Schneider continued. 'The reason the picture on your receiving set does not drift up or down is that the pulses generated within the set synchronize with corresponding pulses generated by the transmitting television station. The receiver is *forced to operate* at a rate controlled by the transmitter and *the picture must obey*.'

'Like the transmitter of a television station, the Brain Wave Synchronizer also produces synchronizing pulses. And through photic stimulation, the waves sent from the synchronizer cause the frequency of the brain waves also to *lock in step*. At this point hypnosis can be achieved. Just compare your brain to a receiving set, and the Brain Wave Synchronizer to a television transmitter.'

And you will see as you continue to read that in addition to comparing your brain to a receiving set, you can compare it to a television transmitter also.

A little knowledge becomes a dangerous thing. We have just explored some of the unseen forces from known physical causes. Now let's proceed further into the realm of the unknown: the thrilling field of psychic phenomena, such as:

1. ESP (extrasensory perception)—awareness of or response to an external event or influence not

apprehended by sensory means. Here are included:
(a) Telepathy—thought transference
(b) Clairvoyance—the power of discerning objects not present to the senses
(c) Precognition—seeing into the future
(d) Postcognition— seeing into the past
2. Psychokinesis— the effect of the mind on an object.

Now let's be realistic and keep our feet firmly on the ground. Let's explore the unknown with common sense! You'll be in danger unless you use good logic and avoid the gathering of cobwebs in your thinking. Facts should be your stepping stones over the river of doubt. Therefore, let an experienced guide direct you along safe paths. And we will introduce you to such a guide. But before we do, let's talk about the past.

Thomas J. Hudson's famous book, *The Law of Psychic Phenomena*, when published in 1893, became a best seller. (The book is published today in paperback by the Hudson-Cohen Publishing Company, Monterey, California.) It contained many thrilling stories of reported psychic experiences. The imaginations of tens of thousands of people who read this book were stimulated. Some were ready. Some were not.

From then on public interest in psychic phenomena made rapid progress. But many persons, not properly prepared, injured themselves by becoming crackpots. This was due to the awesomeness and magnetic interest a little knowledge of psychic powers generated within them. There is a noticeable tendency of some persons who are not properly educated and mature in their thinking and not very well adjusted emotionally to become fascinated with this intriguing study. It is easy to understand why so many religious leaders, scientists, and persons responsible for the welfare of the people found the study of psychic phenomena an anathema:

1. Imaginations ran rampant and threatened the sanity of the people.
2. Fact and fiction seemed to be indistinguishable.
3. Hypnotism by amateurs and vaudeville entertainers, as well as the trickery and frauds practiced by fakirs, mediums, and charlatans abused the minds of the public.
4. Basic religious principles were twisted in a direction that led to evil.

Anything associated with psychic phenomena became repellent. It was taboo.

In spite of the dangers, taboos, and social or professional ostracism, there were courageous, honorable men with good common sense who had the courage to explore for the truth.

But it remained for the long, courageous fight of Dr. Joseph Banks Rhine, formerly of Duke University, inspired and assisted by his wife Dr. Louisa E. Rhine, to clothe the study of psychic phenomena with respectability. This is due to the impeccable character of Dr. Rhine and to his 30 years of controlled laboratory experiments based on mathematical laws. His task was a difficult one because spontaneous psychic phenomena are not apt to occur in a laboratory. Such phenomena occur when least expected, and most often when a person is under the greatest emotional strain, or possessed of an intensified obsessional desire—often simultaneously with the death of a loved one.

Westinghouse invests in ESP communication. It is apparent that any writer on the subject of psychic phenomena today endeavors to have the protection of a part of the cloak of Dr. Rhine's respectability by referring to Dr. Rhine and Duke

University to make his own theories digestible. We are no exception. We urgently suggest that if you are interested further, you read *The Reach of the Mind* and the other books of which Dr. Rhine is the author or co-author. Our recommendation: Let Dr. Joseph Banks Rhine be your guide.

And how successful has Dr Rhine's work been in breaking down the resistance to investigation and belief in these strange mindpowers? A fair test, it would seem to us, lies in the fact that hard-headed businessmen are convinced and are making experiments of their own: In an interview, Dr. Peter A. Castruccio, Director of the Westinghouse Astronautics Institute, confirmed that Westinghouse scientists are engaged in research to find a means of using telepathy and clairvoyance for long distance communication. Dr. Castruccio too had many lengthy visits with Dr. Rhine before a decision was reached to engage in this great experiment.

And will the search for ways and means to harness telepathy and clairvoyance and make them commercially feasible be successful? Let us answer this as follows: Not too long ago people were scoffing at ideas that were unbelievable to them then but are taken for granted *today*: (a) matter being turned into energy and energy into matter; (b) the breaking of the atom; (c) man-made satellites; (d) jet power; or (e) everyday necessities like television, for example.

And what about the electronic computer that was designed from the human computer: the human brain and the nervous system. Every one was conceived, believed and achieved by men with PMA! Machines that operate with the speed of light—186,300 miles per second! Machines that can calculate 40,000 arithmetical operations per second and detect and correct their own errors!

Machines that became a reality because man built into

them electrical circuits which in many respects function like the known electrical activity of the nervous system of your own physical body. Our answer:

What the mind of man can conceive and believe, the mind of man can achieve with PMA!

But no machine or manmade invention is as marvelous as the wonderful human computer you own: your brain and your nervous system, with their power of electrical activity.

Man is more than a body with a brain.

You are a mind with a body—a mind, possessing, and also affected by, powers known and unknown! A mind composed of two parts: the conscious and the subconscious.

Here we have stressed most the concept of the subconscious mind—its powers and the forces known and unknown that affect it. But what about the conscious mind? That is equally important. And you will read about it in the next chapter entitled... *And Something More!*

Now, if your reaction to what you have read has not given you an insight on how you can turn the right knob or push the right button to get what you want from the machine you own, dare to explore the powers of your mind. Be guided by Pilot No 4... *And Something More!*

PILOT NO. 4
Thoughts to Steer By

1. *You are a mind with a body.* Your body is an electrical machine. Your brain is a mechanism that is an electrical marvel.
2. Your mind has two parts: the conscious and the subconscious. They work together.
3. *Conscious autosuggestion* and *self-suggestion* are synonymous, and are contrasted with the word *autosuggestion*, an unconscious activity. Autosuggestion automatically sends messages from the subconscious to the conscious mind as well as to parts of the body. The subconscious mind is the seat of habit, memory, inviolable standards of conduct, etc.
4. *Day by day in every respect I am getting better and better.* Self-affirmations repeated with frequency, rapidity, and emotion affect the subconscious mind and cause it to react. Bill McCall acquired wealth through the use of self-suggestion.
5. Coue's great discovery was: you can use healthful, positive suggestions to help yourself. And you can also refrain from negative, harmful suggestions.
6. Learn to use the proper suggestion in influencing others. Learn to employ the right conscious autosuggestions. When you do, you can have: physical, mental and moral health, happiness and success.
7. *Yow can do it if you have PMA and believe you can.*
8. Hidden persuaders: Take the PMA approach.
9. Your brain sends out energy in the form of brain waves. And this energy is power which can affect another person or an object.
10. A little knowledge may be a dangerous thing. Dare to explore the powers of your mind. When you enter the

dangerous, unexplored territory of psychic phenomena, let Dr. Joseph Banks Rhine be your guide.

DAY BY DAY IN EVERY WAY THROUGH
THE GRACE OF GOD I AM GETTING
BETTER AND BETTER THROUGH PMA

5

... AND SOMETHING MORE

Have you sincerely tried—and still failed?

Perhaps you failed because there was *something more* that was needed to bring you the success you were seeking. Euclid's axiom says: 'The whole is equal to the sum of all the parts and is greater than any of its parts.' This can be related, assimilated, and applied to every result or achievement. Conversely, any part is smaller than the whole. Therefore, it's important that you add all the necessary parts to complete the whole.

A negative mental attitude is one of the primary causes failure. You may be needlessly ignorant of facts, universal laws, and powers. You may know many of them but fail to apply them to a specific need. You may not know how you can affect, use, control, or harmonize with powers known and unknown.

When you seek success with PMA, you keep trying. You keep searching to find *something more.* Failure is experienced by those who, when they experience defeat, stop trying to find the *something more.*

It's easy when you learn the *something more* and experience the know-how! Give a puzzle to a child, and he may not solve it. If he keeps trying and learns how to solve it, he can then work it quickly. You aren't a child.

But perhaps there are several of life's puzzles you would like to solve. You can solve them more easily with PMA. For example, there once was a song writer who wrote a song but couldn't get it published. George M. Cohan bought it and added *something more*. The *something more* made George M. Cohan a fortune. He merely added three little words: *Hip, Hip, Hooray!*

Thomas Edison tried more than ten thousand experiments before he developed a successful incandescent lamp. But after each defeat he kept searching for *something more* until he found what he was looking for. When the unknown became known to him, innumerable electric light bulbs could be manufactured. It was necessary only to apply the universal laws that had always existed but which had not been previously recognized as applicable for the specific invention.

There are many cures and preventatives for diseases. But at a given time they may be unknown. The medical preventative for polio was unknown until Dr. Jonas Edward Salk used principles of universal law that were previously not applied by the medical profession for the prevention of this dreaded disease.

You may make a million dollars by employing a success formula. If you lose your money, you can make another million—and even more! That is, provided you know the formula and apply it. Suppose you didn't recognize the formula that helped you make your first million. You may fail in your second attempt because you deviate from the principles of success that are applicable. On your second attempt, you may need to make adjustments for changing conditions. But the principles will remain the same.

Orville and Wilbur Wright succeeded in flying because they added something more! Many inventors came exceedingly close to inventing the airplane before the Wright brothers. The Wright brothers used the same principles that were employed by the others. But they added—*something more*. They created a new combination. So they succeeded where all others failed.

The *something more* was rather simple. They attached movable flaps of a particular design to the edges of the wings so the pilot could control them and maintain the plane's equilibrium. These flaps were the forerunners of the modem aileron.

You'll notice there's a common denominator to all these success stories. In each case, the secret ingredient was the application of a previously unapplied universal law. That made the difference. So, if you are standing on the threshold of success without being able to pass over, try adding *something more*. It needn't be much. The words '*Hip, Hip, Hooray!*' were all it took to make a hit tune. Tiny flaps were all it took to make an airplane failed. It isn't necessarily the quantity of *something more*, but the 'inspired quality' that counts.

Why did the Supreme Court decide that Alexander Graham Bell invented the telephone? Many persons claimed to have invented the telephone before Alexander Graham Bell. Among those who held prior patents were Gray, Edison, Dolbear, McDonough, Vanderweyde, and Reis. Philipp Reis was the only one who apparently came close to success. The little difference that made the big difference was a single screw. Reis didn't know that it he had turned one screw one quarter of a turn, he would have transformed interrupted current into continuous current. Then he would have been successful!

In a United States Supreme Court case, the court noted:

> That Reis knew what had to be done in order to transmit speech by electricity is very apparent, for in his first paper he said: 'As soon as it is possible to produce, anywhere and in any manner, vibrations whose curves shall be the same as those of any given tone or combination of tones, we shall receive the same impression as that tone or combination of tones would have produced on us.'

The Court further noted:

> Reis discovered how to reproduce musical tones, but he did no more. He could sing through his apparatus, but he could not talk. From the beginning to the end he has conceded this.

As in the case of the Wright brothers, the *something more* Bell added was comparatively simple. He switched from an intermittent to a continuous current, the only type capable of reproducing human speech. The two currents are exactly the same direct current. 'Intermittent' means breaking with a slight pause. Specifically, Bell kept the circuit open instead of breaking the circuit intermittently as Reis had done. The Court concluded:

> Reis never thought of it, and he failed to transmit speech telegraphically. Bell did, and he succeeded. Under such circumstances it is impossible to hold that what Reis did was an anticipation of the discovery of Bell. To follow Reis is to fail, but to follow Bell is to succeed. The difference between the two is just the difference between failure and success. If Reis had kept on he might have found out the way to succeed, but he stopped and failed. Bell took up his work and carried it on to a successful result.

His silent senior partner inspired him to success. R. G. LeToumeau, builder of heavy earth-moving equipment, motivated thousands of persons with his inspirational speeches. In these talks, he referred reverently to 'my Senior Partner'. He told about the inspiration and help he received from the 'Partner'. LeToumeau had little formal education. But he performed feats of engineering that are astounding.

As a sub-contractor on the great Hoover Dam in Nevada, LeToumeau lost a fortune because he ran into an unexpected strata of rock. The cost of drilling through the rock was more than he had calculated in estimating his contract. So he went broke trying to fulfill his end of the bargain.

But instead of brooding over his loss, LeToumeau turned to prayer. How did he pray? By expressing gratitude— profound gratitude—for what he had left: A sound body. A strong pair of hands. A brain that could think. And *something more.*'In my hour of greatest distress,' said LeToumeau, 'I found my greatest asset in the revelation and discovery of a silent Senior Partner. I have since recognized this Partner in my personal and business life. Everything I have—everything I have done that has been worthwhile—I owe to Him.'

Napoleon Hill was associated with Mr. LeToumeau for eighteen months and had an opportunity to observe him closely. By this time LeToumeau had become a well- known inspirational lecturer. He devoted much of his time to traveling around the country in his private plane, preaching his message: 'It's wonderful to be in partnership with God.' One night when the two men were flying home from a speaking engagement in North Carolina, something interesting happened.

Soon after his pilot took off, Mr. LeToumeau went to sleep. In about thirty minutes Napoleon Hill saw him take in it. After the plane landed, Napoleon Hill asked Mr. LeToumeau if he remembered writing in his notebook.

'Why no!' exclaimed LeToumeau. He immediately pulled the notebook from his pocket and looked at it. He said: 'Here it is! I've been looking for this for several months! Here's the answer to a problem that has kept me from completing a machine we are working on!'

When you receive a flash of inspiration, write it down! This may be the *something more* that you are looking for. We believe that communication with Infinite Intelligence is through the subconscious mind. We believe you should establish the habit of immediately writing down flashes of inspiration as they are communicated to you from the subconscious to the conscious.

Albert Einstein developed intricate and profound theories regarding the universe and the natural laws that control it. Yet he used only the simplest—but most important—of instruments ever invented: a pencil and a piece of paper. He wrote down his questions and answers. You will develop your mental powers when you learn and develop the habit of asking yourself questions—when you learn and develop the habit of using pencil and paper to write down your questions, ideas, and answers.

It is unlikely that Einstein and other scientists would have come to their successful conclusions unless they had learned from the recorded knowledge of mathematicians and scientists who preceded them. It is also unlikely that Einstein would have tried unless he had been motivated to search for universal principles after having developed the habit of engaging in thinking time and action. Do you know of any great thinker, or person of achievement, who does not make notes of ideas that occur to him?

Learn creative thinking from the creative thinker! *Your Creative Power and Applied Imagination* by Alex F. Osborn, of the advertising firm of Batten, Barton, Durstine and Osborn, have inspired hundreds of thousands of persons to engage in creative thinking. What is equally important, these people have been motivated to positive, constructive action. Thinking is not creative unless it is followed through with action.

Osborn, like so many creative thinkers, used a notepad and a pencil as favorite working tools. When an idea occurred, he jotted it down. He, like other great men of accomplishment, engaged in thinking, planning, and study time.

Alex Osborn stated an obvious truth when he said: 'Everyone has some creative ability, but most people haven't learned to use it.'

Osbon's brainstorming methods, explained in his easily-read textbook *Applied Imagination*, are being employed in college classrooms, factories, business offices, churches, clubs, and in the home. Brainstorming, as developed by Osborn, is a very simple method whereby two or more persons use their collective imaginations to come up with ideas that flash from their subconscious to their conscious minds in answer to a question incorporating a specific problem. The ideas are written down just as fast as they strike the minds of the participants. No critical judgment is permitted until after many ideas are written down. Later the ideas are screened and judged to determine their practicality and value.

La Salle College in Philadelphia, and many universities throughout the country, teach well-rounded courses in creative thinking which include the methods used by creative thinkers in many phases of business and industry.

It was just such creative thinking that enabled Dr. Elmer Gates to make this world a better place in which to live. Dr. Gates was a great American teacher, philosopher, psychologist, scientist, and inventor. During his lifetime, he developed hundreds of inventions and discoveries in the various arts and sciences.

He did his creative thinking by 'sitting for ideas'. Dr. Gates' own life proved that his methods of brain and body building could develop a healthy body and increase the efficiency of the mind. Napoleon Hill recalls how, armed with a letter of introduction from Andrew Carnegie, he went to visit Dr. Gates at his Chevy Chase laboratory. When Napoleon Hill arrived, Dr. Gates' secretary told him: 'I'm sorry, but... I'm not permitted to disturb Dr. Gates at this time.'

'How long do you think it will be before I can see him?' Napoleon Hill asked.

'I don't know, but it might take as long as three hours.'

'Do you mind telling me why you are unable to disturb him?'

She hesitated and then responded, '*He is sitting for ideas?*'

Napoleon Hill smiled. 'What does that mean—sitting for ideas?'

She returned the smile and said, 'Maybe we'd better let Dr. Gates explain. I really don't know how long it will take, but you're welcome to wait. If you prefer to come again, I'll see if I can make a definite appointment for you.'

Mr. Hill decided to wait. It was a valuable decision. What he learned was well worth waiting for. This is how Napoleon Hill tells what happened:

> When Dr. Gates finally came into the room and his secretary introduced us, I jokingly told him what his secretary had said. After he read the letter of introduction from Andrew Carnegie, he responded pleasantly, 'Would you be interested in seeing where I sit for ideas and how I go about it?'
>
> He led me to a small, soundproof room. The only furniture in the room consisted of a plain table and a chair. On the table were pads of paper, several pencils, and a push-button to turn the lights off and on.
>
> In our interview Dr. Gates explained that when he was unable to obtain an answer to a problem, he went into the room, closed the door, sat down, turned off the

lights, and engaged in deep concentration. He applied the success principle of controlled attention, asking his subconscious mind to give him an answer to his specific problem, whatever it might be. On some occasions ideas didn't seem to come through. At other times they would immediately flow into his mind. And in some instances it would take as long as two hours before they made an appearance. As soon as ideas began to crystalize, he would turn on the lights and begin to write.

Dr. Elmer Gates refined and perfected more than two hundred patents which other inventors had undertaken but which had fallen just short of success. He was able to add the missing ingredients— the *something more.* His method was to begin by examining the application for the patent and its drawings until he found its weakness, the *something more* that was lacking. He would bring a copy of the patient application and drawings into the room. While sitting for ideas, he would concentrate on finding the solution to a specific problem.

When Napoleon Hill asked Dr. Gates to explain the source of his results while *sitting for ideas*, he gave the following explanation: 'The sources of all ideas are:

1. Knowledge stored in the subconscious mind and acquired through individual experience, observation, and education.
2. Knowledge accumulated by others through the same media, which may be communicated by telepathy.
3. The great universal storehouse of Infinite Intelligence, wherein is stored all knowledge and all facts, and which may be contacted through the subconscious section of the mind.

'When I sit for ideas, I may tune in to one or all of these sources. If other sources of ideas are available, I do not know what they are.'

Dr. Elmer Gates found the time to concentrate and think in his search for *something more.* He knew specifically what he was looking for. And he followed through with positive action!

In Chapter Seven, we will discuss how you can *'Learn To See'* so that your search for *something more* will be made easier. In your search, you may fail. But in failing you may succeed in discovering something even greater. Ask yourself, 'Why?' Be observant. Think! Get into action!

The Bible and both a good, comprehensive dictionary and an encyclopedia should, we believe, be in every home. They also can help in your search for *something more.*

YOU DON'T NEED TO BE ASHAMED TO BE A FAILURE LIKE CHRISTOPHER COLUMBUS!

Look in your *Encyclopaedia Britannica* and you'll find the thrilling, exciting story of Christopher Columbus. He studied astronomy, geometry, and cosmography at the University of Pavia. *The Book of Marco Polo*, theories of geographers, reports and traditions of mariners, as well as floating works of art and craftsmanship of non-European origin cast up by the sea—all these stimulated his imagination.

Step by step over the years he came to the firm belief, through inductive reasoning, that the world was a sphere. Having reached this conclusion, he was convinced through deductive reasoning, that the Asiatic continent could be reached by sailing westward from Spain just as well as Marco Polo had reached it by traveling east. He developed a burning desire to prove his theory. He sought the necessary financial backing, ships, and men to explore the unknown *and find something more.*

He got into action! He kept his mind on his objective. Over a period of ten years he was often on the verge of receiving the necessary help. But the deception of a king... the ridicule, suspicion, and fear of subordinate government officials... the disbelief of those who wanted to help him but who at the last moment refused because of the skepticism of their scientific advisors... all brought defeat after defeat. *He kept trying.*

In 1492 he received the help for which he had so persistently searched and prayed! In August of that year he sailed westward for India, China, and Japan. He was on the right course and headed in the right direction.

You know the story. After he landed on the islands in the Caribbean, he returned to Spain with gold, cotton, Parrots, curious arms, mysterious plants, unknown birds and beasts, and several natives. He thought he had achieved his objective and had reached the islands off India. He had failed. He had not reached Asia. But, without being aware of it immediately, Columbus had found *something more*! Quite a bit more!

You, like Christopher Columbus, may fail to reach your major objectives, or your magnificent obsessions. You, like him, may fail in your efforts to reach a destination in the realm of the unknown. But you may discover *something more*—something equaling the wealth of the Americas. You, like him, may inspire and direct those who follow you to head in the right direction, on the right course, and to continue further into the unknown until they achieve the worthwhile objectives you conceived. You, like Columbus, have the time and the power to think. You, like him, can persistently strive with a positive mental attitude to achieve your definite major aims to find *something more.*

You don't need to be ashamed to be a failure like Christopher Columbus.

...And something more! How can you apply it? By now you should be in a position to extract principles from specific illustrations so that you can relate, assimilate, and use them. We agree with Admiral H. G. Rickover in the fundamental truths of his statement:

> Among the young engineers we interview we find few who have received thorough training in engineering fundamentals or principles; but most have absorbed quantities of facts. . . much easier to learn than principles but of little use without application of principles. Once a principle has been acquired it becomes a part of one and is never lost. It can be applied to novel problems and does not become obsolete as do all facts in a changing society.

Learn the principles. Apply them. If you're not making satisfactory progress toward achieving your aims, look for the *something more*! It may be known or unknown. But you'll find it, if you take the necessary time to study, think, plan, and search for it.

Now this chapter would not be complete without reference to *Cosmic Habit Force. Use cosmic habit force* is one of the 17 success principles.

And the concept of cosmic habit force is easy to understand. For it is a name that we have given to *applied power* of any natural, or universal, principle or law, known or unknown.

Cosmic habit force can be simply defined as: the use of universal law, whether it is known or unknown to you.

As an example, it's easy to understand that when an object falls to the ground, the law of gravity is being applied. And, therefore, if you want an object to fall from a given height, you use cosmic habit force. And in this particular instance— the law of gravity.

But *the law of gravity, or any other law, is not in itself a power.* Yet when you properly use the principle, then power is employed according to universal law.

And thus: the breaking of the atom, every invention, every chemical formula, every psychic phenomenon, every individual action and reaction—be it physical, mental, or spiritual —is the result of the use of natural law. For every result there is a cause. And the result is brought about through the use of cosmic habit force.

Again, *man is a mind with a body.* And he can think. It is through thinking that he learns how to use cosmic habit force. And his thinking can bring the thoughts he thinks into reality.

This concept is not difficult to comprehend, for in 1905 Albert Einstein gave to the world his now famous formula: **$E=mc^2$.** This formula explains the relationship between energy and matter. When matter approaches the speed of light, we call it energy, and as the velocity slows down to zero, it remains matter. In the formula: E is energy, m is mass or matter, and c represents the velocity of light.

And thus we see that Einstein's formula is a word symbol of one of the laws of cosmic habit force. And by understanding and applying this formula man has been able to turn matter into energy and energy into matter, and to use atomic power for constructive purposes such as: to light an entire city, to power ships, or even for such everyday affairs as to develop heat for cooking.

... And something more—we can now see that because matter and energy are the same thing, everything in the universe is related.

Now 'You've Got a Problem? That's Good!' And you'll learn in the next chapter how to adapt many of the lessons learned in this chapter to your own life. And then you will be able successfully to meet the problems created by the universal law of change, which—like all natural law—is the result of cosmic habit force.

PILOT NO. 5
Thoughts to Steer By

1. ... *And something more.* What does the important principle contained in this chapter mean to you and how can you apply it?
2. If you have failed in an endeavor, could it be because you lack *something more*—a missing number for a correct, winning combination for success?
3. The whole is equal to the sum of all the parts and is greater than any of its parts. Are any missing parts keeping you from success?
4. The little difference between success and failure is often *something more*: Hip, Hip, Hooray! A movable wing flap. A quarter- turn of a screw.
5. Are you in partnership with your silent Senior Partner?
6. Use the simplest, but most important, of instruments ever invented—paper and pencil—to write down flashes of inspiration when they occur.
7. How does the technique of brainstorming differ from that of 'sitting for ideas'? What is the value of each?
8. Use the success principle of *Controlled Attention.*
9. Don't be afraid to be a failure like Christopher Columbus.
10. Have you established the habit of learning fundamental principles, or do you merely absorb quantities of facts?
11. Do you understand and can you apply in your own experience the fundamental truths and principles of Admiral H. G. Rickover's statement?

Among the young engineers we interview we find few who have received thorough training in engineering fundamentals or principles; but most have absorbed quantities of facts. . .

much easier to learn than principles but of little use without application of principles. *Once a principle has been acquired it becomes a part of one and is never lost.* It can be applied to novel problems and does not become obsolete as do all facts in a changing society.

YOU DON'T NEED TO BE ASHAMED TO BE A FAILURE LIKE CHRISTOPHER COLUMBUS

PART II

FIVE MENTAL BORNBSHELLS FOR ATTACKING SUCCESS

6

YOU'VE GOT A PROBLEM? THAT'S GOOD!

So you've got a problem? That's good! Why? Because repeated victories over your problems are the rungs on your ladder of success. With each victory you grow in wisdom, stature, and experience. You become a better, bigger, more successful person each time you meet a problem and tackle and conquer it with PMA.

Stop and think about it for a moment. Do you know of a single instance where any real achievement was made in your life, or in the life of any person in history, that was not due to a problem with which the individual was faced?

Everyone has problems. This is because you and everything in the universe are in a constant process of change. Change is an inexorable natural law. What is important to you is that your success or failure to meet the challenges of change are dependent upon your mental attitude.

You can direct your thoughts and control your emotions, and thus regulate your attitude. You can choose whether your attitude will be positive or negative. You can decide whether you will affect, use, control, or harmonize with the changes in yourself and your environment. You can ordain your destiny. When you meet the challenges of change with PMA, you can intelligently solve each problem with which you are confronted.

How do you meet a problem with PMA? If you know and believe the first principal element of a positive mental attitude: *God is always a good God*—then you can effectively use the following formula and meet your problems:

When you are faced with a problem that needs a solution, regardless of how perplexing it may be:

1. Ask for Divine Guidance. Ask for help in finding the right solution.
2. Engage in thinking time for the purpose of solving your problems. Remember that every adversity has the seed of an equivalent or greater benefit for those who have PMA.
3. State the problem. Analyze and define it.
4. State to *yourself* enthusiastically: 'That's good!'
5. Ask yourself some specific questions, such as:
   (a) What's good about it?
   (b) How can I turn this adversity into a seed of equivalent or greater benefit; or how can I turn this liability into a greater asset?
6. Keep searching for answers to these questions until you find at least one answer that *can work*.

Now the problems that will confront you will, broadly speaking, be of three kinds: personal problems—emotional, financial, mental, moral, physical; family problems; and business or professional problems. Because personal problems are the most immediate problems experienced by all of us, we would like to tell you the story of a man who met some of the most severe problems a human being can experience. As you read this story, see how he applied PMA to the solution of each difficulty until he achieved ultimate victory.

He met his challenge to change with PMA at Leavenworth

Penitentiary. This man was born in poverty. While in grade school, he sold newspapers and sinned shoes in and around the saloons on Seattle's waterfront to help his mother meet expenses. Later he became a cabin boy on an Alaskan freighter during the summer months. After he finished high school at the age of seventeen, he left home.

He became one of the horde of hobos that rode the rails and traveled to every part of the United States.

His companions were hard-bitten men. He gambled, associated with riffraff—men of the so-called 'Border Legion'. Soldiers of fortune, fugitives, smugglers, cattle thieves, and the like were his companions. He joined the forces of Pancho Villa in Mexico. 'You can't skate close to those extra-legal operations without knowing about them, even if you have nothing to do with them,' Charlie Ward said. 'My mistake was being with the wrong companions. My major sin was associating with people who were bad.'

From time to time he won large sums gambling, and then lost them. Finally he was arrested for narcotics smuggling. He was tried and convicted. Yet throughout his life Charlie Ward maintained his innocence of the charge on which he was convicted.

Charlie Ward was thirty-four years old when he entered Leavenworth. He had never been in jail before in spite of his associates. And he was embittered. He vowed that no prison was strong enough to hold him. He looked for a chance to make a break.

Then something happened! Charlie chose to change his attitude from negative to positive. He met the challenge to change with PMA. Something within him told him to stop being hostile and to become the best prisoner in the prison. From that very moment the entire tide of his life began to flow in the direction most favorable for him. By the simple *change from negative to positive thinking,* Charlie Ward began to master himself.

He changed the direction of his aggressive personality. He forgave the federal agents who had brought about his plight. He quit hating the judge who sentenced him.

He took a real good look at the Charlie Ward of the past. And he resolved to avoid the very appearance of evil in the future. He looked around for ways to make his stay in prison as pleasant as possible.

First, he asked himself some questions. And for the first time in his adult life he found his answer in books, particularly *The Bible.* In his prison cell he began to read *The Bible.* He read it and reread it. Thereafter, and up to the date of his death at the age of seventy-three, he read *The Bible* every day for inspiration, guidance and help.

Because of his change in attitude, and consequently in behavior, he began to attract favorable notice from the prison officials. And one day a convict clerk told him that a trusty in the power plant was to be released in three months. Charlie Ward knew little about electricity, but there were books on electricity in the prison library. So he studied. He learned what these books could teach him.

At the end of three months, Charlie was ready. He applied for the job. Something about his mannerism and his tone of voice impressed the deputy warden. That *something* was the earnestness and sincerity of Charlie Ward's positive mental attitude. He got the job!

Because he continued to study and work with PMA, Charlie Ward became superintendent of the prison power plant with one hundred and fifty men under him. He tried to inspire each one of them to make the best of his situation.

When Herbert Hughes Bigelow, president of Brown & Bigelow of St. Paul, Minnesota, arrived at Leavenworth on a conviction of income tax evasion, Charlie Ward also befriended him. In fact, he went out of his way to motivate Bigelow to adjust himself to his environment. Mr. Bigelow was so appreciative of Charlie's friendship and help that as his prison term approached its end, he told Charlie, 'You have been good to me. When you get out, come to St. Paul. We will have a job for you.'

Five weeks later Charlie was released from prison and went to St. Paul. As he had promised, Mr. Bigelow gave Charlie a job. He was given work as a laborer at $25 a week. Because Charlie worked with PMA, he became a foreman within two months. After a year, he became a superintendent. Finally Charlie was made vice president and general manager. And when Mr. Bigelow died, Charlie was made president of Brown & Bigelow; he continued in this capacity until his own death many years later. Under Charlie's management, sales rose from less than three million dollars to over fifty million dollars annually. Brown & Bigelow became the largest company of its kind.

Because of Ward's positive mental attitude and his desire to help those less fortunate, he himself received peace of mind, happiness, love, and the better things in life. By presidential decree, his rights as a citizen were restored in acknowledgment of his exemplary life. Those who knew him held him in the highest esteem, and were themselves inspired to help others.

Perhaps one of his most unusual and commendable activities was his employment of over five hundred men and women who had come from prisons. They continued their rehabilitation under his stem and understanding guidance and inspiration. He never forgot that he too had been a convict. He wore a tag on his bracelet with his old prison number as a symbol.

Charlie Ward had been sentenced to prison. That was good!

Why? Who knows what might have become of Charlie Ward had he continued in the direction in which he was headed. But in prison he met the challenge to change. And there he learned to use PMA to solve his personal problems. He made his world a better world to live in. He became a bigger and better man. No one will ever know the exact number of the needy who have prayed for blessings to Charlie Ward in response to their inner thoughts:

> I was naked and ye clothed me; I was sick and ye visited me. I was in prison and ye came unto me.

Fortunately not everyone is faced with problems as severe as those which Charlie Ward was called upon to meet and solve. But there is a lesson in Charlie's story, in addition to the fact that he changed his attitude from negative to positive. You will recall, Charlie himself said: 'My greatest mistake was being with the wrong companions.' Negative attitudes are often contagious, and bad habits are contagious. Let each of us look to our own associations and be certain to keep them on the highest possible level. One of the greatest services you can render to children is to motivate them to motivate themselves to select the right kind of friends and associates. Remember:

> Vice is a monster of such awful mien That to be hated
> needs but to be seen;
> Yet, seen too oft, familiar with his face,
> We first endure, then pity, then embrace.

Another force with which every human being has to contend, and which, if not met with PMA, can cause physical, moral, and mental destruction is the power of sex. Sex presents the greatest challenge of change! Each human being has the power to choose for himself whether he will use the tremendous power of sex for good or for evil. Each human being must contend with the problems that will arise in his life because of sex.

You can transmute sex into virtue or vice. One of God's greatest gifts to mankind is the power to procreate a human being. Sex is the means of procreation. It is power! Like all power, it can be used for good or for evil.

Sex is a physical function of the body under the control of the subconscious and conscious mind. It is inherited. The physical sex organs, works of God, like all His creations, are good. The little difference that makes the big difference between the power of sex being a virtue or a vice is *mental attitude*.

The inherent emotion of sex is one of the most powerful forces of the subconscious mind. The effects of its motivating power can be observed long before adolescence. This power blends with and intensifies the driving force of all other emotions.

When it is in conflict with the will of the conscious mind, the power of imagination, as it affects the emotion of sex, has a tendency to win unless the conscious mind uses its power to affect, use, control or harmonize with the powers of the subconscious. You have the power to choose. Choose wisely—with PMA. Transmute sex into virtue! Thus, you will win over one of the greatest problems you win ever have to face in your personal life. And you will be physically, mentally, and morally better.

And what are the seven virtues? Virtue is moral practice or action, moral excellence; rectitude; valor; chastity. *The seven virtues are: prudence, fortitude, temperance, justice, faith, hope, and charity.*

1. *Prudence*—the ability to govern and discipline one's self by the exercise of reason.

2. *Fortitude*—strength of mind that enables a person to encounter danger or bear pain or adversity with courage. It is the possession of the stamina essential to face that which repels or frightens one, or to put up with the hardships of a task imposed. It implies triumph. Synonyms are grit, backbone, pluck and guts.
3. *Temperance*—habitual moderation in the indulgence of the appetites and passions.
4. *Justice*—the principle or ideal of just dealing or right action; also conformity to this principle or ideal; integrity.
5. *Faith*—trust in God.
6. *Hope*—the desire with expectation of obtaining what is desired, or belief that it is obtainable.
7. *Charity*—the act of loving all men as brothers because they are sons of God. It stresses benevolence and goodwill in giving and in the broad understanding of others with kindly tolerance.

How can you transmute the power of sex into the good and the beautiful? A crystal-clear answer can be found by you if you search for it as you read and study this entire book. Results will be achieved when you relate and assimilate the principles into your own life.

But one must gain knowledge for himself. The following suggestions may be helpful as you search for your answer while reading:

1. Keep your mind on the things you want and off the things you don't want. This means that you keep your mind on immediate, intermediate, and distant desirable objectives. The instinct of sex in the subconscious mind will be patient if it has hope that you will fulfill life's

mission. The boy or girl who is truly in love and plans to marry will not have the sex problems he or she might otherwise have.

2. If there were more and often earlier marriages, there would be fewer sex problems. Life's mission to procreate is fulfilled in marriage; however, marry for love beyoud the sex instinct.
3. Lead a well-balanced, four-square life.
4. Work long hours at a labor of love. It will keep you busy, occupy your thoughts, and use up surplus energy.
5. Develop a *Magnificent Obsession*. Study the significance to be found in Chapter Fifteen.
6. Relate and assimilate into your own life the concepts in Chapter Two, *'You Can Change Your World!'* and Chapter Seven, *'Learn to See!'*
7. Select environment that will develop you best towards your objectives.
8. Choose the self-motivators for self-suggestion that you believe will help you. Memorize them. Make sure they will flash from your subconscious mind to your conscious mind as autosuggestion.

Not all the problems of one's personal life, however, are of so deep and penetrating a nature. Many times all that it takes to meet an immediate problem is quick thinking, adaptability, and taking a second look at the situation which is causing the problem. It often takes only one idea, followed by action, to turn failure into success.

It takes only one idea, followed by action, to succeed when others fail. In 1939 on Chicago's North Michigan Avenue, in an area now known as The Magnificent Mile, office space was going begging. Building after building had empty floors: one that was half-rented was considered lucky. It was a bad year for business and NMA hung over Chicago real estate like a cloud. You heard such comments as, 'No sense in advertising, there just isn't the money around,' or 'What can you do? You can't fight the times.' Then into this gloomy picture came a building manager with PMA. He had an idea. And he got into action!

This man was hired by Northwestern Mutual Life Insurance Company to run a large building on North Michigan Avenue which they had acquired in a mortgage foreclosure. When he took the job the building was only ten per cent occupied. Within one year it was 100 per cent rented, with a long waiting list. What was the secret? The new manager accepted the problem of no-demand-for-offices as a challenge rather than a misfortune. Here is what he did as he explained in an interview.

I knew precisely what I wanted. I wanted to have the premises 100 per cent occupied with choice, substantial tenants. I knew that under the prevailing conditions it was likely that the offices would not be rented for possibly several years. I therefore concluded that we had everything to gain and nothing to lose by doing the following:

1. I would seek out desirable, prospective tenants of my choice.
2. I would stimulate the imagination of each prospect. I would offer him the most beautiful offices in the city of Chicago.
3. I would offer him these superior offices at a rental no higher than the one he was now paying.
4. Furthermore, I would assume responsibility for his present lease, provided he paid us the same monthly rental under a one-year lease.
5. In addition to all this, I would offer redecoration

without cost to the tenant. I would employ creative architects and interior decorators and remodel the offices of my building to suit the personal taste of each new tenant.

I reasoned:

1. If an office were not rented during the next few years, we would receive no income from that office. So we had nothing to lose by going into such arrangements as are above described. We might come out at the end of the year with no income, but we would be no worse off than we would have been if we had not acted. And we would be better off because: we would have satisfied tenants who would in future years supply dependable rentals.
2. Furthermore, it is an established custom to rent offices on a one-year basis only. In most cases, there would be only a few months left to run on the old lease of my new tenant. Promising to assume these rentals was therefore not too great a risk.
3. If a tenant should vacate at the end of his year, it would be comparatively easy to re-rent in a well-filled building. The redecoration of his office would not be money lost, as it would have increased the equity value of the entire building.

The result was marvelous. Each newly redecorated office seemed to be more beautiful than the one that had preceded it. The tenants were so enthused that many expended additional sums. In one instance, a tenant spent an additional $22,000 in remodeling.

So at the end of a year the building which had started off only ten per cent rented was 100 per cent rented. None of the tenants wanted to leave after

> his lease expired. They were happy with their new, ultramodern offices. And we gained their permanent goodwill by not raising the rents at the expiration of their first one- year's lease.

We would like you to think back over this story. Here was a man faced with a most serious problem. He had a giant office building on his hands that had nine empty offices in it for every one that was occupied. And yet within a year, his building was 100 per cent rented. Now right next door, up and down The Magnificent Mile, there were dozens of office buildings standing idle and practically empty.

The difference of course was the mental attitude which each individual building manager brought to the problem. One man said, 'I have a problem. That's awful!' The other said, 'I have a problem. *That's good!*'

A man who seizes upon his problems as opportunities in disguise and scmtinizes them for the good element that is going to be there, is the man who understands the very core of PMA. The man who develops an idea that can work and follows it with action will turn failure into success.

Time after time the pattern repeats itself: problems and difficulties turn out to be the best things that could have happened to us—*provided* we translate them into advantages.

As you recognize, the problem which the building manager faced occurred during the Depression. Things were still plenty tough in 1939 when he solved this problem. But they had been much worse.

Now the economic problems of the nation and of the world arose as the result of the Depression. Depressions are caused by cycles in the economic life of a nation or nations. But it is not necessary to sit idly by. There is no need to be beaten and tossed to and fro by the cycles of life. You can meet the problem of cycles and conquer it intelligently. In so doing, you can often acquire a fortune.

Make a fortune or achieve your aims by understanding cycles and trends. Many years ago Paul Raymond, Vice President in charge of loans for the American National Bank and Trust Company of Chicago, rendered a service bank's customers. He sent them Dewey and Dakin's book *Cycles*. Subsequently many of these clients made fortunes. They learned and understood the theory of business cycles and trends. Some of them will be among those who won't lose the fortunes they acquired regardless of economic trends and changes.

Edward R. Dewey, who has been the director for The Foundation for the Study of Cycles for many years, points out that every living organism, be it an individual, business, or nation, grows to maturity, levels off, and dies. What is equally important, he indicates a solution whereby, regardless of the trend or cycle, you, as an individual, can do something about it. You can meet the challenge of change successfully.

You can change the trend as far as you and your interests are concerned, regardless of the general trend, with new life, new blood, new ideas, new activity.

He anticipated a downward cycle and prepared to go upward. Before newspapers publicized the recession that began in the latter part of 1957, one of the bank's clients got into action. His organization went after business aggressively with a positive mental attitude. In 1958, his company developed a premium increase of over 30 per cent compared to the previous year which had shown a 25 per cent increase. The entire industry, however, had a downward trend.

Sometimes the cycle that presents a problem is not a cycle that affects an industry, or an entire nation. It may be a cycle within an individual business only. This problem, too, can be anticipated and met. Witness the continual growth of many American corporations, in spite of the fact that in the normal course of events they would have grown to maturity, leveled off, and died. E. I. du Pont de Nemours & Co., Inc., is an outstanding example.

They met the challenge with new life, new blood, new ideas, new activity. It is unnecessary to point out that E. I. du Pont de Nemours & Co., Inc. has continued to grow. But what is the cause of its success? Why has it not followed the natural cycle of growing to maturity, leveling off, and dying?

Du Pont has met the challenge of change with new life, new blood, new ideas, new activity. Its executives have met this problem with PMA and the determination to overcome it. They have continued to engage in research and are constantly making new discoveries, developing new products, and perfecting their previous products. They inject new blood into their management, and study and improve their sales methods.

Learn from their success!

The owner of a small business, or you as an individual, can study and experiment. You can relate and assimilate the principles used by such a large corporation. You too can continue to grow with booster shots of new ideas, new life, new blood, new activity.

You can change a downward trend into an upward one. You can be different! When others float downstream, you can move upstream!

So many of the stories you have read and will read in this book indicate that 'if you have a problem —that's good!' It's good if you *learn to see* how to turn adversity into seeds of equivalent or greater benefit. You may still not see the principle; however, the next chapter entitled 'Learn to See' can help you.

PILOT NO. 6
Thoughts to Steer By

1. So you've got a problem? That's good! Why? Because every time you meet a problem and tackle and conquer it with PMA, you become a better, bigger and more successful person.
2. Everyone has problems. Those with PMA turn their adversities into seeds of equivalent or greater benefits.
3. Your success, or failure, in meeting the problems presented by the challenges of change will be determined by your mental attitude.
4. You can direct your thoughts, control your emotions and ordain your destiny by recognizing, relating, assimilating and applying the principles that are applicable to you to be found in this book.
5. *God is always a good God.*
6. When you have a problem: (a) ask for Divine Guidance; (b) think; (c) state the problem, and (d) analyze it; (e) adopt the PMA attitude 'That's good!' (f) then change the adversity into seeds of greater benefit.
7. Charlie Ward is an outstanding example of a man who successfully met the challenges of change. Prepare to meet the challenges of change by developing PMA.
8. Sex is the greatest challenge of change. Transmute the emotion of sex into virtue.
9. The seven virtues are: prudence, fortitude, temperance, justice, faith, hope, and charity. *Success Through a Positive Mental Attitude* indicates how you can relate and assimilate these qualities into your own life.
10. One good idea followed by action can change failure into success.

YOU'VE GOT A PROBLEM?
THAT'S GOOD!
FOR IT'S THE SEEDS OF
GREATER BENEFITS FOR
THOSE WHO HAVE PMA

7

LEARN TO SEE

When he was born, George W. Campbell was blind. 'Bilateral congenital cataracts,' the doctor called it.

George's father looked at the doctor, not wanting to believe. 'Isn't there anything you can do? Wouldn't an operation help?'

'No,' said the doctor. 'As of now, we know of no way to treat this condition.'

George Campbell couldn't see, but the love and faith of his parents made his life rich. As a very young boy, he did not know that he was missing anything.

And then, when George was six years old, something happened which he wasn't able to understand. One afternoon he was playing with another youngster. The other boy, forgetting that George was blind, tossed a ball to him. 'Look out! It'll hit you!'

The ball did hit George—and nothing in his life was quite the same after that. George was not hurt, but he was greatly puzzled. Later he asked his mother: 'How could Bill know what's going to happen to me before I know it?'

His mother sighed, for now the moment she dreaded had arrived. Now it was necessary for her to tell her son for the first time: 'You are blind.' And here is how she did it:

'Sit down, George,' she said softly as she reached over and took one of his hands. 'I may not be able to describe it to you, and you may not be able to understand, but let me try to explain it this way.' And sympathetically she took one of his little hands in hers and started counting the fingers.

'One—two—three—four—five. These fingers are similar to what is known as the five senses.' She touched each finger between her thumb and index finger in sequence as she continued the explanation.

'This little finger for hearing; this little finger for touch; this little finger for smell; this one for taste,' and then she hesitated before continuing: 'this little finger for sight. And each of the five senses, like each of the five fingers, sends messages to your brain.'

Then she closed the little finger which she had named 'sight' and tied it so that it would stay next to the palm of George's hand.

'George, you are different from other boys,' she explained, 'because you have the use of only four senses, like four fingers: one, hearing—two, touch—three, smell— and four, taste. But you don't have the use of your sense of sight. Now I want to show you something. Stand up,' she said gently.

George stood up. His mother picked up his ball. 'Now hold out your hand as if you were going to catch this,' she said.

George held out his hands, and in a moment, he felt the hard ball hit his fingers. He closed them tightly around it and caught it.

'Fine. Fine,' said his mother. 'I never want you to forget what you have just done. You can catch a ball with four fingers instead of five, George. You can also catch and hold a full and happy life with four senses instead of five—if you get in there and keep trying.' Now George's mother had used a metaphor, and such a simple figure of speech is one of the quickest and most effective methods of communicating ideas between persons.

George never forgot the symbol of 'four fingers instead of five'. It meant to him the symbol of hope. And whenever he became discouraged because of his handicap, he used the symbol as a self-motivator. It became a form of self- suggestion to him. For he would repeat 'four fingers instead of five' frequently. At times of need it would flash from his subconscious to his conscious mind.

And he found that his mother was right. He was able to catch a full life, and hold it with the use of the four senses which he did have.

But George Campbell's story doesn't end here.

In the middle of his junior year at high school the boy became ill, and it was necessary for him to go to the hospital. While George was convalescing, his father brought him information from which he learned that science had developed a cure for congenital cataracts. Of course, there was a chance of failure but—the chances for success far outweighed those for failure.

George wanted so much to see that he was willing to risk failure in order to see.

During the next six months four delicate surgical operations were performed—two on each eye. For days. George lay in the darkened hospital room with bandages over his eyes.

And finally, the day came for the bandages to be removed. Slowly, carefully, the doctor unwound the gauze from around George's head and over his eyes. There was only a blur of light.

George Campbell was still technically blind!

For one awful moment he lay thinking. And then he heard the doctor moving beside his bed. Something was being placed over his eyes.

'Now, can you see?' came the doctor's question.

George raised his head slightly from the pillow. The blur

of light became color, the color a form, a figure.

'George!' a voice said. He recognized the voice. It was his mother's voice.

For the first time in his 18 years of life George Campbell was seeing his mother. There were the tired eyes, the wrinkled, 62-year-old face, and the knotted and gnarled hands. But to George she was most beautiful.

To him—she was an angel. The years of toil and patience, the years of teaching and planning, the years of being his seeing eyes, the love and affection: that was what George saw.

To this day he treasures his first visual picture: the sight of his mother. And, as you will see, he learned an appreciation for his sense of sight from this first experience.

'None of us can understand,' he says, 'the miracle of sight, unless we have had to do without it.'

Seeing is a learned process. But George also learned something that is very helpful to anyone interested in the study of PMA. He will never forget the day he saw his mother standing before him in the hospital room, and did not know who she was—or even what she was—until he heard her speak. 'What we see,' George points out, 'is always an interpretation of the mind. We have to train the mind to interpret what we see.'

This observation is backed up by science. 'Most of the process of seeing is not done by the eyes at all,' says Dr. Samuel Renshaw, in describing the mental process of seeing. 'The eyes act as hands which reach 'out there' and grab meaningless 'things' and bring them into the brain. The brain then turns the 'things' over to the memory. It is not until the brain interprets in terms of comparative action that we really *see* anything.'

Some of us go through life 'seeing' very little of the power and the glory around us. We do not properly filter the information that our eyes give us through the mental processes of the brain. As a result, we often behold things without really *seeing* them at all. We receive physical impressions without grasping their meaning to us. We do not, in other words, put PMA to work on the impressions that are sent to our brain.

Is it time to have your mental vision checked? Not your physical vision—that is a matter for the medical specialists. But mental vision, like physical vision, can become distorted. When it does you can grope in a haze of false concepts. . . bumping and hurting yourself and others unnecessarily.

The most common physical weaknesses of the eye are two opposite extremes—nearsightedness and farsightedness. These are the major distortions of mental vision, too.

The person who is mentally nearsighted is apt to overlook objects and possibilities that are distant. He pays attention only to the problems immediately at hand and is blind to the opportunities that could be his by thinking and planning in terms of the future. You are nearsighted if you do not make plans, form objectives, and lay the foundation for the future.

On the other hand, the mentally farsighted person is apt to overlook possibilities that are right before him. He does not see the opportunities at hand. He sees only a dream-world of the future, unrelated to the present. He wants to start at the top rather than move up step by step—and he does not recognize that the only job where you can start at the top is the job of digging a hole.

They looked and recognized what they saw. So, in the process of learning to see, you will want to develop both your near sight and your far sight. The advantages to the man who knows how to see what is directly in front of him are enormous. For years the people in the little town of Darby, Montana, used to look up at what they called Crystal Mountain. The mountain was given this name because erosion had exposed a ledge of a lightly sparkling crystal that looked something like rock salt. A pack trail was built directly across the outcropping as early as 1937. But it wasn't until the year 1951—14 years later—that anyone bothered to stoop down, pick up a piece of the sparkling material, and really look at it.

It was in this year 1951 that two Darby men, Mr. A. E. Cumley and Mr. L. I. Thompson, saw a mineral collection displayed in the town. Thompson and Cumley became very excited. There in the mineral display were specimens of beryl which, according to the attached card, was used in atomic energy research. Immediately, Thompson and Cumley staked claims on Crystal Mountain. Thompson sent a specimen of the ore to the Bureau of Mines office in Spokane, together with a request to send an examiner to see a 'very large deposit' of the mineral. Later that year the Bureau of Mines sent a bulldozer up the mountain and scraped off enough of the outcropping to determine that here indeed was one of the world's greatest deposits of extremely valuable beryllium. Today, heavy earthmoving trucks struggle up the mountain and work their way back down again, weighted down with the extremely heavy ore, while at the bottom, virtually waiting with dollar bills in their hands, are representatives of the United States Steel Company and the United States Government, each anxious to buy the highly valued ore. All because one day two young men not only observed with their eyes, but took the trouble to see with their minds. Today these men are well on their way to being multimillionaires.

A mentally farsighted person could not have done what Thompson and Cumley did—if his mental vision were distorted. For he is the man who can see only far-off values while the advantages that he at his feet go unclaimed. Are there fortunes right at your doorstep? Look about you. As you go about your daily chores are there small areas of irritation? Perhaps you can think of a way to overcome them—a way that will be helpful not only to yourself but to others. Many a man has made a fortune by meeting such homely needs. This was so of the man who invented the bobby pin and the one who devised the paper clip. It was so of the man who invented the zipper, and the metal pants-fastener. Look about you. Learn to see. You may find in your own backyard.

But mental nearsightedness can be just as much of a problem as mental farsightedness. The man with this problem sees only what is under his nose, while more distant possibilities go unclaimed. He is the man who does not understand the power of a plan. He does not understand the value of thinking time. He is so busy with the problems that immediately confront him that he does not free his mind to range into the distance, reaching for new opportunities, seeking trends, getting the big picture.

Being able to see into the future is one of the most spectacular accomplishments of the human brain. Down in the heart of the citrus belt in Florida there is a little town called Winter Haven. The surrounding country is farmland. Certainly, it would be considered by most people as an area entirely unsuited for a large tourist attraction. It is isolated. It has no beach, no mountains, only mile after mile of gently rolling hills with little lakes and cypress swamps down in the valleys.

But to this region came a man who 'saw' these cypress swamps with an eye that others had not used. His name was Richard Pope. Dick Pope bought one of these old cypress swamps, put a fence around it, and has turned down offers of at least a million dollars for the world-famous Cypress Gardens.

Of course, it really wasn't as simple as that. All along the line Dick Pope had to 'see' opportunities in his situation.

For instance, there was the question of advertising. Pope knew that the only way he would be able to draw the public into such an isolated place was through a barrage of advertising. But ads cost money. So what Dick Pope did was quite simple. He went into the popular photography business. He set up a photo supply house at Cypress Gardens, sold his visitors film and then taught them how to take spectacular shots of the Garden. He hired skilled water skiers. He put them through intricate performances while over a loudspeaker he announced to the public exactly what camera settings they should use in order to catch the action. And then, of course, when these travelers went back home, the very best trip pictures were always of Cypress Gardens. They gave Dick Pope the very best kind of advertising there is—word-of-mouth recommendations, with pictures!

This is the kind of creative seeing that we all need to develop. We need to learn how to look at our world with fresh eyes—seeing the opportunities that lie all about us, but simultaneously looking into the future for the chances that are there.

Seeing is a learned skill. But like any skill it must be exercised.

See another person's abilities, capacities and viewpoint. We may think we recognize our own talents; yet in this respect we may be blind. Let's illustrate with an example of a teacher who needed to have her mental vision checked. She was both nearsighted and farsighted. For she could not see either the present or the future potential abilities and capacities of her students, or their points of view.

Now everyone —the great and the near great—had to have a starting point. They weren't born brilliant and successful. As a matter of fact, some of our greatest men were regarded as quite stupid at times during their lives. It was not until they grasped a positive mental attitude and learned to comprehend their capabilities and envision definite goals that they started their climbs to success. But there was one young man, in particular, whom his teachers thought 'a stupid, muddle-headed blockhead'.

The youngster sat and drew pictures on his slate. He looked about and listened to everybody else. He asked 'impossible questions' but refused to reveal what he knew, even under the threat of punishment. The children called him 'dunce,' and he generally stood at the foot of his class.

And this boy was Thomas Alva Edison. You will be inspired when you read the life story of Thomas A. Edison. He attended primary school for a total period of less than three months. The teacher and his schoolmates told him that he was stupid. Yet, he became an educated man after an incident in his life prompted him to turn his talisman from NMA to PMA. He developed into a gifted person. He became a great inventor.

What was that incident? What happened to Edison that changed his whole attitude? He told his mother about hearing the teacher tell the inspector at school that he was 'addled' and it wouldn't be worthwhile to keep him in school any longer. His mother marched off to school with him and told all within range of her voice that her son, Thomas Alva Edison, had more brains than the teacher or the inspector.

Edison called his mother the most enthusiastic champion a boy ever had. And from that day forward he was a changed boy. He said, 'She cast over me an influence which has lasted all my life. The good effects of her early training I can never lose. My mother was always kind, always sympathetic, and she never misunderstood or misjudged me.' His mother's belief in him caused him to view himself in an entirely different light. It caused him to turn his talisman to PMA and take a positive mental attitude regarding studying and learning. This attitude taught Edison to view things with deeper mental insight, that enabled him to comprehend and develop inventions which benefited mankind. Perhaps the teacher didn't see because the teacher wasn't genuinely interested in helping the boy. His mother was.

You have a tendency to see what you want to see.

To hear does not necessarily imply attention or application. To listen always does. Throughout *Success Through a Positive Mental Attitude* we urge you to listen to the message. This means: to see how you can relate and assimilate the principle into your own life.

Perhaps you'd like to see how you can relate the principle of the following experience into your own life:

Dr. Roy Plunkett, a DuPont chemist, made an experiment. He failed. When he opened the test tube after the experiment, he observed that it apparently contained nothing. He was curious. He asked himself, 'Why?' He didn't throw the tube away as others might have done under similar circumstances. Instead, he weighed the tube. And, to his surprise, it weighed more than a tube of like make and design. So, again, Dr. Plunkett asked himself, 'Why?'

In searching for the answer to his questions, he discovered that marvelous transparent plastic, tetrafluoroethylene, commonly known as Teflon. During the Korean War, the United States government contracted for Du Pont's entire output.

When there is something you don't understand, ask yourself: 'Why?' Look at it more closely. You may make a great discovery.

Ask yourself questions. Asking yourself or others questions about things that puzzle you may reward you richly. This very procedure led to one of the world's greatest scientific discoveries.

A young Englishman, while vacationing on his grandmother's farm, was relaxing. He was lying on his back under an apple tree and engaging in thinking time. An apple fell to the ground. This young man was a student of higher mathematics.

'Why does the apple fall to the ground?' he asked himself. 'Does the earth attract the apple? Does the apple attract the earth? Does each attract the other? What is the universal principle involved?'

Isaac Newton used his power to think and he made a discovery. To see mentally is to think. He found the answers he was looking for; the earth and the apple attracted each other, and the law of attraction of mass to mass applies to the entire universe.

Newton discovered the law of gravitation because he was observant and sought the answers to what he observed. Another man, because he exercised his powers of observation and acted upon what he perceived, found happiness and great wealth.

Newton asked himself questions. The other man sought expert advice.

He became wealthy because he accepted advice. In Toba, Japan, in the year 1869, when he was just eleven years old, Kokichi Mikimoto continued his father's business as the village noodle maker. His father had developed an illness that prevented him from working. The youngster supported his six brothers, three sisters, and his parents. In addition to making the noodles daily, young Mikimoto had to sell them. He proved to be a good salesman.

Mikimoto had previously been tutored by a Samurai who taught:

Exemplification of true faith consists of acts of kindness and love for one's fellowmen, not mere formal prayers uttered by rote.

And with this basic PMA philosophy of positive action, Mikimoto became a *doer*. He developed the habit of converting ideas into reality.

At the age of twenty he fell in love with the daughter of a Samurai. The young man knew that his future father-in- law would not bless his daughter's marriage with a noodle maker. Therefore, he was motivated to harmonize with this known power. He changed his occupation and became a pearl merchant.

Like many persons who achieve success in any part of the world, Mikimoto kept searching for specific knowledge that would help him in his new activity. He, like the great industrialists of our day, sought help from a university. Professor Yoshikichi Mizukuri told Mikimoto of a theory of one of the laws of nature that had never been proved.

The professor said: 'A pearl is formed in an oyster when a foreign object, like a grain of sand, is stuck in the oyster. If the foreign object does not kill the oyster, nature covers the object with the same secretion that forms the mother-of-pearl in the lining of the oyster's shell.'

Mikimoto was thrilled! He could hardly wait to get the answer to the question he asked himself, 'Can I raise pearls by deliberately planting a tiny foreign object in the oyster and letting nature take its course?'

He converted a theory into a positive action once he learned to see.

Mikimoto had been taught to see by that university professor. And then he used the power of his imagination. He engaged in creative thinking. He used deductive reasoning. He decided that if all pearls were formed only when a foreign object entered the oyster, he could develop pearls by using nature's laws. He could plant foreign objects in the oysters and force them to produce pearls. He learned to observe and act and he became a successful man.

Now a study of Mikimoto's life indicates that he employed all the 17 success principles. For knowledge doesn't make you successful. But application of the knowledge will. Action!

Many of the ideas which come to us as we learn to see with fresh eyes will strike others as bold. These ideas can either frighten us or, if we act on them, make our fortunes. Here is another true story of pearls. This time the hero is a young American, Joseph Goldstone. He sold jewelry to Iowa farmers, door-to-door.

Then one day in the heart of the Depression he learned that the Japanese were producing beautiful cultured pearls. Here was quality, and it could be sold at a fraction of the cost of natural pearls!

Joe 'saw' a great opportunity. In spite of the fact that it was a Depression year, he and his wife, Esther, converted all their tangible assets into cash and set out for Tokyo. They landed in Japan with less than $1000—but they had their plan and lots of PMA.

They obtained an interview with Mr. K. Kitamura, head of the Japanese Pearl Dealers Association. Joe was aiming high. He told Mr. Kitamura of his plan for merchandising Japanese cultured pearls in the United States, and asked Mr. Kitamura for an initial credit of $100,000 in pearls. This was a fantastic sum, especially in a period of depression. After several days, however, Mr. Kitamura agreed.

The pearls sold well. The Goldstones were well on their way to becoming wealthy. A few years later, they decided they wanted to establish their own pearl farm, which they did with the help of Mr. Kitamura. Once again they 'saw' opportunity where others had seen nothing. Experience proved that the mortality rate of oysters into which a foreign object had been artificially inserted was over 50 per cent.

'How can we eliminate this great loss?' they asked themselves.

After much study, the Goldstones began to use on the oysters the methods employed in hospital rooms. The outside shells were scraped and scrubbed to reduce the danger of infection to the oyster. The 'surgeon' used a liquid anesthetic that relaxed the oyster. Then he slipped a tiny clam pellet into each oyster as a nucleus for the pearl that was to be formed. The incision was made with a sterilized scalpel. Then the oyster was put into a cage, and the cage was dropped back into the water. Every four months cages were raised and the oysters were given a physical checkup. Through these techniques, 90 per cent of the oysters lived and developed pearls, and the Goldstones went on to acquire a fabulous fortune.

Time and again we see how men and women have become successful after they learned to apply mental perception. The ability to see is much more than the physical process of taking light rays through the retina of the eye. It is the skill of interpreting what you see and applying that interpretation to your life and the lives of others.

Learning to see will bring to you opportunities that you never dreamed existed. However, there is more to success through PMA than learning mental perception. You must also learn to act on what you learn. Action is important because through action you get things done.

Don't wait any longer. Read *The Secret of Getting Things Done* in the next chapter and move another rung up the ladder of success through PMA.

PILOT NO. 7
Thoughts to Steer By

1. Learn to see! *Seeing is a learned process.* Nine- tenths of seeing takes place in the brain.
2. *Four fingers instead of five:* This was the symbol whereby George Campbell, the blind boy, could catch and hold a full and happy life. How can you use this symbol?
3. *Seeing* is learned through association. George Campbell's first sight of his mother became meaningful to him only when he recognized her voice.
4. Is it time to have your mental vision checked? When it is distorted, you can grope around in a haze of false concepts, bumping and hurting yourself and others unnecessarily. Does your mental vision become clearer year by year?
5. Take a look—& good look—and recognize what you see. There may be in your own backyard!
6. Don't be nearsighted—look to the future. Cypress Gardens became a reality because Richard Pope saw it as a definite future objective.
7. *See* another person's abilities, capacities, and viewpoint. You may be overlooking a genius. The story of Thomas Edison is a good example.
8. Do you see how you can relate and assimilate the principles of *Success Through a Positive Mental Attitude* into your own life?
9. Learn from nature. How? Ask yourself some questions, as Isaac Newton did. If you don't know the answers, get expert advice.
10. Convert what you see into reality by action. Mikimoto converted a theory into a fortune in pearls. Goldstone recognized, related and applied the principles and methods

used in hospitals to save human lives as being applicable to saving the lives of oysters in producing cultured pearls.

OPEN YOUR MIND AND LEARN TO SEE

8

THE SECRET OF GETTING THINGS DONE

In this chapter you will find the secret of getting things done. You will also receive a self-motivator so powerful that it will subconsciously force you to desirable action, for it is in reality a *self-starter*. Yet you can use it at will. When you do, you overcome procrastination and inertia.

If you do the things you don't want to do, or if you don't do the things that you do want to do, then this chapter is for you.

Those who achieve greatness employ this secret of getting things done. Take, for example, Maryknoll Father James Keller. Father Keller had been developing an idea for quite some time. He hoped to motivate 'little people to do big things by encouraging each to reach beyoud his or her own little circle to the outside world'. The Biblical command, *'go ye forth into all the world'* was to him the symbol of an idea whereby the mission he had in mind could be fulfilled.

When he responded to this command, he employed the secret of getting things done. And when he did, he went into action. This happened in 1945. It was then that he organized the Christophers —an organization most unusual.

It has no chapters, no committees, no meetings, no dues. It doesn't even have a membership in the usual sense of the word. It simply consists of people—no one can say how many—

dedicated to an ideal. The Christophers operate on the concept that it is better for people to 'do something and pay nothing' than to 'pay dues and do nothing'.

What is the ideal to which each is dedicated?

Each Christopher is dedicated to carry his religion with him wherever he goes throughout the day—into the dust and heat of the market place, into the highways and byways, into the home. And thus, he brings the major truths of his faith to others.

The thrilling story is told by the Rev. James Keller in *You Can Change the World*. It came about because he conceived and believed in an ideal. But he did little or nothing about it until he responded to the secret of getting things done.

You get the feel of this secret from the statement of E. E. Bauermeister, supervisor of education and correctional counselor at California Institution for Men, Chino, California, who told the authors:

'I always tell the men in our self-adjustment class that too often what we read and profess becomes a part of our libraries and our vocabularies, instead of becoming a part of our lives.'

Remember the Biblical statement: *For the good that I would, I do not; hut the evil which l would not, that I do.* Now how can you train yourself to get into action immediately when it is desirable?

And then we told Mr. Bauermeister how the good things we read and profess can become a part of our lives. We gave him the self-starter for getting things done.

How do you make the secret of getting things done a part of your life? By habit. And you develop habit through repetition. 'Sow an action and you reap a habit; sow a habit and you reap a character; sow a character and you reap a destiny,' said the great psychologist and philosopher William James. He was saying that you are what your habits make you. And you can choose your habits. You can develop any habit you wish when you use the self-starter.

Now what is the secret of getting things done and what is the self-starter that forces you to use this great secret?

The secret of getting things done is to act. The self-starter is the self-motivator *DO IT NOW!*

As long as you live, never say to yourself, *'DO IT NOW!'* unless you follow through with desirable action. Whenever action is desirable and the symbol *DO IT NOW!* flashes from your subconscious mind to your conscious mind, immediately act.

Make it a practice to respond to the self-starter *DO IT NOW!* in little things. You will quickly develop the habit of a reflex response so powerful that in times of emergency or when opportunity presents itself, you will act. Say you have a phone call that you should make but you have a tendency to procrastinate. And you have put off making that phone call. When the self-starter *DO IT NOW!* flashes from your subconscious to your conscious mind: *Act.* Make that phone call immediately.

Or suppose, for example, that you set your alarm clock for 6:00 A.M. Yet when the alarm goes off, you feel sleepy, get up, turn off the alarm, and go back to bed. You will have a tendency to develop a habit to do the same thing in the future. But if your subconscious mind flashes to the conscious, *DO IT NOW!* then come what may—*DO IT NOW!* Stay up! Why? You want to develop the habit of responding to the self-starter *DO IT NOW!*

In Chapter Thirteen you will read how one of the authors bought a company with one million six hundred thousand dollars in net liquid assets with the seller's own money. This became a reality because at the proper time the buyer responded to the self-starter *DO IT NOW!*

Now H. G. Wells learned the secret of getting things done. And H. G. Wells was a prolific writer because he did. He tried never to let a good idea slip away from him. While an idea was fresh, he immediately wrote down the thought that occurred to him. This would sometimes happen in the middle of the night. No matter. Wells would switch on the light, reach for the pencil and paper that were always beside his bed and scribble away. And then he would drop off to sleep again.

Ideas that might have been forgotten were recalled when he refreshed his memory by looking at the flashes of inspiration that had been written down immediately when they occurred. This habit of Wells' was as natural and effortless to him as smiling is to you when a happy thought occurs.

Many persons have the habit of procrastination. Because of it, they may miss a train, be late for work, or even more important—miss an opportunity that could change the whole course of their lives for the better. History has recorded how battles have been lost someone put off taxing desirable action.

New students in our PMA Science of Success course sometimes state that the procrastination habit is the one they would like to eliminate. And then we reveal to them the secret of getting things done. We give them the self-starter. We may motivate them by telling them the true story of what the self-starter meant to a war prisoner in World War II.

What the self-starter meant to a war prisoner. Kenneth Erwin Harmon was a civilian employee for the Navy at Manila when the Japanese landed there. He was captured and held in a hotel for two days before he was sent to a prison camp.

On the first day, Kenneth saw that his roommate had a book under his pillow. 'May I borrow it?' he asked. The book was *Think and Grow Rich*. Kenneth began to read. As he read, he met the most important living person with the invisible talisman imprinted with PMA on one side and NMA on the reverse.

Before he started to read it, he had the feeling of despair. He fearfully looked ahead to possible torture-even death— in the prison camp. But now as he read his attitude became one inspired by hope. He had a craving to own the book. He wanted it with him during the dread days ahead. In discussing *Think and Grow Rich* with his fellow prisoner, he realized that the book meant a great deal to the owner.

'Let me copy it,' he said.

'Sure, go ahead,' was the response.

Kenneth Harmon employed the secret of getting things done. He swung into immediate action. In a fury of activity, he began typing away. Word by word, page by page, chapter by chapter. Because he was obsessed with the possibility that it would be taken away at any moment, he was motivated to work night and day.

It was a good thing that he did for within an hour after the last page was completed, his captors led him away to the notorious Santo Tomas prison camp. He had finished in time because he started in time. Kenneth Harmon kept the manuscript with him during the three years and one month he was a prisoner. He read it again and again. And it gave him food for thought. It inspired him to: develop courage, make plans for the future, and retain his mental and physical health Many prisoners at Santo Tomas were permanently injured physically and mentally by malnutrition and fear—fear of the present and fear of the future. 'But I was better when I left Santo Tomas than when I was interned—better prepared for life—more mentally alert,' Kenneth Harmon told us. You get the feel of his thinking in his statement: 'Success must be continually practiced, or it will take wings and fly away.'

Now is the time to act.

For the secret of getting things done can change a person's attitude from negative to positive. A day that might have been ruined can become a pleasant day.

The day that might have been wasted. Jorgen Juhldahl, a student at the University of Copenhagen, worked one summer as a tourist guide. Because he cheerfully did much more than he was paid to do, some visitors from Chicago made arrangements for him to tour America. The itinerary included a day of sightseeing in Washington, D. C., while he was en route to Chicago.

On arriving in Washington, Jorgen checked in at the Willard Hotel, where his bill had been pre-paid. He was sitting on top of the world. In his coat pocket was his Plane ticket to Chicago; in his hip pocket was his wallet with his passport and money. Then the young man was dealt a shocking blow!

While getting ready for bed, he found that his wallet was missing. He ran downstairs to the hotel desk.

'Well do everything we can,' said the manager.

But the next morning the wallet had still not been located. Jorgen Juhldahl had less than two dollars change in his pockets. Alone in a foreign country, he wondered what he should do. Wire his friends in Chicago and tell them what had happened? Go to the Danish embassy and report the lost passport? Sit at police headquarters until they had some news?

Then, all of a sudden, he said: 'No! I won't do any of these things! I'll see Washington. I may never be here again. I have one precious day in this great capital. After all, I still have my ticket to get me to Chicago tonight, and there'll be plenty of time then to solve the problem of the money and the passport.

But if I don't see Washington *NOW* I may never see it. I've walked miles at home, I'll enjoy walking here.

'Now is the time to be happy.

'I am the same man that I was yesterday before I lost my wallet. I was happy then; I should be happy now—just to be in America—just to have the privilege of enjoying a holiday in this great city.

'I won't waste my time in futile unhappiness over my loss.'

And so, he headed off, on foot. He saw the White House and the Capitol, he visited the great museums, he climbed to the top of the Washington Monument. He wasn't able to take the tour of Arlington and some other places he'd wanted to see. But what he did see, he saw more thoroughly. He bought peanuts and candy and nibbled on them to keep from getting too hungry.

And when he got back to Denmark, the part of his American trip he remembered best was that day on foot in Washington—a day that might have gotten away from Jorgen Juhldahl if he had not employed the secret of getting things done. For he knew the truth in the statement. *NOW* is the time. He knew that *NOW* must be seized before it becomes: yesterday-I-could-have...

Incidentally, to round off his story, five days after that eventful day Washington police found both wallet and passport and sent them to him.

Are you scared of your own best ideas? One of the things that often prevents us from seizing the *NOW* is a certain timidity in the face of our own inspirations. We're a little bit afraid of our ideas when they first occur to us. They may seem novel or farfetched. There's no doubt about it: It takes a certain boldness to step out on an untested idea. Yet it's exactly this kind of boldness that often produces the most spectacular results. The well-known writer, Elsie Lee, tells about Ruth Butler and her sister Eleanor, the daughters of a nationally-known New York furrier.

'My father was a frustrated painter,' says Ruth, 'He had talent, but the need to earn a living left him no time to build a reputation as an artist. So he collected paintings. Later, he started buying paintings for Eleanor and me. Thus, the girls developed a knowledge and appreciation for fine art, along with an impeccable sense of taste. As they grew older, friends would consult them on what types of paintings they should buy for their homes. Often, they would loan pieces from their collection for brief periods.

One day Eleanor woke Ruth up at 3 A.M. 'Don't start arguing, but I have a terrific idea! We're going to form a Master Mind alliance.'

'Now what in the world is a Master Mind alliance?' Ruth asked.

'A Master Mind alliance is coordination of knowledge and effort, in a spirit of harmony, between two or more people, for the attainment of a definite purpose. And that's just what we're going to do. We're going into the business of renting paintings!'

And Ruth agreed. It was a terrific idea. They set to work the same day —although friends tried to warn them of dangers: Their valued paintings might be lost or stolen; and there might be law suits and insurance problems. But they went right on working—accumulating $300 in capital and talking their father into loaning them the basement of his fur shop, rent free.

'We hauled 1,800 paintings from our own collections in among the coat forms,' Ruth recalls, 'and ignored father's sad and disapproving eyes. The first year was grim—a real struggle.'

But the novel idea paid off. Their company, known as the New York Circulating Library of Paintings, became a success—

with about 500 paintings constantly on rental to business firms, doctors, lawyers and for use in homes. One valued client was an inmate of the Massachusetts Penitentiary for eight years. He wrote humbly that perhaps the Library wouldn't rent to him, considering his address. The paintings went to him rent free except for transportation costs. In return Ruth and Eleanor received a letter from prison authorities telling how the paintings were used in an art appreciation course that benefited many hundreds of prisoners. Ruth and Eleanor started their business with an idea. And then they backed their idea up with immediate action. The results were a profit to themselves and increased pleasure and happiness for many others.

Are you ready to double your income? W. Clement Stone toured the Asiatic and Pacific areas as one of seven executives serving as representatives of the National Sales Executives International. On a Tuesday, Stone gave a talk on motivation to a group of businessmen at Melbourne, Australia. The following Thursday evening, he received a phone call. It was from Edwin H. East, manager of a firm that sold metal cabinets. Mr. East was excited: 'Something wonderful has happened! You'll be as enthusiastic as I am when I tell you about it!'

'Tell me about it. What did happen?'

'An amazing thing! You gave your talk on motivation Tuesday. In your talk you recommended ten inspirational books. I bought *Think and Grow Rich* and started to read it that evening. I read for hours. The next morning, I started reading it again and then I wrote on a piece of paper:

'My major definite aim is to double last year's sales this year. The amazing thing is: I did it in forty-eight hours.'

'How did you do it?' Mr. Stone asked East. 'How did you double your income?'

East responded: 'In your speech on motivation, you told

how Al Allen, one of your Wisconsin salesmen, tried to sell cold- canvass in a certain block. You said that Al was lucky because he worked all day and didn't make a sale.

'That evening, you said, Al Allen developed *inspirational dissatisfaction*. He determined that the following day he would again call on exactly the same prospects and sell more insurance policies that day than any of the other representatives in his group would sell all week.

'You told how Al Allen completely canvassed the same city block. He called on the same people and sold 66 new accident contracts. I remembered your statement: 'It can't be done some may think, but—Al did it.' I believed you. I was ready.

'I remembered the self-starter you gave us: *DO IT NOW!*

'I went to my card records and analyzed ten 'dead' accounts. I prepared what might previously have seemed to be an enormous program to present to each. I repeated the self-starter *DO IT NOW!* several times. And then I called on the ten accounts with a positive mental attitude and made eight large sales. It is amazing—truly amazing—what PMA will do for the salesmen who use its power!'

Now Edwin H. East was ready when he heard the talk on motivation. He listened to the message that was applicable to him. He was searching for something. And he found what he was looking for. Our purpose in relating this particular story is that you, too, have read about Al Allen. But you may not have seen how you could apply the principle to your own experience. Edwin H. East did. And you can, too. You can apply the principles in each of the stories you read in *Success Through a Positive Mental Attitude*.

Now, however, we want you to learn the self-starter, *DO IT NOW!*

Sometimes a decision to act immediately can make your

wildest dreams come true. It worked that way for Manley Sweazey.

You can mix business and pleasure. Manley loved hunting and fishing. His idea of the good life was to hike fifty miles into the woods with his pole and his rifle, and hike back a couple of days later exhausted, muddy, and very happy.

The only trouble with this hobby was that it took too much time out from his work as an insurance salesman. Then one day as he reluctantly left a favorite bass lake and headed back to his desk, Manley had a wild idea. Suppose, somewhere, there were people living in a wilderness—people who needed insurance. Then he could work and be out-of- doors at the same time! And indeed, Manley discovered, there was such a group of people: The men who worked for the Alaska Railroad. They lived in scattered section-houses strung out along the 500-mile length of the track. What if he were to sell insurance to these railroad men, and to the trappers and gold miners along the route?

The same day that the idea came to him, Sweazey began making positive plans. He consulted a travel agent and began packing. He didn't pause to let doubts creep in and frighten him into believing that his idea might be scatterbrained... that it might fail. Instead of picking the idea apart for its flaws, he took a boat to Seward, Alaska.

He walked the length of the railroad many, many 'Walking Sweazey,' as he was called, became a welcome sight to these isolated families, not only because he sold insurance when no one else had thought them worth bothering with, but because he represented the outside world. He went the extra mile. For he taught himself how to cut hair, and did it free of charge. He taught himself how to cook, too. Since the single men ate mostly canned foods and bacon, Manley, with his culinary skills, was a welcome guest. And all the while he was doing what came naturally. He was doing what he wanted to do: tramping the hills, hunting, fishing and—as he puts it, 'living the life of Sweazey!'

In the life insurance business, there is a special place of honor reserved for men who sell over a million dollars' worth of business in one year. It is called the Million Dollar Round Table. Now the remarkable and almost unbelievable part of Manley Sweazey's story is that: having acted on his impulse, having taken off for the wilds of Alaska, having walked the railroad where no one else had bothered to go, he did his million dollars of business, and more, in a single year, to take his place at the Round Table.

And none of it would have happened if he had hesitated to employ the secret of getting things done when his 'wild' idea came to him.

Memorize the self-starter *DO IT NOW!*

DO IT NOW! can affect every phase of your life. It can help you do the things you should do, but don't feel like doing. It can keep you from procrastinating when an unpleasant duty faces you. But it can also help you as it did Manley Sweazey, to do those things that you want to do. It helps you seize those precious moments which, if lost, may never be retrieved. The endearing word to a friend, for example. The telephone call to an associate, just telling him that you admire him. All in response to the self-starter *DO IT NOW!*

Write yourself a letter. Here is an idea to help you get started. Sit down and write yourself a letter, telling the things you always intended to do as though they had already been accomplished—some personal, some charitable, and others community projects. Write the letter as if a biographer were writing about the wonderful person, you really are when you come under the influence of PMA. But don't stop there. Use the secret of getting things done. Respond to the self-starter *DO IT NOW!*

Remember, regardless of what you have been or what you are, you can be what you want to be if you act with PMA.

The self-starter *DO IT NOW!* is an important self-motivator. It is the important step towards understanding and applying the principles of the next chapter entitled, *'How to Motivate Yourself.'*

PILOT NO. 8
Thoughts to Steer By

1. It is better for people to do something and pay nothing, than to pay dues and do nothing.
2. 'Too often what we read and profess becomes a part of our libraries and our vocabularies, instead of becoming a part of our lives.' Stop and think about this. You have knowledge of principles that could help you achieve any worthwhile goal in life you might desire—but do you make these principles a part of your life?
3. 'Sow an action and you reap a habit; sow a habit and you reap a character; sow a character and you reap a destiny.' What habits of thought or action, in any human activity, would you like to acquire? What habits would you like to eliminate? You should know how to acquire desirable habits and eliminate the undesirable if you have learned how to recognize principles revealed to you in this book and apply them.
4. The secret of getting things done is: *DO IT NOW!*
5. As long as you live, when the suggestion *DO IT NOW!* flashes from your subconscious to your conscious mind to do that which you ought to do, immediately follow through with desirable action. It's a habit that will make you an outstanding achiever.
6. The burden of learning is upon the person who wants to learn. If you want to learn how you can achieve anything in life that doesn't violate the laws of God or the rights of your fellow men, now is the time to begin to study and learn the concepts that can teach you how to achieve your goals. Study and apply the principles contained in *Success*

Through a Positive Mental Attitude—don't only read what is written.

7. Now is the time to act.

DO IT NOW!

9

HOW TO MOTIVATE YOURSELF

What is motivation?

Motivation is that which *induces action or determines choice.* It is that which *provides a motive.* A motive is the 'inner urge' *only within the individual* which incites him to action, such as an instinct, passion, emotion, habit, mood, impulse, desire or idea.

It is the hope or *other force* which starts an action in an attempt to produce specific results.

Motivating yourself and others. When you know principles that *can* motivate you, you will then know principles that *can* motivate others. Conversely, when you know principles that *can* motivate others, you will then know principles that *can* motivate you.

How to motivate yourself is the purpose of this chapter. How to motivate others is the purpose of Chapter Ten. How to motivate yourself and others with a positive mental attitude is the purpose of *Success Through a Positive Mental Attitude.* In essence, this is a book on motivation.

Our purpose in illustrating specific experiences of the success and failures of others is to motivate you to desirable action.

Now, therefore, to motivate yourself, try to understand principles that motivate others—to motivate others, try to understand principles that motivate you.

Establish the habit of motivating yourself with PMA... at will. And then you can direct your thoughts, control your emotions and ordain your destiny.

Motivate yourself and others with the magic ingredient. What is the magic ingredient?

One man, in particular, found it. Here is his story.

Some years ago, this man, a successful cosmetic manufacturer, retired at the age of sixty-five. Each year thereafter his friends gave him a birthday party, and on each occasion, they asked him to disclose his formula. Year after year he pleasantly refused; however, on his seventy-fifth birthday his friends, half-jokingly and half seriously, once again asked if he would disclose the secret.

'You have been so wonderful to me over the years that I now will tell you,' he said. 'You see, in addition to the formulas used by other cosmeticians, I added the magic ingredient'

'What is the magic ingredient?' he was asked.

'I never promised a woman that my cosmetics would make her beautiful, but I always gave her hope.'

Hope is the magic ingredient!

Hope is a desire with the expectation of obtaining what is desired and belief that it is obtainable. A person consciously reacts to that which to him is desirable, believable, and attainable.

And he also subconsciously reacts to the inner urge that induces action when environmental suggestion, self-suggestion, or autosuggestion cause the release of the powers of his subconscious mind. His response to suggestion may develop obedience that is direct, neutral, or in reverse action to a specific symbol. In other words, there may be various types and degrees of motivating factors.

Every result has a given cause. Your every act is the result of a given cause—your motives.

Hope, for example, motivated the cosmetic manufacturer to build a profitable business. Hope also motivated women to buy his cosmetics. Hope will motivate you, too.

The ten basic motives which inspire all human action. Every thought you think, every act in which you voluntarily engage, can be traced back to some definite motive or combination of motives. There are ten basic motives which inspire all thoughts, all voluntary actions. No one ever does anything without having been motivated to do it.

When it comes to learning how to motivate yourself for any given purpose, or how to motivate others, you should have a clear understanding of these ten basic motives. Here they are:

1. The desire for SELF-PRESERVATION
2. The emotion of LOVE
3. The emotion of FEAR
4. The emotion of SEX
5. The desire for LIFE AFTER DEATH
6. The desire for FREEDOM OF BODY AND MIND
7. The emotion of ANGER
8. The emotion of HATE
9. The desire for RECOGNITION AND SELF-EXPRESSION
10. The desire for MATERIAL GAIN

As you have been reading this chapter, perhaps you felt that it contains food for thought. A good sandwich contains nine-tenths bread and one-tenth meat. Unlike a sandwich, this chapter is nine-tenths meat. That is the way the authors planned it. We hope you will chew and digest it carefully.

Are negative emotions good? As you read *Success Through a Positive Mental Attitude* you clearly see that negative emotions, feelings, and thoughts are harmful to the individual. But are there times when these are good?

Yes, negative emotions, feelings, thoughts and attitudes are good —at the proper time and under the right circumstances.

For that which is good for the species of man is good for the individual. It is clear that in the process of evolution, negative thoughts, feelings, emotions, and attitudes protected the individual. In fact, these negatives prevented the species of man from becoming extinct. And these negatives in a person, like the negative forces of a bar magnet, effectively repelled the forces of the other negative powers. This has been. And because it is a universal law, it will continue to be.

Now culture, refinement, and civilization, like man himself, have also evolved from a primitive state. And the more cultured, refined, and civilized a society or environment may be, the less need there is for the individual to use these negatives. But in a negative, antagonistic environment, a person with common sense will use these negative forces with PMA to oppose the evil with which he is faced.

And because you live in a country with laws designed to bring the greatest good to the greatest number; because the rights of that individual are protected, because you are in a society and environment of culture, refinement, and the highest form of civilization: those negative thoughts, feelings, emotions, and passions which lie dormant within you from your hereditary past are not now necessary to solve the problems which primitive man could not otherwise have solved. For he was a law unto himself. And the law of the individual has become subservient to the law of society for his benefit.

Now let's clarify these concepts. Let's take anger, hate, and fear as examples.

Anger and hate. Righteous indignation against evil is a form of anger and hate. The desire to protect one's nation when attacked by an enemy, or the desire to protect the weak against the criminal attack of the madman to save human life is good. To kill to accomplish this, when necessary, is an example of the worst form of all negative feelings and emotions used to achieve a worthy purpose. In our society the patriotism of a soldier or the fulfillment of duty by a police officer are virtues.

Fear. With every new experience and in every new environment nature protects you from potential danger by alerting you through some shade of the emotion of fear. You can be assured that the bravest individual will, in a new environment, at first, experience an awareness that is a conscious or subconscious feeling of timidity or fear. If he finds that the fears are not beneficial to him, the person with PMA will neutralize an undesirable negative emotion by substituting a positive one.

What can you do about it? Man is the only member of the animal kingdom who, through the functioning of his conscious mind, can voluntarily control his emotions from within, rather than be forced to do so by external influences.

And he alone can deliberately change habits of emotional response. The more civilized, cultured and refined you are, the *more easily* you can control your emotions and feelings if you choose to do so.

Emotions are controlled through the combination of reason and action. When fears are unwarranted, or harmful, they can and should be neutralized.

How?

While your emotions are not always immediately subject to reason, nonetheless they are immediately subject to action. For you can use reason to determine the needlessness of the negative emotion and thus motivate yourself to action. You can substitute fear with a positive feeling. How do you do this?

One effective means is through self-suggestion, in fact self-command, with a one-word symbol that incorporates what you want to be. Thus, if you are afraid and want to be courageous, give the self-command be courageous with rapidity several times. Follow this with action. If you want to be courageous, act courageously.

How?

Use the self-starter *Do It Now!* then get into action.

In this and the next chapter you will see how to control your emotions and actions by using self-suggestions. In the meantime:

Keep your mind on the things you should and do want and off the things you shouldn't and don't want.

A success formula that always succeeds when applied. Are you among the hundreds of thousands of persons throughout the world who have read the *Autobiography of Benjamin Franklin*, or among the tens of thousands who have read Frank Bettger's book *How I Raised Myself from Failure to Success in Selling*? If not, we recommend that you read both. These books contain a formula that always succeeds when applied with PMA.

In his autobiography, Franklin indicates that he endeavored to help Benjamin Franklin just as the most important living person wants to help you. He wrote (language modernized):

> 'My intention being to acquire the habit of all these virtues, I judged it would be well not to distract my attention by attempting the whole at once, but to fix it on one of them at a time; and when I should be master of that, then to proceed to another, and so on, until I should have gone through the thirteen, and, as the previous acquisition of some might facilitate the acquisition of

certain others, I arranged them with that view... '

The names of these virtues as Franklin fitted than, together with the precepts (self-motivators for self-suggestion) he gave each one, are:

1. TEMPERANCE: Eat not to dullness; drink not to elevation.
2. SILENCE: Speak not but what may benefit others or yourself, avoid trifling conversation.
3. ORDER: Let all your things have their places; let each part of your business have its time.
4. RESOLUTION: Resolve to perform what you ought; perform without fail what you resolve.
5. FRUGALITY: Make no expense but to do good to others or yourself, that is, waste nothing.
6. INDUSTRY: Lose no time; be always employed in something useful; cut off all unnecessary actions.
7. SINCERITY: Use no hurtful deceit; think innocently and justly, and, if you speak, speak accordingly.
8. JUSTICE: Wrong none by doing injuries, or omitting the benefits that are your duty.
9. MODERATION: Avoid extremes; forbear resenting injuries so much as you think they deserve.
10. CLEANLINESS: Tolerate no uncleanliness in body, clothes, or habitation.
11. TRANQUILITY: Be not disturbed at trifles, or at accidents, common or unavoidable.
12. CHASTITY: Rarely use venery but for health or offspring, never to dullness, weakness, or the injury of your own or another's peace or reputation.
13. HUMILITY: Imitate Jesus and Socrates.

Franklin wrote further: 'Conceiving then that, agreeably to the advice of Pythagoras in his Golden Verses, daily examination would be necessary, I contrived the following method for conducting that examination.

'I made a little book, in which I allotted a page for each of the virtues. I ruled each page with red ink, so as to have seven columns, one for each day of the week, marking each column with a letter for the day. I crossed these columns with thirteen red lines, making the beginning of each line with the first letter of one of my virtues, on each line, and in its proper column, 1 might mark, by a little black spot, every fault I found upon examination to have been committed respecting that virtue upon that day.' Here is the chart:

TEMPERANCE Eat not to dullness; drink not to elevation.							
	S.	M.	T.	W.	T.	F.	S.
T.							
S.	*	*				*	
O.	**	*	*		*	*	*
R.			*				*
F.			*				
I.			*				
S.							
J.							
M.							
C.							
T.							
C.							
H.							

Form of the pages

Now it is as important to know how to use a formula as it is to know the formula. Here's how to use your Knowledge:

A FORMULA IN ACTION

1. *Concentrate on one principle for an entire week,* every day of the week. Respond by proper action every time an occasion arises.
2. And then, start the second week on the second principle of virtue. Let the first be taken over by your subconscious mind. Should an occasion arise when the employment of a previous principle flashes into your conscious mind, use the self-starter *DO IT NOW!* and then *ACT!* Continue to concentrate on one principle at a time each week and leave the others to be executed by the habits established in your subconscious as the occasion arises.
3. When the series is completed, start over again. Thus, at the end of a year, you will have completed the entire cycle four times.
4. When you have acquired a desired characteristic, substitute a new principle for a new virtue, attitude, or activity that you may wish to develop.

Now you have just read the method Benjamin Franklin used to help Benjamin Franklin. As *Success Through a Positive Mental Attitude* is a self-help book, it would be wise for you to study Franklin's method and see how you can apply the principles. In the chapter entitled 'How to Motivate Others' you will see how Frank Bettger raised himself from failure to success by employing Benjamin Franklin's plan.

If you decide to start your own plan, and don't know exactly what principles to start with you could begin with the 13 virtues used by Benjamin Franklin; or you may prefer the 17 success principles described in Chapter Two.

Now for some bread for your sandwich. Let's tell about the first Fuller Brush man.

Alfred C. Fuller, the first of the 'Fuller Brush men,' came from a poor farm family living in Nova Scotia. He couldn't seem to hold a job. In fact, during the first two years of trying to earn a living, he lost three jobs.

But then a radical change came into Fuller's life. For he tried selling brushes. Right then Fuller was motivated. He began to realize that his first three jobs were not the kind of work suited to him.

He didn't like them.

The work didn't come to him naturally. But selling did. And he saw immediately that he would do well as a salesman. He liked his work. So, he conditioned his mind to do the best-selling job in the world. He was terrific.

And having succeeded as a salesman' he set a goal in his climb up the ladder of success. It was: to go in business for himself. Now this goal fitted nicely with his personality, provided he was in sales.

Alfred C. Fuller did quit selling brushes for someone else. And he had more fun than ever before. He manufactured his own brushes in the evening, then sold them the next day. And when his sales began to mount, he rented space in an old shed for eleven dollars a month and hired an assistant who made the brushes for him while he concentrated on sales. The end result from the boy who lost his first three jobs—the Fuller Brush Company, with thousands of door-to-door salesmen and millions of dollars in annual income! You see, you are more apt to succeed if you do what comes naturally.

But there are greater motivating factors than losing a job, making money, or success in business. The desire for self-preservation is the strongest on the list.

Seven came through. Capt. Edward V. Rickenbacker was one of the most successful and highly esteemed men in the United States.

Capt. Eddie, as he was affectionately called, is a symbol of faith, integrity, the joy of hard work and common sense.

Those who met him, heard his lectures or read his book *Seven Came Through* are themselves inspired by the symbol he represents.

The airplane carrying Capt. Eddie and his crew fell into the Pacific. No trace of the wreckage or the men could be found the first week. Nor the second week. But the world was thrilled with the news that Capt. Eddie was saved on the 21st day.

Just picture Capt. Eddie and his crew on three rafts in the Pacific with nothing in sight but the sea and the sky. Picture these men these men, if you will, suffering from the shock of hitting the water when their plane crash landed, suffering from the heat of the burning sun, hungry, thirsty. Then picture the three rafts tied together each morning and evening, with each member of the crew bowing his head in prayer or listening intently as the 23rd Psalm or the verses from Matthew 6:31-34 were read: 'Therefore take no thought, saying, What shall we eat? or, What shall we drink? or, Wherewithal shall we be clothed? (For after all these things do the Gentiles seek:) for your heavenly Father knoweth that ye have need of these things. But seek ye first the kingdom of God, and his righteousness; and all these things shall be added unto you. Take therefore no thought for the morrow: for the morrow shall take thought for the things of itself. Sufficient unto the day is the evil thereof.'

Now, you have the picture, so let's hear directly from Capt.

Eddie himself as he wrote in his book:

'As I have already stated, there was no time that I lost faith in our ultimate rescue, but the others did not seem to share this state of mind fully with me. My companions clearly began to think of what lay beyoud death and to think of it in terms of their own lives.

'I say in all truth that at no time did I ever doubt we would be saved.

'I tried to impart my own philosophy to these men hoping to stimulate their desire to carry on. It was based upon the simple observation that the longer I have had to suffer under trying circumstances, the more certain I was to appreciate my deliverance. This is part of the wisdom that comes to older men.'

Should you ask us how to motivate yourself, we would list the basic motives. They are repeated here!

First, the desire for self-preservation; then the emotion of: love, fear, sex. The desire for: life after death; and freedom of body and mind would follow. And after that, the emotion of: anger; and hate. Then the desire for recognition and self-expression. And last in the list of the ten basic motives would be the desire for material wealth.

In the following chapter you will see how any one of these, or a combination, motivates others.

PILOT NO. 9
Thoughts to Steer By

1. Motivation is that which induces action or determines choice. It is the hope or other force which starts an action in an attempt to produce specific results.
2. Motivate yourself with PMA. Remember: what the mind of man can conceive and believe the mind of man can achieve with PMA. Recognize the possibility of the improbable.
3. Hope is the magic ingredient in motivating yourself and others.
4. Negative emotions, feelings, thoughts, and attitudes are good at the proper time and under the right circumstances.
5. The 10 basic motives are: self-preservation, love, fear, sex, desire for life after death, freedom of body and mind, anger, hate, desire for recognition and self-expression, and the desire for material wealth.
6. Motivate yourself as Benjamin Franklin motivated himself. Develop your own chart. *DO IT NOW!* If you have difficulty listing 13 virtues you would like to acquire or goals you would like to reach, you can start with one and then add to your list as you realize what virtues or goals you desire. Like Benjamin Franklin, have a self-motivator for each. Important: Inspect your progress daily.
7. Capt. Eddie Rickenbacker had developed a strong faith that came to his rescue in time of need. How can you strengthen your faith to help you at the time of your greatest need?
8. Are you prepared so that you can and will apply your faith at the time of your greatest need?

HOPE IS THE MAGIC INGREDIENT IN MOTIVATING YOURSELF AND OTHERS

10

HOW TO MOTIVATE OTHERS

It is important to know how to motivate others in an effective manner and in a desirable direction. Throughout life you play dual parts in which you motivate others and they motivate you: parent and child, teacher and pupil, salesman and buyer, master and servant—you take each part.

How a child motivated his father. A boy two-and-one-half years of age was walking with his father after a very heavy Christmas Day dinner. When they had walked about a block and a half, the youngster stopped, looked up at his father with a smile, and said: 'Daddy...' then hesitated. His father responded, 'Yes?' The boy paused for a second or two and continued, 'If you say please, I'll let you carry me,' Now, who could resist this type of motivation? Even a newborn baby motivates his parents to action.

And, of course, a parent motivates a child. We saw this illustrated by Thomas Edison and his mother. Having confidence in a youngster gives him confidence in himself. When the child feels that he is wrapped in the warm, secure belief that he will do well; he is actually able to do better than he knows. His defenses are relaxed; his guard down: he is able to stop spending emotional energy protecting himself from the possible hurts of failure; instead, he spends his energy reaching for the probable rewards of success. He is relaxed. Confidence has had a measurable effect on his ability—it has brought out the best in him. 'My mother was the making of me,' said Edison. And Napoleon Hill himself had an experience in this direction. He speaks about it in this way:

When I was a youngster, I was considered to be a hellion. Whenever a cow was let loose from her pasture, or a dam broken, or a tree cut down mysteriously, it was young Napoleon Hill that everyone suspected.

And, furthermore, there was some justification for all of this suspicion. My own mother was dead, and my father and brothers thought I was bad, so I really was pretty bad. If people considered me this way, I was not going to disappoint them.

And then one day, my father announced that he was going to remarry. All of us were worried about what kind of a new 'mother' we were going to have, but I in particular was bound and determined that no new mother coming into our home would be able to find a place in my heart. The day finally came when this strange woman entered our home. My father stood back and let her handle the situation in her own way. She went around the room and greeted each of us cheerfully—that is, until she came to me. I stood straight as a ramrod, with my hands folded over my chest, and glared at her without the least suggestion of welcome in my eyes.

'And this is Napoleon,' my father said. 'The worst boy in the hills.'

And with that I'll never forget what my stepmother did. She put both hands on my shoulders and looked me straight in the eye with a twinkle in her own eyes that I shall hold dear forever. 'The worst boy?' she said. 'Not at all. He's just the brightest boy in these hills, and all we have to do is bring that out in him.'

My stepmother was always the one who encouraged me to strike out on my own with such bold schemes as later proved the backbone of my career. I will never forget the great lesson she taught me in how to motivate others by giving them confidence in themselves.

For my stepmother was the making of me. Her deep love and unshakeable faith motivated me to try to become the kind of a boy she believed me to be.

So, you can motivate others by having faith in them. Faith, rightly understood, is active, not passive. Passive faith is no more a force than sight is in an eye that does not observe. Active faith steps out on its belief and risks failure because it assumes it will succeed.

When you motivate others by having faith in them, then you must have an active faith. You must commit your belief. You must say, 'I know that you are going to succeed in this job, so I have committed *myself and others* to your success. We are here, waiting for you...'

When you have that kind of faith in another man, he will succeed.

Now faith can be expressed in a letter. In fact, a letter is an excellent tool for expressing one's thoughts and motivating another person.

A letter can change a life for the better. Anyone who writes a letter affects the subconscious mind of the receiver through suggestion. And the power of this suggestion is, of course, dependent upon several factors.

If you are a parent, for example, and your son or daughter is away at school, you can accomplish that which you might not otherwise achieve. You can grasp the opportunity: (a) to mold the character of your child; (b) to discuss matters that you might hesitate or never take the time to discuss in conversation; and (c) to express your inner thoughts.

Now a boy or girl may not readily accept advice when it

is given verbally. For environment and emotions involved at the time of the conversation might prevent this. And yet the same boy or girl would treasure the same advice received in a carefully written, sincere letter.

To a son or daughter away from home a letter with all of its contents, including advice, is most welcome. And if it is properly written, it may be read frequently, studied, and digested.

And the executive or sales manager who writes the right type of letter to his salesmen can motivate them to break all previous records. Likewise the salesman who writes his sales manager will benefit from this tool of motivation.

Now to write a letter, one must think. Therefore, the writer should crystallize his ideas on paper. And he can ask questions to direct the recipient's mind in the desired channels. In fact, he can ask a question to obtain a letter in return. Or when the person he would like to hear from does not write, he, like an advertising expert, can use a bait. That's what J. Pierpont Morgan did.

One way to motivate a college student to write. J. Pierpont Morgan proved there is at least one way to get college students to answer a letter. His sister had complained that her two college sons just wouldn't write home. Mr. Morgan said that he could get the boys to respond immediately if he sent a letter. And then his sister challenged him to prove it. So. he wrote each nephew and received an immediate reply from both.

Surprised, his sister asked, 'How did you do it?'

Morgan handed the letters to her and she saw that both contained interesting information about college life and thoughts of home. But the postscript on each was similar. One read: 'The ten dollars you said was enclosed in your letter wasn't received!'

Motivate by example. A successful sales manager knows

that one of the most effective means to motivate a salesman is to set an example when working with him in the field. W. Clement Stone has inspired many people with the story he tells about how he trained a salesman who lived at Sioux City, Iowa. Here's the way he tells it:

I listened to one of our salesmen at Sioux City, Iowa, gripe for over two hours one evening. Now he kept on telling how he had worked for two days at Sioux Center without making a sale. He said: 'It's impossible to sell at Sioux Center because the people there are Holland Dutch, they're clannish and they won't buy from a stranger. Besides, the territory has had a crop failure for five years.'

I suggested that we sell the next day at Sioux Center, the town where he had worked for two days without making a sale. So, the next morning we drove to Sioux Center. For there I intended to prove that the salesman with PMA who believed in and used our company's system could sell regardless of the obstacles.

And while the salesman was driving, I closed my eyes, relaxed, meditated, and conditioned my mind. I kept my mind on the reasons why I should and would sell these people rather than why I wouldn't or couldn't.

Here's what I thought: He says that they are Holland Dutch and clannish; therefore, they won't buy. That's good! What's so good about it? It's a well-known fact that if you sell one of a clan, particularly a leader, you can sell the entire clan. Now all I have to do is to make the first sale to the right person. I'll do it even if it takes a long time.

Again, he claims that the territory has had a crop failure for five years. What could be more wonderful? The Holland Dutch are marvelous people and they save their money. Also, they are responsible and want to protect their families and property.

And, as a matter of fact, they probably have not purchased accident insurance from any other insurance salesman because other salesmen wouldn't even try. For they, like the salesman with whom I am driving, would have a negative mental attitude. Our policies offer excellent protection at a low cost. Actually I'll find no competition!

I then engaged in what I term 'mind conditioning'. I repeated to myself with reverence, sincerity, expectation, and emotion, 'Please God help me sell! Please God help me sell! Please God help me sell!' Over and over again I repeated, 'Please God help me sell!' Then I took a nap. And when we arrived at Sioux Center, we called at the bank. Now the personnel consisted of a vice president, a cashier and a teller. Within twenty minutes the vice president had purchased the most protection our company was willing to sell, a full unit. And the cashier purchased a full unit. But the teller will never be forgotten by me because he didn't buy.

And starting with the first place of business next to the bank, we began cold canvassing systematically, store after store, office after office; we interviewed every individual in each establishment.

An amazing thing happened: every person we called on that day purchased the full unit. And there was no exception.

While riding back to Sioux City I thanked the Divine Power for the assistance I had received.

Now why did I succeed in selling in the same place where the other man had failed? Actually, I experienced success for exactly the same reasons that he had experienced failure, except for the—*something more.* He said it was impossible to sell them because they were Holland Dutch and clannish. That's NMA. Now I knew they would buy because they were Holland Dutch and clannish. That's PMA.

Again, he said it was impossible to sell them because they had had a crop failure for five years. That's NMA.

I knew they would buy because they had had a crop failure for five years. And that's PMA.

Now the *something more* was the difference between PMA and NMA. For I had asked for Divine Guidance and help. What's more, I believed that I was receiving it. Now this salesman returned to Sioux Center and stayed for a long tune. And each day that he was there was a record day in sales for him.

This illustrates the value of motivating another person by example, for this salesman also succeeded where he had failed because he learned the value of working with a positive mental attitude.

There are many ways to motivate a person, but a most effective way is through an inspirational book.

When you want to motivate, say it with an inspirational, self-help action book. The most important factors to success in selling are, in order of importance: (a) inspiration to action; (b) knowledge of a successful sales technique for the particular product or service—which is termed know-how; and (c) knowledge of the product or service itself, activity knowledge. Now, these same three principles can be related to success in any business or profession.

In the story that you have just read you can assume that the salesman had knowledge of the sales know-how and knowledge of the service he was selling. But he did lack the most important ingredient—inspiration to action.

Many years ago, Morris Pickus, a well-known sales executive and sales counselor, gave W. Clement Stone a copy of *Think and Grow Rich*. Since then, he has used inspirational books such as those mentioned in *Success Through a Positive Mental*

Attitude to help salesmen develop inspiration to action. Mr. Stone knows that inspiration and enthusiasm are the life of a sales organization. And because the flame of inspiration and enthusiasm will be extinguished unless the fuel that feeds it is kept replenished, Mr. Stone has made it a habit to see that his representatives receive inspirational, self- help action books frequently. And this is in addition to weekly and monthly publications that are intended to act as mental vitamins.

If you know what motivates a person, you can motivate him. As a boy Walter Clarke of Walter Clarke Associates, Providence, Rhode Island, intended to be a doctor. But when he grew older, he thought he wanted to become an engineer. And he studied engineering.

At Columbia University, however, he found the study of the functioning of the human mind so interesting and challenging that he changed from engineering to psychology. And finally, he received his Master's Degree.

Walter Clarke worked as a personnel officer in Macy's Department Store and several other well-known concerns. At that tune the known psychological tests developed the specific information for which they were intended: an applicant's

I. Q., aptitude, and personality. But something important was missing!

Walter endeavored to find the missing factor. He thought: 'An engineer can select the proper part and put it in its place so that a machine will function efficiently. And that is exactly what I want to do with people. I want to select the right person for the right job.'

You see, Walter, like many personnel officers, found: people fail on their job even though their psychological tests indicated that they had sufficient intelligence, aptitude and personality to succeed on the job. 'Why then do we have so much absenteeism, turn-over, and failure?' he asked himself. 'What's the missing factor?'

Now the answer to this question became so simple and obvious that it is truly amazing that other psychologists had not discovered it. For you see a person is more than a mechanical body. He is a mind with a body. He succeeds or fails because he is—or is not—motivated.

Therefore, Walter endeavored to develop an analysis technique that would:

(a) Indicate the individual's tendencies in behavior in either a pleasant or antagonistic environment;
(b) Show the sort of environment that attracts and repels him under favorable or unfavorable situations;
(c) In essence—indicate 'what comes naturally' to the individual.

Also, he endeavored to develop a technique that could be used to analyze the requirements of a given job successfully.

And because he worked hard and continued to search, Walter Clarke found and recognized exactly what he was looking for. For he developed what he called *Activity Vector Analysis*, better known as AVA. It is based on semantics, specifically: the reaction of the individual to word symbols. From the answers given, by the applicant, Clarke designed a chart. And he likewise came up with a formula for designing a similar diagram for any specific job.

Now when the diagram of the applicant corresponded with that of the job, he had a perfect combination.

Why?

For then the applicant would have a job doing the kind of work that came naturally to him. And a person will do what he likes to do—it's fun.

Now the sole purpose of AVA as conceived by Walter Clarke is to help business management in: (a) the selection of personnel; (b) management development; (c) cutting the high cost of absenteeism; (d) personnel turnover.

Walter Clarke achieved a definite major aim. Now for many years W. Clement Stone kept searching for a scientific working tool that could aid him in his efforts to help the representatives under his supervision to achieve success in solving their personal, family, social, and business problems. He was looking for a simple, accurate and usable formula that would eliminate guesswork and save time when applied to a specific individual in a given environment.

Therefore, when he heard of AVA, Mr. Stone investigated and immediately recognized that it was the working tool that he had so long been looking for. He could see that AVA might be used for purposes far beyoud that for which it was conceived. And when he studied under Walter Clarke, his conclusions were confirmed.

For when you know: (a) what the personality traits of the individual are; (b) what his environment is; (c) what motivates him, you then can motivate that individual.

How to motivate another person. While reading *Success Through a Positive Mental Attitude*, you have seen the importance of: semantics, word symbols, suggestion, self- suggestion, and autosuggestion. This was particularly true when you read Chapter Four. Now, Mr. Stone combined this knowledge with what he learned from AVA.

And thus, he made what to him was a great discovery in the technique of motivating other persons.

For the discovery was: with PMA you can be what you want to be, if you are willing to pay the price. This is true regardless of your past experiences, aptitude, I.Q. or environment.

Remember—you have the power to choose.

Now you don't have to study AVA to learn how to motivate yourself and others. But it could certainly help you. For you can use the proper technique when you know what motivates an individual.

And the simple technique that you can use to help you motivate yourself and others is based on the use of suggestion, self-suggestion, and autosuggestion. Let's be specific:

1. If for example a salesman is timid and his job requires him to be aggressive, then:
   (a) The sales manager uses reason to point out that timidity and fear are natural. He proves that others have overcome timidity. He then recommends that the salesman state to himself frequently a word or self-motivator that would symbolize what the salesman wants to be.
   (b) And in this instance, the salesman would repeat every morning and other times throughout the day the following words with rapidity and frequency: 'Be aggressive! Be aggressive!' He would particularly do so if he had a feeling of timidity in a specific environment where it was necessary to act. In such an instance he would act on the self-starter: *Do It Now!*
2. When a sales manager discovers that one of his men is deceitful or dishonest, he will have a talk with his representative. And if he sees the representative wants to cure the fault, then:
   (a) The sales manager tells how others have solved this difficulty. He gives the salesman an inspirational book, article, poem or recommends specific *Bible*

passages. We have found that books like *I Can* by Ben Sweetland and *I Dare You* by William Danforth are particularly effective.

(b) And in such an instance, as in 1(b) above, the salesman would repeat 'Be truthful! Be truthful!' with rapidity every morning and at frequent intervals throughout the day. He would particularly do so at the time that he was tempted to be dishonest or engage in deception in a specific environment where it was necessary for him to make a decision. He would act on the self-motivator: 'Have the courage to face the truth' as well as the self-starter: *Do It Now!*

Now this plan should be easy for you to understand as it is illustrated frequently throughout this book.

And because you understand its effectiveness, you yourself will use it.

And in addition, you, unlike the hundreds of thousands of persons who have read Benjamin Franklin's *Autobiography*, will now immediately use Franklin's method to achieve success. You, unlike them, have been *given The Secret of Getting Things Done: DO IT NOW!*

Use Franklin's method to achieve results! Yes, many hundreds of thousands of persons have read Benjamin Franklin's *Autobiography*. Yet they didn't learn how to use the success principles contained in it. But at least one man did: Frank Bettger.

He listened to the messages that were applicable to him. For he had a problem: he was a failure in business. And he was searching for a workable, down-to-earth formula that would help him help himself. And because he knew what he was looking for, he discovered Franklin's secret.

Franklin indicated that he owed all of his success and happiness to just one idea: a formula for personal achievement. Now Bettger recognized that formula and used it. What happened? He raised himself from *failure to success.* He tells us about it in his great, motivating book, *How I Raised Myself from Failure to Success in Selling.*

Now, why shouldn't you use Franklin's formula for personal achievement? You can, if you will. If the authors of this book succeed in motivating you to use this one idea, you too will, like Bettger, be able to raise yourself from failure to success. Or, if you are not a failure, then you will—through the use of Franklin's method—be able to obtain what you seek: be it wisdom, virtue, happiness, health, or wealth.

Now Bettger wrote out his objectives on thirteen separate cards. The first one is entitled 'Enthusiasm'. The self-motivator is: *To be enthusiastic ACT enthusiastic.* As the great teacher and psychologist, William James, has so conclusively proved: the emotions are not immediately subject to reason, but they are always immediately subject to action.

And the action can be physical or it can be mental. A thought can be just as stimulating and effective as a deed in changing an emotion from negative to positive. In such an instance the act, be it physical or mental, precedes the emotion.

See how the plan works. Because the purpose of *Success Through a Positive Mental Attitude* is to help you help yourself, and because the authors want you to get into action, we shall now illustrate how we motivate individuals in an audience to action through the Franklin-Bettger System.

Here's how we have motivated many thousands of students to apply the Franklin-Bettger plan using the card 'Enthusiasm' and the self-motivator: To be enthusiastic act enthusiastic. We call a student to the front of the class and give him a simple yet effective lesson that he will learn immediately. Here's how we do it—try it. Here is the dialogue that would take place between the instructor and student:

(Note: The dialogue of the instructor is in bold-face type. The student's answers are set in italics.)

Do you want to feel enthusiastic?

Yes.

Then learn the self-motivator: To be enthusiastic act enthusiastic. Now repeat this phrase.

To be enthusiastic act enthusiastic.

Right! What is the key word in the affirmation?

Act.

That's right Let's paraphrase the message and thus you will learn the principle and be able to relate and assimilate it into your own life. If you want to be sick, what do you do?

Act sick.

You're right. If you want to be melancholy, what do you do?

Act melancholy.

Right again! And if you want to be enthusiastic, what do you do?

To be enthusiastic—act enthusiastic.

We then proceed to point out that you can relate this self-motivator to any desirable virtue or personal aim. Thus, we might take justice as an example, and a card could read: ***To be just, ACT just.***

And then the instructor would proceed:

Remember, when someone else's idea is accepted by you, it becomes *your* idea for *your* use. You own it! Now I want you to talk in an enthusiastic tone of voice. I want you to act enthusiastically. To speak enthusiastically, do the following:

1. *Talk loudly!* This is particularly necessary if you are emotionally upset, if you are shaking inside when you stand before an audience, if you have 'butterflies in your stomach'.
2. *Talk rapidly!* Your mind functions more quickly when you do. You can read two books with greater understanding in the time you now read one if you concentrate and read with rapidity.
3. *Emphasize!* Emphasize important words, words that are important to you or your listening audience—a word like you, for example.
4. *Hesitate!* When you talk rapidly, hesitate where there would be a period, comma, or other punctuation in the written word. Thus, you employ the dramatic effect of silence. The mind of the person who is listening catches up with the thoughts you have expressed. Hesitation after a word which you wish to emphasize accentuates the emphasis.
5. *Keep a smile in your voice!* Thus, in talking loudly and rapidly, you eliminate gruffness. You can put a smile in your voice by putting a smile on your face, a smile in your eyes.
6. *Modulate!* This is important if you are speaking for a long period. Remember, you can modulate both pitch and volume. You can speak loudly and intermittently change to a conversational tone and a lower pitch if you wish.
7. When the butterflies stop flying around in your stomach, you can then speak in an enthusiastic, conversational tone of voice.

Do it now! Now in the previous chapter you have read the thirteen principles used by Benjamin Franklin. And here you have been told that *enthusiasm* is the first of the thirteen principles used by Frank Bettger. And you know that a Positive Mental Attitude is the first of the 17 Success Principles.

Therefore, if you have not already done so, start the first of your own 17 cards with the heading 'Develop a Positive Mental Attitude'. Follow through with a card for each of the 17 Success Principles and—use Franklin's method to achieve results.

Your action on the self-starter *DO IT NOW* at this time would prove conclusively that you can motivate yourself. You can! And if you purposely motivate yourself, you will find it easy to motivate others.

And now that you know how to motivate yourself; and others, you are ready to receive the Key to the Citadel of Wealth. The next chapter answers the question: *Is There a Shortcut to Riches?*

PILOT NO. 10
Thoughts to Steer By

1. Throughout life you play dual parts in which you motivate others and they motivate you. Learn and apply the art of motivation with PMA.
2. Motivate others to have confidence in themselves by showing them that you have faith in them and faith in yourself.
3. A letter can change a life for the better. Start the habit of motivating your loved ones by writing letters containing wholesome, good suggestions.
4. Motivate others by example.
5. When you want to motivate, say it with an inspirational, self-help action book.
6. If you know what motivates a person—you can motivate him if you learn the art of motivation with PMA.
7. Motivate others by suggestion. Motivate yourself by self-suggestion.
8. While your emotions are not always subject to reason, nonetheless they are subject to action. If there is an instance you recall in which you might experience the emotion of fear, what action do you think you could take to neutralize it?
9. To become enthusiastic, act enthusiastically!
10. To speak enthusiastically and overcome timidity and fear:
    (a) talk loudly;
    (b) talk rapidly;
    (c) emphasize important words;
    (d) hesitate where there is a period, comma or other punctuation in the written word;
    (e) keep a smile in your voice so that it isn't gruff; and
    (f) use modulation.

11. Start the first of your 17 PMA success cards. *DO IT NOW!*

ANYTHING IN LIFE WORTH
WORKING FOR IS WORTH
PRAYING FOR!

PART III

YOUR KEY TO THE CITADEL OF WEALTH

11

IS THERE A SHORTCUT TO RICHES?

Is there a shortcut to riches?

A shortcut is defined as: a way of accomplishing *something more* directly and quickly than by ordinary procedure. It is a route more direct than that ordinarily taken.

And the man who takes the shortcut knows his destination. He knows the route that is more direct. Yet he will never arrive at his destination unless he starts and continues toward it regardless of the interruptions he encounters or the obstacles he meets.

In Chapter Two we listed the 17 success principles as:

1. A Positive Mental Attitude
2. Definiteness of purpose
3. Going the extra mile
4. Accurate thinking
5. Self-discipline
6. The mastermind
7. Applied faith
8. A pleasing personality
9. Personal initiative
10. Enthusiasm
11. Controlled attention
12. Teamwork
13. Learning from defeat

14. Creative vision
15. Budgeting time and money
16. Maintaining sound physical and mental health
17. Using cosmic habit force

Now why do we repeat the 17 success principles?

We want to show you the shortcut to riches. We want you to take the most direct route.

Now to take the most direct route, *you* must necessarily *think with PMA*... and a positive mental attitude results from the application of these success principles.

The word *think* is a symbol. Its meaning for you depends upon who *you* are.

Who are *you*?

You are the product of your: heredity, environment, physical body, conscious and subconscious mind, experience, and particular position and direction in time and space, and *something more*, including powers known and unknown.

When *you think with PMA*—you can affect, use, control, or harmonize with all of them.

Now only you can think for you.

Therefore, the shortcut to riches for you can be expressed in a six-word symbol:

Think with PMA and Grow Rich!

For if you really think with PMA, you will automatically follow through with action. You will employ the PMA principles expressed in this book—principles that will help you achieve any goal that doesn't violate the laws of God or the rights of your fellow men.

PILOT NO. 11
A Thought to Steer By

A shortcut to riches: Think with PMA and Grow Rich!

IF YOU HAVE PMA,
YOU CAN DO IT IF YOU
BELIEVE YOU CAN.

12

ATTRACT—DON'T REPEL—WEALTH

Whoever you are—regardless of your age, your education, or your occupation—you can attract wealth. You can also repel it. We say: 'Attract—don't repel—wealth.'

This chapter tells you how you can make money. Would you like to be rich? Be truthful with yourself. Of course, you would. Or—are you afraid to be rich?

Perhaps you're sick and because of this, you don't try to acquire wealth. If this be the case, just remember the experience of Milo C. Jones about whom you read in Chapter Two.

Or, if you are a, patient in a hospital, you can attract wealth by engaging in study, thinking, and planning time as George Stefek did.

In a hospital bed—think! Time after time as we have studied the careers of successful men, we have discovered that they date their own success from the day they picked up a self-improvement book. Never underestimate the value of a book. Books are tools, providing inspiration which can launch you onto a bold new program and which can also light the dark days that any such program entails.

George Stefek was convalescing at the Veterans Administration Hospital in Hines, Illinois. There he discovered by accident the value of thinking time. Financially—he was broke. While George was convalescing, he had a great deal of time on his hands. There wasn't too much to do except read and think. He read *Think and Grow Rich*. And he was ready.

An idea occurred to him. Many laundries, George knew, fold their newly ironed shirts over a piece of cardboard to keep the shirts stiff and free from wrinkles. By writing a few letters, George learned that these shirt boards cost the laundries about $4.00 per thousand. His idea was to sell the boards for $1.00 a thousand; however, each one would carry an advertisement. The advertisers would, of course, pay for the space, and George would make a profit.

George had an idea and he tried to make it work.

When he left the hospital, he got into action!

New in the advertising field, he had his problems. But he finally developed successful sales techniques through what others term 'trial and error' and we term 'trial and success'.

George continued the custom he had started in the hospital to engage in study, thinking and planning time each day.

Even when George's business was moving ahead swiftly, he decided to increase his sales by increasing the efficiency of his service. The shirt boards, when withdrawn from the shirts, were not retained by the laundries' customers.

Now, he asked himself the question: 'How can I get families to keep these shirt boards with the advertisements on them?' The solution flashed into his mind.

What did he do? On one side of the shirt board, he continued to print an advertisement in black and white or in colors. On the other side he added something new—an interesting game for the children, a delicious recipe for the wife, or a provocative crossword puzzle for the whole family. George tells about one husband who complained that his laundry bill had gone up in a sudden, unaccountable way. Then he discovered that his wife was sending in shirts to the laundry which ordinarily he could have worn another day, just to get more of George's recipes!

But George didn't stop there. He was ambitious. He wanted to expand his business still further. Again, he asked himself the question: 'How?' And he found the answer.

George Stefek gave the entire $1.00 per thousand he received from the laundries to the American Institute of Laundering. The Institute, in turn, recommended that each member help himself and his trade association by using George Stefek's shirt boards exclusively.

And thus George made another important discovery: *the more you give of that which is good and desirable—the more you get!*

Now a carefully planned thinking time session brought George Stefek considerable wealth. He discovered that a time apart is essential to any successful attraction of riches.

It is in quiet that our best ideas occur to us. Don't make the mistake of believing that by a frantic kind of dashing around you are being your most effective and efficient self. Don't assume that you are wasting time when you take time out for thought. Thought is the foundation upon which all else is built by man.

Now it isn't necessary for you to go to a hospital to establish the habit of reading good motivating books, to think or to make plans. And your thinking, study, and planning sessions need not be too lengthy. If you invest only one per cent of your time in a study, thinking, and planning session it will make an amazing difference in the speed with which you reach your goals.

Your day has 1,440 minutes in it. Invest one per cent of that time in a study, thinking and planning session. And you will be astounded at what those fourteen minutes do for you. For it may surprise you to find that when you develop this habit you will receive constructive ideas almost any time or anywhere you might be: while doing the dishes, or riding the bus, or while taking a bath.

Be certain to use two of the greatest, yet simplest working tools ever invented—tools used by a genius like Thomas Edison—a pencil and a piece of paper. For he always had handy—paper and pencil. And thus you, like him, will record the ideas that come to you day or night.

Another requirement to attract wealth is to learn how to set your goal. It is important for you to understand this. Few people, even when they realize its importance, really understand how to set a goal.

Learn how to set your goals. There are four important things to keep in mind.

(a) Write down your goal. You will then begin to crystallize your thinking. The very act of thinking as you write will have a tendency to create an indelible impression in your memory.

(b) Give yourself a deadline. Specify a time for achieving your objective. This is important in motivating you: set out in the direction of your goal and keep moving towards it.

(c) Set your standards high. Now there seems to be a direct relationship between ease in achieving a goal and the strength of your motives. You have discovered for yourself in Chapter Nine how to motivate yourself at will and in Chapter Ten how to motivate others.

And the higher you set your major goal, generally speaking, the more concentrated will be the effort you make to achieve it. The reason: logic will make it mandatory that you at least aim at an intermediate objective as well as an immediate one. So, aim higher. And then have immediate and intermediate steps leading towards its achievement.

The following question should stimulate your thinking: Where will you be and what will you be doing ten years from today if you keep doing what you are doing now?

(d) Aim high. It is a peculiar thing that no more effort is required to aim high in life, to demand prosperity and abundance, than is required to accept misery and poverty.

I bargained with life for a penny,
And life would pay no more,
However, I begged at evening when I counted my scanty store.
For life is a just employer, it gives you what you ask,
But once you have set the wages,
Why, you must bear the task.
I worked for a menial's hire, only to learn, dismayed,
That any wage I had asked of life,
Life would have willingly paid.

You have to be bold enough to ask of life more than you may, right now, feel you are worth because it is an observable fact that people tend to rise to meet demands that are put upon them.

While it is exceedingly desirable that you blueprint your program from beginning to end, this is not always feasible. One doesn't always know all the answers between the beginning of a great enterprise or journey and its ending. But if you know where you are and where you want to be and you start from where you are to get to where you want to be, you will, if you keep properly motivated, move forward step by step until you get there.

Take that first step. The important thing after setting a goal is taking action. A sixty-three-year-old grandmother,

Mrs. Charles Philipia, decided that she was going to walk from New York City to Miami, Florida. She reached Miami and, while there, was interviewed by newspapermen. They wanted to know if the idea of such a long journey on foot hadn't frightened her. How did she ever summon courage to make such a journey with her feet as her only mode of travel?

'It doesn't take courage to take one step,' replied Mrs. Philipia. 'And that's all I did really. I just took one step. And then I took another step. And then another and another and here I am.'

Yes, you must take that first step. It makes no difference how much thinking and study time you spend, it will avail you little unless you also act.

One of the authors was introduced to a man in Phoenix, Arizona, by a friend. It was a rather odd introduction.

'Meet the man who received a million dollars cash for a gold mine and now has the million dollars and also owns the mine.'

'How in the world did you manage such a thing?' came the question, asked with considerable awe.

'Oh, I had an idea, but I didn't have any money. I did have a pick and a shovel. So I took my pick and my shovel and went out to make my idea a reality,' he responded.

'And then it occurred to me: if I would search for a gold mine and dig around the vein, should I find a mine, one of the large mining corporations could afford to work the mine whereas I wouldn't have the necessary capital. You know, mining machinery costs money today.

'So, I searched for and found a vein of gold. Every indication was that I had made a very rich strike. I sold it for two million dollars. The terms were a million dollars in cash and a first mortgage of a million dollars. While mining operations were underway the vein ran out. I informed the owners of the mining company that if they wanted to abandon the mine, I would take it back and cancel their mortgage. They accepted. So you see, I got a million dollars cash for the mine and still have the million dollars and the mine.'

Wealth repelled with NMA. A positive mental attitude will attract wealth but a negative mental attitude will do just the opposite.

With a positive mental attitude, you will keep trying until you achieve the wealth you are seeking. Now you might start with a positive mental attitude and make your first step forward. Yet you may become influenced by the negative side of your talisman and stop when you are just one step from reaching your destination. You may fail to employ one of the 17 success principles. Here's a very good example:

Let's call our man Oscar. In the latter part of 1929, he was at the railroad station in Oklahoma City where it was necessary for him to wait several hours for a train connection east. He had spent months in the western deserts in temperatures as high as 110 degrees. He was seeking oil for an eastern concern. And he was successful.

Oscar was a graduate of M.I.T. It is said that he had combined the old divining rod, galvanometer, magnetometer, oscillograph, radio tubes, and other instruments, into a Doodle Bug for detecting oil deposits.

Now Oscar had received word that the company he represented was insolvent. It had become bankrupt because the president had used the firm's large cash resources in speculation in the stock market. The market crashed in late 1929. Oscar was on his way home. He was out of a job, and the outlook was rather dismal.

The influence of NMA began to exert a powerful influence on him.

Because he had to wait several hours, he decided to occupy himself by setting up his instrument in the railroad station. The reading on his instrument was so high in its positive indication of oil deposits that Oscar in a rage impulsively kicked the instrument and destroyed it.

You see, Oscar was frustrated.

'There couldn't be that much oil! There couldn't be that much oil!' he shouted repeatedly in disgust.

But Oscar was frustrated. He was under the influence of a negative mental attitude. The opportunity for which he had been searching lay at his very feet. He only had to make one step to reach it. But, because of the influence of NMA, he refused to recognize it

He lost faith in his own invention. Had he been under the influence of PMA, he would have attracted wealth, not repelled it. Applied faith is one of the important 17 success principles. The test of your faith is whether you apply it at the time of your greatest need.

NMA had led Oscar to believe that many of the things that he had faith in were wrong. As you recall: the Depression brought a fear consciousness into the minds of many persons—Oscar was one. He had worked hard and sacrificed, yet he was out of a job through no fault of his own. The president of his company had been held in high esteem by Oscar, yet this man whom he trusted embezzled the company's funds. Now the machine that had proved its value in the past seemed to have gone haywire. Yes—Oscar was frustrated.

When Oscar boarded the train at the Oklahoma City railroad station that day, he left his Doodle Bug behind. And he also left one of the nation's richest oil deposits.

A short time later, Oklahoma City was found to be literally ***floating on oil.*** Oscar has become a living demonstration of the application of two principles:

A positive mental attitude attracts wealth and a negative mental attitude repels it.

Wealth can be acquired on a modest salary. But you may say: 'All this about positive and negative mental attitudes is very fine for someone who's out to make a million dollars. But I'm not really interested in making a million.

'Of course, I want security. I want enough to live well and take care of the needs I will have some day when I retire.

'What about me if I am an office employee? What about me when I have just a fair salary?' Now here's our answer:

You too can acquire wealth. Wealth enough for security. Or, even wealth enough to become rich in spite of what you say. Just let the PMA influence of your talisman affect you favorably.

We'll prove that this can be done.

And if for some reason you aren't fully convinced, just read a book: *The Richest Man in Babylon.* And then make your first step forward. Keep going and you'll have the financial security or wealth you are seeking. Now that's exactly what Mr. Osborn did.

Mr. Osborn was a salaried employee, yet he acquired wealth. It wasn't so many years ago that he retired with the statement: 'I now spend my time having my money make money for me while I do what I want to do.'

Again, the principle used by Mr. Osborn is so obvious that it is often unseen.

The principle he learned and the one that you also can employ will now be stated in a very few words. In reading *The Richest Man in Babylon,* Mr. Osborn found that wealth could be acquired if you:

(a) Just save one dime out of every dollar you earn;
(b) Each six months, invest your savings and interest or dividend returns from these savings and investments; and
(c) When you invest, seek expert advice on safe investments and thus you won't gamble and lose your principal.

Let us repeat: that's exactly what Mr. Osborn did. Just think of it. You can have security or wealth by saving only a dime out of each dollar you earn and investing it safely.

When should you start? *Do It Now!*

Now let's contrast Mr. Osborn's experience with that of a man who had good physical health and read an inspirational book. He was fifty years old when he was introduced to Napoleon Hill.

This man smiled when he said, 'I read your book *Think and Grow Rich* many years ago—but I'm not rich.'

Napoleon Hill laughed and then replied seriously:

'But you can be rich. Your future is ahead of you. You must prepare yourself to be ready. And in making yourself ready for the opportunities that are available to you, you must first develop a positive mental attitude.' And the interesting thing is that this man did heed the author's advice. Five years later, the man wasn't rich, but he had developed a positive mental attitude. And he was on his way to wealth. He had been many thousands of dollars in debt. Within the five-year period, he had gotten completely out of debt and had begun making investments with the money he had saved.

He developed PMA as he studied the book *Think and Grow Rich*. He did not only read it. He had learned to recognize principles and apply them.

When the NMA side of his talisman was influencing him, he was like those workmen who blame their tools for poor craftsmanship.

Have you ever blamed your tools?

Where does the fault lie: If you own a perfect camera and use the right film; if you have the proper set of rules to take perfect pictures under all types of circumstances; if someone else takes perfect photographs with your camera but—yours are failures?

Does the fault lie with the camera?

Could it be that you have read the rules but haven't taken the time to understand them? Or, if you do understand them, that you don't apply the rules?

Could it be that you will read *Success Through a Positive Mental Attitude*—a book that could change the entire course of your life for the better—without taking the time to understand, memorize self-motivators, learn the principles that will guarantee success—and apply them? Your answer will be evident to you by your action.

Now, it's not too late to learn.

If you haven't learned by now, you might as well learn now: you will not succeed consistently unless you know and understand the rules; you will not continuously succeed unless you apply the rules. Therefore, take the time to understand and apply what you are reading in this book. PMA will help you.

'The home of my dreams.' Remember, the thoughts that you think and the statements you make regarding yourself determine your mental attitude. If you have a worthwhile objective, find the one reason why you can achieve it rather than hundreds of reasons why you can't.

One of the rules in obtaining what you want through PMA is to *act* once you have your sights on a goal. Another is: 'Go the extra mile.' W. Clement Stone tells of the following experience which illustrates both rules.

> One April evening, while I was visiting Frank and Claudia Noonan in Mexico City, Claudia commented, 'I wish we could have a home in the Jardines del Pedregal de San Angel.' (This is the most desirable section of that beautiful city.) 'Why don't you?' I asked.
>
> Frank laughed and answered, 'We don't have the money.'
>
> 'Does that make any difference, if you know what you want?' I inquired, and then, without waiting for a response, I asked a question that I might ask of you.
>
> 'By the way, have you ever read an inspirational, motivating book like *Think and Grow Rich, The Power of Positive Thinking, I Can, I Dare You, TNT, Applied Imagination, Turn on the Green Lights in Your Life, Acres of Diamonds,* or *The Magic of Believing?*
>
> 'No,' was the response.

Thereupon I told of several experiences of those persons who: knew what they wanted; read an inspirational book; listened to its message; and then got into action.

And I even told how years ago I purchased a new $30,000 home on my own terms—with a $1500 down payment and how in due course it was completely paid for. I promised to send one of the recommended books. I did.

Frank and Claudia Noonan were ready.

It was the following December, while studying in my library that I received a telephone call from Claudia who said, 'We just arrived from Mexico City, and the first thing Frank and I wish to do is to thank you.' 'Thank me for what?'

'We want to thank you for our new home in the Jardines del Pedregal de San Angel.'

A few days later at dinner Claudia explained, 'Late one Saturday afternoon Frank and I were relaxing at home. Some friends from the States telephoned and asked if we would drive them to the Jardines del Pedregal de San Angel.

'It just so happened we were both rather exhausted. And besides, we had taken them there earlier in the week. Frank was ready to 'beg off' when an expression used in the book flashed through his mind—*Go the extra mile.*

'While driving them through this man-made paradise, I saw the home of my dreams—even the swimming pool I longed for.' (Claudia is the swimming champion, Claudia Eckert.)

'Frank bought it.'

Frank said, 'You might like to know that although the property cost in excess of a half million pesos, I only made a deposit of five thousand pesos. It costs less for our family to live in the Jardines del Pedregal de San Angel than in our former home.'

'Why is this?' I asked in surprise.

'Well, we bought the two homes that were on the property instead of one. The rent from the one house is enough to make payments on the entire enterprise.

Now this wasn't so surprising after all. It's quite common for a family to buy a duplex apartment and rent one and live in the other. What is surprising to a person without experience is how easy it is to get what you want by understanding and applying the success principles to be found in an autobiography or self-improvement book.

'Attract wealth with PMA,' we say. You say: 'Money makes money and I have no money.' This is a negative mental attitude. If you don't have money, use OPM. That's what the next chapter is all about.

PILOT NO. 12
Thoughts to Steer By

1. If you know your specific destination and take the first step, you're on your way!
2. The test of your faith is whether you apply it when you are not in difficulty, as well as at the time of your greatest need.
3. If you don't succeed when you finally read and study *Success Through a Positive Mental Attitude*, with whom does the fault lie?
4. The house of your dreams: You can have it! Like Frank and Claudia Noonan, you may buy two houses and rent one to pay for both.
5. Do you need to be in an accident or get sick and land in a hospital to establish the habit of regularly engaging in study, thinking and planning time regarding your personal, family or business life?
6. Have you made a start toward achieving desirable goals by: (a) writing down each goal, (b) setting deadlines for reaching them, (c) setting high goals, and (d) inspecting your written statements daily?
7. Where will you be and what will you be doing ten years from today if you keep on doing what you are doing now?
8. *The Richest Man in Babylon*: This book gives you a proven formula of success:
   (a) Just save one dime out of every dollar you earn.
   (b) Each six months invest your savings, and the interest or dividend returns from these savings and investments.
   (c) Before you invest, seek expert advice on safe investments.
   (d) If you need the money you are saving for living expenses or necessities, then work an extra hour (or

more) so that you have no excuse for not saving 10 per cent of your earnings.

ENGAGE IN: STUDY...THINKING... AND PLANNING TIME WITH PMA

13

IF YOU DON'T HAVE MONEY—USE OPM!

Business? It is quite simple. It is other people's money!' said Alexander Dumas the Younger in his play, *The Question of Money.*

Yes, it's that simple: use OPM—*other people's money.* That's the way to acquire great wealth. Benjamin Franklin did it, William Nickerson did it, Conrad Hilton did it, Henry J. Kaiser did it, Colonel Sanders did it, and Ray Kroc did it. And if you are wealthy, the chances are you did it too.

Now, if you are not wealthy, learn to read what is unwritten. In fact—rich or poor: read what is unwritten into every platitude, axiom, or self-motivator. The basic unwritten premise in 'Use OPM' is: that you will operate on the highest ethical standards of integrity, honor, honesty, loyalty, consent, and the Golden Rule and *apply these* in your business relationships.

The dishonest man is not entitled to credit.

And the self-motivator *Use OPM* implies repayment in full as agreed with an advantageous consideration or profit to those whose money is used.

Credit and the use of OPM are one and the same thing. It is the lack of a satisfactory credit system within country that keeps backward nations back. Whereas it is the credit system as practiced in the United States that has developed such great wealth and progress in this nation. It has been singularly American.

Now the person, corporation or nation that does not have credit—or does not use it for expansion and progress if they do have it—is missing an important number in the combination for success. Therefore, take the advice of a wise and successful businessman like Benjamin Franklin.

Good advice. *Advice To a Young Tradesman* written in 1748 by Franklin, discusses the use of OPM as follows:

'Remember, that money is of the prolific, generating nature. *Money can beget money*, and its offspring can beget more,' and so on.

Also, Franklin said:

'Remember, that six pounds a year is but a groat a day. For this little sum (which may be daily wasted either in time or expense unperceived) a man of credit may, on his own security, have the constant possession and use of an hundred pounds.'

Now this statement of Franklin's is a symbol of an idea. His advice is as good today as when it was written. You can start with a few cents and have constant possession of $500 by employing it. Or you can expand the idea and have constant possession of millions of dollars. That is what Conrad Hilton does. He is a *man of credit.*

The Hilton Hotels Corporation obtained credit of millions of dollars to build luxurious motels for air travelers at large airports. The corporation's collateral: mostly, Hilton's name for honest dealing.

Honesty is one thing for which a satisfactory substitute has never been found. It is something which reaches deeper into a human being than most traits of personality. Honesty, or the lack of it, writes itself indelibly into every word one speaks, into every thought and deed, and often reflects itself in one's face so that the most casual observer can sense the quality of sincerity immediately. The dishonest person, on the other hand, may announce his weakness in the very tone of his voice, the expression on his face, in the nature and trend of his conversations, or in the type of service he renders.

So, while this chapter might seem to be one about the use of other people's money, it also has strong overtones about character in it. Honesty and reputation, credit and success in business are all intermixed. The man who has the first of them is well on his way to gaining the other three.

Make investments with OPM. William Nickerson was another man of credit and reputation who found: 'Money can beget money, and its offspring can beget more,' and so on. He tells about it in his book. The title tells what he did. The book tells how he did it.

Nickerson's book is aimed specifically at how to make money with OPM in your spare time in the real estate field. But almost everything he has to say also applies to you in your efforts to acquire wealth by making investments with OPM.

How I Turned $1000 Into $3 Million in My Spare Time is the title of the book.

'Show me a millionaire,' he says, 'and I will show you almost invariably a heavy borrower.' To back up his statement, he points to wealthy men such as Henry Kaiser, Henry Ford, and Walt Disney.

And we will point to Charlie Sammons who, with bank credit, developed a forty-million-dollar business in ten years. But, before we do, let's talk about the people who help men like Conrad Hilton, William Nickerson, and Charlie Sammons by loaning them the money they need.

Your banker is your friend. Banks are in business to loan money. The more they loan to honest men, the more money they make for themselves. Commercial banks loan money primarily for business purposes. Thus, loans for luxuries are not encouraged.

Your banker is an expert. And more important, he is your friend. He wants to help you. For he is one of the people eager to see you succeed. If the banker knows his business, listen to what he has to say.

For a person with common sense never underestimates the power of a borrowed dollar or the advice of an expert. It was the use of OPM and a successful plan—plus the PMA success principles of initiative, courage, and common sense— that resulted in an average American boy named Charlie Sammons becoming wealthy.

Like some Texans, Charlie Sammons of Dallas is a millionaire. In fact, like some other Texans, he is a multimillionaire. Yet at the age of 19, he was no better off financially than most teenage boys except that he had worked and saved some money.

One of the officers in the bank where Charlie regularly deposited his savings each Saturday took an interest in him. For the banker felt: now here's a boy of character and ability— and he knows the value of money.

So, when Charlie decided to go in business for himself, buying and selling cotton, the banker gave him credit. And this was the first experience Charlie Sammons had in the use of OPM. As you will see, it was not the last. He learned then, and has seen it confirmed since:

Your banker is your friend.

About a year and a half after he became a cotton broker, the young man became a horse and mule trader. It was then that he learned much about human nature.

And his understanding of people in addition to his knowledge of money soon developed in Charlie Sammons a very sound philosophy of a brand commonly observed in persons who are, or will be, successful. Charlie learned this philosophy at an early age. He has never lost it. Today he still maintains it.

This brand of philosophy is known as: *common sense.*

After he had operated a few years as a horse and mule trader, two men came to Charlie and asked him to go to work for them. These two men had developed a reputation for themselves as being outstandingly successful in the sale of insurance. They had come to Charlie because they had learned a lesson from defeat. Here's how it happened...

It seems that after these two salesmen had successfully sold life insurance over a period of many years, they were motivated to form a company of their own. They were good salesmen all right. But they were poor business administrators. In fact, they were such good salesmen that they sold their company out of business.

Now it is not uncommon for salesmen to assume that financial success in a business is contingent only on sales. But this is a false premise. A poor administration can lose money as fast, or faster, than a good sales management and sales force can bring it in. Their trouble was that neither one of these men was a good administrator.

But they had learned their lesson—the hard way. On the day they went to see Charlie, one of the salesmen told their story of defeat and said:

'Since our company went broke, we have paid off our losses from the commissions we have since made selling insurance. We also had to pay for our living. It has taken a mighty long time but—we have done it.

'We know we are good salesmen. And we also know now that we should keep to our own specialty—selling.' He hesitated, looked into the eyes of the young man and continued:

'Charlie, you have your feet on the ground. You have good common horse sense and we need you. Together we can succeed.'

And they did.

A plan and OPM developed a $40,000,000 volume. A few years later Charlie Sammons bought all of the shares of the company he and these two men had formed. How did he get the money? He used OPM plus what he had saved.

Where did he get the large amount of money that he needed? He borrowed it from a bank, of course. Remember: he had learned early that his banker was his friend.

And then in the year that his company had produced an annual premium volume of almost $400,000, the insurance executive finally found the success formula for rapid expansion that he had long been looking for.

He was ready.

It was this formula plus OPM that developed a forty-million-dollar premium volume in a single year. Sammons had seen that an insurance company in Chicago had successfully developed a sales plan through 'leads'.

Now for many years sales managers had used what is termed the 'lead system' to promote a new business. And with sufficient good leads salesmen often earn exceedingly large incomes. Inquiries from individuals who indicate an interest are called 'leads'. These are generally obtained from some form of promotional advertising program.

Perhaps you know from experience that with human nature being what it is, many salesmen are timid or afraid to try to sell persons whom they don't know or with whom they have had no previous personal contact or communication. Because of this fear, they waste a lot of time that could be used in selling prospects.

But even an ordinary salesman will be motivated to call on as many prospects as he has leads. For he knows that many sales can be made even though he himself may have little sales training or experience—when he is furnished good leads. And besides he has an address and a specific person to see there. He believes the prospect is somewhat interested before he interviews him.

Therefore he is not as fearful as he would be if he were forced to try to sell a person without any preconditioning whatsoever. Some companies build their entire sales program on such leads. And advertising is used to obtain them.

But advertising costs money.

Charlie Sammons knew where to go to get the money when he had a good bankable idea—the Republic National Bank of Dallas. For it is well known in Texas that this bank helped build Texas. And it is in the business to loan money to men of integrity like Charlie Sammons who have a plan and know how to work it.

Now while it is true that some bankers won't take the time to learn their client's business, Oran Kite and other officers of the Republic National do. Charlie explained his plan to them. And, as a result, he was able to employ unlimited credit to build his insurance business through the lead system.

You see, it was because of the American credit system that Charlie Sammons was able to build the Reserve Life Insurance Company. And under such a system he was able to develop a premium volume from four hundred thousand dollars to over forty million within the short space of ten years. Again because he used OPM in his investments, he is able to invest and own controlling interest in hotels, office buildings, manufacturing plants and other enterprises.

But you don't need to go to Texas to use OPM. W. Clement Stone bought an insurance company with one million six hundred thousand dollars in assets, using the seller's own money. He went to Baltimore.

How W. Clement Stone bought a $1,600,000 company with the seller's own money. This is how he describes the purchase:

> It was the year-end, and I was engaging in study, thinking, and planning time. I determined that my major objective for the following year would be to own an insurance company that was licensed to operate in several states. I set a deadline as to when this was to be accomplished: December 31st of the next year.
>
> Now I knew what I wanted and a date was set for its achievement. But I didn't know how I could get it. This wasn't really important, for I believed that I could find a way. Therefore I must, I thought, look for a company that would fulfill my requirements: (1) that it have a charter to sell accident and health insurance, and (2) that it be licensed to operate in nearly all the states. I didn't need established business, just a vehicle.
>
> Of course, there was the problem of money. But I would face that problem when it arose. Even then it occurred to me that I was a salesman by vocation and therefore I could, if it should become necessary, work out a three-way deal: a contract to buy the company; reinsure the entire business with some large company; and thus own everything but the insurance in force. These other insurance companies were willing to pay a good price for established business. I didn't need established business. I had the experience and ability to build an accident

and health business as long as I had the vehicle. I had already proved this by building a national insurance sales organization.

And then I made the next step: I asked for Divine guidance and help.

While analyzing the immediate problems with which I might be faced, it occurred to me that I should let the world know what I wanted, and the world would help me. (Now this conclusion was not in conflict with the principles laid down by Napoleon Hill in *Think and Grow Rich* wherein he states that you keep your definite objectives a secret except to members of your mastermind alliance. When I found the company that I wished to buy, I would, of course, follow his suggestion and keep the negotiations a secret from the world until I closed the deal.)

So I let the world know what I wanted. Every time I met a person in the industry who might give me information, I told him what I was looking for.

Joe Gibson of Excess Insurance was such a person. I had met him on just one occasion.

The new year was started with enthusiasm as I had a big objective and I set out to reach it. One month passed. Two. Six months passed. At last ten months had gone by. And although I had checked into many possibilities, none fulfilled my two basic requirements.

Then one Saturday in the month of October when I was seated at my desk with my papers pushed back, engaged in study, planning, thinking time, I checked off the list of my objectives for the year. All had been achieved but one—the important one.

Just two months to go, I said to myself. There is a way. While I don't know what it is, I know I'll find it. For it never occurred to me that my aim could not be reached or that it wouldn't be reached within the time limit specified. There is always a way, I said to myself. Again, as on similar occasions, I asked for Divine guidance and help.

Now two days later something unexpected happened. I was again seated at my desk. This time I was busy dictating. The telephone rang a disturbing note at my elbow. I picked up the receiver and a voice said: 'Hello, Clem. This is Joe Gibson.' Our conversation was short, and I will never forget it. Joe talked rapidly:

'I thought you would be interested in knowing that the Commercial Credit Company of Baltimore will probably liquidate the Pennsylvania Casualty Company because of its tremendous losses. Of course, you know Commercial Credit owns Pennsylvania Casualty. There will be a meeting of the Board of Directors next Thursday in Baltimore. All the Pennsylvania Casualty Company's business is already being reinsured by two other insurance companies owned by Commercial Credit. The name of the executive vice president of Commercial Credit is E. H. Warheim.'

I thanked Joe Gibson warmly, asked him one or two more questions, and then hung up the phone. After a few minutes of thought it flashed into my mind that if I could conceive a plan whereby Commercial Credit Company would accomplish its objectives more quickly and with greater certainty than under its proposed plan, it shouldn't be difficult to persuade the directors to accept such a plan.

I didn't know Mr. Warheim, and therefore was hesitant to call him, but I felt that speed was of the essence. And then two self-motivators forced me to act.

Where there is nothing to lose by trying and everything to gain if successful, by all means try. *Do It Now!*

And without a second's further hesitation, I picked up the phone and placed a long-distance call to E. H. Warheim in Baltimore. 'Mr. Warheim,' I began with a smile in my voice. 'I have some good news for you!'

And then I introduced myself and explained that I had heard of the possible action to be taken regarding the Pennsylvania Casualty Company and that I thought I would be in a position to help them reach their objectives more quickly. Then and there I made an appointment to see Mr. Warheim and his associates the following day at 2 p.m. in Baltimore.

At 2 p.m. the next day W. Russell Arlington, my attorney, and I met with Mr. Warheim and his associates.

Pennsylvania Casualty Company fulfilled my needs. It had a charter permitting it to operate in 35 states. It had no insurance in force as the business had already been reinsured by other companies. By making the sale, Commercial Credit Company accomplished its objectives quickly and with certainty. In addition, they received $25,000 from me for the charter.

Now the company had $1,600,000 in liquid assets: negotiable securities and cash. How did I get the one million six hundred thousand dollars? I used OPM. It happened this way:

'What about the one million six hundred thousand

dollars in assets?' Mr. Warheim asked.

I was ready for the question and immediately responded: 'Commercial Credit Company is in the business of lending money. I will just borrow the one million six hundred thousand dollars from you.'

We all laughed, and then I continued: '*You have everything to gain and nothing to lose.* For everything I own will be behind the loan, including the one million six hundred-thousand-dollar company that I am now buying.

'Besides, you are in the business of lending money. And what better security could you have than the pledge of the company you are selling me? In addition, you will receive interest on the loan.

'What is most important to you is that this way you will solve your problem swiftly and with certainty.'

When I hesitated, Mr. Warheim asked another very important question: 'How are you going to repay the loan?'

And I was ready for that question too. My response was: 'I will repay the entire loan in sixty days.

'You see, I don't need more than a half million dollars to operate an accident and health company in the 35 states in which Pennsylvania Casualty Company is licensed.

'As the company will be wholly owned by me, all I need to do is to reduce the capital and surplus of Pennsylvania Casualty Company from one million six hundred thousand dollars to five hundred thousand dollars, which I can then apply to my loan with you.

'You and I know that a businessman is faced with the matter of income taxes on any transaction involving

> income or expenditures. But no income tax payments will be required on this transaction for the simple reason that the Pennsylvania Casualty Company has not made profits, and no part of the money I receive when I reduce the capital will, therefore, be from profits.'
>
> And then another question was asked me: 'What about your plans to repay the balance of the half million dollars?'
>
> Again, I was prepared to answer and said: 'This should be easy. The Pennsylvania Casualty Company has assets consisting only of cash, government bonds, and high-grade securities. I can borrow the half million dollars from the banks with which I have been doing business by pledging my interest in Pennsylvania Casualty Company and my other assets as additional security to back the loan.'
>
> When Mr. Arrington and I left the office of Commercial Credit Company at 5:00 p.m., the deal was closed.

Now this experience is related in detail here to illustrate the steps one takes to achieve his aims through the use of OPM. If you will refer to Chapter Eleven entitled 'Is There a Shortcut to Riches?' you will see how the principles mentioned there were applied here.

While this story indicates how the use of OPM can help a person, credit can sometimes be harmful.

Warning—credit can hurt you. So far we have been talking about the benefits of the use of credit. We have been talking about the practice of borrowing money for the purpose of making money. This is capitalism. This is good.

But that which is good can be harmful to a person with

a negative mental attitude. Credit is no exception. And credit may make a person who has been honest become dishonest. The abuse of credit is one of the main sources of worry, frustration, unhappiness, and dishonesty.

Now we are talking about credit given voluntarily by a creditor. He gives credit to a person who he thinks has the quality of being worthy, on whose truthfulness he can rely. The one who betrays such a trust is dishonest. Such a person is the one who will borrow money or purchase merchandise without the intent to make the payments agreed upon or to pay the loan in full.

Likewise, the honest person can become dishonest when he neglects to repay the loans *he* makes, or pay for the merchandise *he* buys, even though circumstances may prevent him from making a payment on the due date.

For the man under the influence of the PMA side of his talisman will have the courage to face the truth. He will have the courage to notify his creditors as far in advance as possible when circumstances prevent him from making a payment. And then he will work out some satisfactory arrangement by mutual consent with his creditor. Above everything else, *he will sacrifice until his obligation is finally fully paid.*

The honest man with common sense does not abuse credit privileges.

The honest man who *lacks common sense* will borrow or purchase on credit indiscriminately. And then because he sees no way to pay his creditors, the NMA influence of his talisman exerts such a terrific force on him that he may become dishonest. He may feel his situation is hopeless and he can do nothing about it. He realizes that he won't be thrown into jail for owing borrowed money. Although he thinks he is not going to be punished, in reality his worries, fears, and frustrations are a very real punishment.

And he remains dishonest until he comes under the strong influences of the PMA side of his talisman—influences strong enough to cause him to clear his obligations in full.

The abuse of credit privileges has literally brought on physical, mental, and moral illness. Remember *Necessity, NMA, and Crime* in Chapter Three entitled *'Clear the Cobwebs From Your Thinking.'*

Warning—OPM and cycles. As a very young salesman in the early part of 1928, W. Clement Stone called on an officer at the Continental Illinois National Bank and Trust Company in Chicago. The banker was talking to a customer or friend. While the young salesman was waiting, he overheard him say, 'The market just can't keep going up forever. I'm selling my shares.'

Some of the keenest investors in the country lost fortunes when the stock market crashed the following year—all because they lacked the knowledge of cycles, or, if they had the knowledge, they, unlike the banker, failed to act.

Tens of thousands of individuals engaging in all forms of business enterprises, including farming, lost their wealth—even though they were honest, prudent persons. Their wealth was acquired through OPM. As their securities increased in value, they borrowed more money to purchase more securities, farmland or other assets.

When the market value of their securities fell, they were unable to pay when the banks were forced to call in their loans.

Cycles repeat with regularity. So, in the first half of the 1970s, thousands of honest, prudent persons again lost their wealth because they didn't clear their loans in time by selling a portion of their securities—or didn't refrain from going further into debt to make additional purchases. When you use OPM, be certain to calculate how you can and will pay the individual or institution that loaned you the money.

Important: If you have lost a portion or all of your wealth, remember that cycles repeat. Don't hesitate to start over again at the proper time. Many wealthy persons today lost fortunes previously. But because they didn't lose their PMA, they had the courage to learn from their experiences and, subsequently, acquired even greater wealth.

If you would like to learn more about cycles, refer to *Cycles—The Mysterious Forces That Trigger Events*, by Edward R. Dewey and Og Mandino. You may find it exceedingly profitable. You can keep abreast of the theories and experiments on cycles by subscribing to Cycles magazine (write to 124 S. Highland Ave., Pittsburgh, Pennsylvania.)

In business, there are very few numbers necessary in the combination to success, but if one or more of the numbers are missing, you will fail until you find the missing numbers.

The use of other people's money has been the means whereby honest men who were poor became rich. Money or credit is an important number in the combination to business success.

The missing number. A young sales manager, whose yearly earnings are in excess of $35,000, wrote:

'I have a feeling: the type of feeling one would have if he were standing in front of a safe which held all the wealth, happiness, and success in the world, and he had all the numbers to the combination—*except one.* Just one number! If he had it, he could open the door.'

Often the difference between poverty and wealth lies in the employment of all principles in a formula but one. Just that one missing number makes the difference!

This can be illustrated in the experience of another man who had been successful in selling cosmetics for a manufacturer before he went into business for himself.

In his own business Leonard Lavin, like any man who starts from the bottom, was faced with problems. As you will see later, that was good. It was good because he had to study, think, plan, and work hard before he found a solution to each problem.

Bernice, his wife, and he formed a perfect mastermind alliance. And they worked together in perfect harmony. They manufactured one cosmetic item and acted as distributors for other companies. But they lacked working capital so they were forced to do the work themselves.

As their business grew, Bernice became an expert in *office management and purchasing*, and an excellent *administrator*. Leonard became a *successful sales manager* and efficient *production manager*. And when the business grew, they were wise enough to employ the services of a *lawyer* with good common sense—the kind that gets things done. And they also benefited from the services of an expert in *accounting* and *taxes*.

The way to *make a fortune* is to *manufacture or sell* a product or service (preferably a necessity at a low cost) that repeats. They did both.

Every dollar that could be spared was plowed back into the business. Necessity motivated them to: study, think, and plan; make one dollar do the part of many; obtain maximum results from every working hour; eliminate waste.

Month by month their sales moved forward as Leonard aggressively sought to break each previous sales record.

He became known in the industry as a man who knew his business. To many, he became known as a man who learned to go the extra mile.

Going the extra mile in two instances completely changed the course of his career for the better.

In the one instance his banker introduced him to three

of the bank's clients who had made an investment in another cosmetic company. They needed expert advice from someone with *good common sense*. And Leonard took the time to help them.

Leonard went the extra mile in doing a good turn for a buyer in a drug store in Los Angeles. And then one day the buyer showed his appreciation by confidentially informing Leonard that the firm manufacturing VO-5, a quality hair dressing, might be for sale. Leonard got excited. For here was a 15-year-old company with a quality product that had leveled off. He knew, from his cosmetic experience and from the *study of cycles and trends*, that all this company needed was new life, new blood, new activity.

He acted on the self-starter *Do It Now!* In fact, that very evening he was in conference with the owner. Now ordinarily in a transaction of this type, where the buyer and seller don't know each other, it takes weeks and sometimes months to negotiate—before there is a meeting of the minds. A *pleasing personality* and *good common sense* on the part of the buyer or seller often eliminate unnecessary delays. Because of Leonard's pleasing personality and his good common sense, the owner agreed to sell the company for $400,000 that same night.

Now it is true that Leonard had been doing well but it was also true that every dollar he could spare was being plowed back into his business. Where could he get $400,000?

In his hotel room that night he realized that he had all of the combinations to real wealth but one. Just one—money.

The next morning, as he awakened, he had a flash of inspiration. Again he reacted to the self-starter *Do It Now!* For he made a long-distance telephone call to one of the three men to whom he was introduced by his banker. He had helped them and perhaps they could give him the right advice. For they knew more about financing than he. Because they had invested in another cosmetic company, perhaps they would invest in his. They did.

And because these men were experienced in investing, they employed a successful investment formula which made it necessary for Leonard to agree to: (a) Consolidate all his operations; (b) devote his entire efforts to one corporation; (c) have the corporation pay back the loan on quarterly installments over a five-year period; (d) pay at the going rate of interest on the loan; and (e) give 25% of the corporation's stock as a premium for the investment gamble.

Leonard did agree. He saw the value of the use of OPM. The three men used OPM, too. They borrowed the $400,000 from their banks.

The missing number—now Leonard and Bernice had it! They worked long hours. They put their: hearts into the business. They found it a thrilling game.

It wasn't long before VO-5 was being used in every part of the United States and in many foreign countries.

December is usually the slowest month of the year for the cosmetic manufacturer. But in December, a year and a half after Leonard and Bernice took over the management of VO-5 and another product which was acquired—*Rinse Away*—the factory had a dollar volume of more than $870,000. That was as much as VO-5 and *Rinse Away* together had received during their past years under previous management.

And Bernice and Leonard found the missing number. With it they found the combination to acquire wealth. For it was only three years after the acquisition of VO-5 that their equities in their company were valued in excess of a million dollars.

Now the numbers in Leonard Lavin's combination for success were:

No. 1: A product or service that repeats.
No. 2: A company that is making money with an exclusive product or trade name, but which has leveled off.
No. 3: A good experienced production manager who operates the factory with maximum efficiency,
No. 4: A successful experienced sales manager who constantly increases sales (at a profit to the company) by adhering to a successful sales formula and simultaneously seeking better sales methods.
No. 5: A good administrator with PMA.
No. 6: An expert accountant who understands cost accounting and income tax law.
No. 7: A good lawyer with common sense and PMA who gets things done.
No. 8: Sufficient working capital or credit to operate the business and expand it at the right time.

You, too, can use OPM for: 'Business? It is quite simple. It is other people's money.'

Now if you choose to learn the principles in this chapter as well as those in Chapter Twelve entitled *'Attract—Don't Repel—Wealth,'* you, like Leonard and Bernice Lavin, can find the missing numbers to unlock the door to riches for yourself.

But to be healthy and happy, you must find satisfaction in your job. When you read the next chapter, you will learn how.

PILOT NO. 13
Thoughts to Steer By

1. 'Business? It is quite simple. It is other people's money!'
2. OPM: other people's money is the way to acquire wealth. The basic unwritten premise in 'Use OPM' is: operate on the highest ethical standards *of integrity, honor, honesty, loyalty, consent, and the Golden Rule.*
3. The dishonest man is not entitled to credit.
4. Your banker is your friend.
5. Where there is nothing to lose by trying, and a great deal to gain if successful, by all means try!
6. When you want to make a deal with someone, develop a plan that will give him what he wants, and in doing so get what you want. A good deal is mutually advantageous.
7. Credit used indiscriminately can hurt you. Abuse of credit is the cause of much frustration, misery and dishonesty.
8. To unlock the combination to success, you must know all the necessary numbers. Just one missing number may keep you from achieving your goal.
9. You too can find the missing numbers and unlock the door to riches for yourself.
10. Learn about cycles in order to know when to expand, and when to make and pay off loans.

HAVE THE COURAGE
TO FACE THE TRUTH!

14

HOW TO FIND SATISFACTION IN YOUR JOB

No matter what your job may be—boss or employee; plant manager or factory worker; doctor or nurse; lawyer or secretary; teacher or student; housewife or maid—you owe it to yourself to find satisfaction in your job as long as you have it.

You can, you know. Satisfaction is a mental attitude. Your own mental attitude is the one thing you possess over which you alone have complete control. You can determine to find satisfaction in your job, and discover the way to do so.

You are more apt to find satisfaction in your job if you do 'what comes naturally'—that for which you have a natural aptitude or liking. When you take a job that doesn't 'come naturally' you may experience mental and emotional conflicts and frustrations. You can, however, neutralize and eventually overcome such conflicts and frustrations—if you use PMA, and if you are motivated to gain experience to become proficient in the job.

Jerry Asam has PMA. And Jerry Asam loves his work. He finds satisfaction in his job.

Who is Jerry Asam? What does he do?

Jerry is a descendant of the Hawaiian kings. The job he loves so much is that of sales manager for the Hawaiian office of a large organization.

Jerry loves his work because he knows his work well and is very proficient in it. Thus, he is doing what comes naturally. But even so, Jerry has days when things could be a little rosier.

In sales work, days like this can be disturbing—if one does not study, think, and plan to correct difficulties and to maintain a positive mental attitude. So Jerry reads inspirational, self-help action books.

Jerry had read such inspirational books and learned three very important lessons:

1. You can control your mental attitude by the use of self-motivators.
2. If you set a goal, you are more apt to recognize things that will help you achieve it than if you don't set a goal. And the higher you set your goal; the greater will be your achievement if you have PMA.
3. To succeed in anything, it is necessary to know the rules and understand how to apply them. It is necessary to engage in constructive thinking, study, learning and planning time with regularity.

Jerry believed these lessons. He got into action. He tried them out himself. He studied his company's sales manuals, and practiced what he learned in actual selling, He set his goals—high goals—and achieved them. And each morning he said to himself: 'I feel healthy! I feel happy! I feel terrific!' And he did feel healthy, happy, and terrific. And his sales results were terrific too!

When Jerry was sure he himself was proficient in his sales work, he gathered about himself a group of salesmen and taught them the lessons he had learned. He trained the men in the latest and best-selling methods as set forth in his company's training manuals. He took them out personally and demonstrated how easy it is to sell if one uses the right methods, has a plan, and approaches each day with a positive mental attitude. He taught them to set high sales goals and to achieve them with PMA.

Every morning Jerry's group meets and recites enthusiastically, in unison: 'I feel healthy! I feel happy! I feel terrific!' Then they laugh together, slap one another on the back for good luck, and each one goes his way to sell his quota for the day. Each man sets a goal and he sets it so high that older, more experienced salesmen and sales managers on the mainland are amazed.

At the end of each week every salesman turns in a sales report that makes the president and sales manager of Jerry's organization smile big, broad smiles.

Are Jerry and the men under him happy and satisfied in their jobs? You bet they are! And here are some of the reasons they are happy:

1. They have studied their work well; they know and understand the rules and techniques and how to apply them so well that what they are doing comes naturally to them.
2. They set their goals regularly and they believe they will make them. They know that what the mind of man can conceive and believe, the mind of man can achieve with PMA.
3. They keep a positive mental attitude continually by using self-motivators.
4. They enjoy the satisfaction that comes with a job well done.

'I feel healthy! I feel happy! I feel terrific!' Another young salesman in the same organization on the mainland learned to control his mental attitude through the use of Jerry Asam's self-motivator. He was an eighteen-year-old college student who was working during his summer vacation selling insurance on a cold-canvass basis in stores and offices. Some of the things he had learned during his two-week theoretical training period were:

1. The habits that a salesman develops within the first two weeks after leaving the sales school will follow him throughout his career.
2. When you have a sales target—keep trying until you hit it.
3. Aim higher.
4. In your moment of need, use self-motivators such as: *I feel healthy! I feel happy! I feel terrific!* to motivate yourself to positive action in the desired direction.

After he had a few weeks' selling experience, he set a specific target of achievement. He aimed to win an award. To qualify, it was necessary to make a minimum of one hundred sales in a single week.

By Friday night of that week, he had succeeded in making eighty sales—twenty short of his target. The young salesman was determined that nothing would stop him from achieving his objective. He believed what he had been taught: *What the mind of man can conceive and believe, the mind of man can achieve with PMA*. Although the other salesmen in his group closed their week's work on Friday night, he was back on the job early Saturday morning.

By three o'clock in the afternoon, he hadn't made a sale. He had been taught that sales are contingent upon the attitude of the salesman—not the prospect.

He remembered the Jerry Asam self-motivator and repeated it five times with enthusiasm. *I feel healthy! I feel happy! I feel terrific!*

About five o'clock that afternoon he had made three sales. He was only seventeen from his goal. He remembered that *Success is achieved by those who try and maintained by those who keep trying with PMA!* Again, he repeated several times with enthusiasm, *I feel healthy! I feel happy! I feel terrific!* About eleven o'clock that night—he was tired, but he was happy! He had made his twentieth sale for the day! He had hit his target! He had won the award and learned that failure can be turned into success by—keeping on trying.

Mental attitude makes the difference. So, it was mental attitude that motivated Jerry Asam and the salesmen under him to find satisfaction in their jobs. It was a controlled positive mental attitude which helped the young student earn the reward and satisfaction he sought.

Just look about you. Notice those people who enjoy their work and those who don't. What's the difference between them? Happy, satisfied persons control their mental attitude. They take a positive view of their situation. They look for the good, and when something isn't so good, they look first to themselves to see if they can improve it. They try to learn more about their work so that they can become more proficient and make their work more satisfying to themselves and their employer.

But those who are unhappy clutch their NMA tightly. Indeed, it is almost as if they want to be unhappy. They look for everything about which they can complain: the hours are too long; lunch hours are too short; the boss is too crabby; the company doesn't give enough holidays or the right kind of bonuses. Or maybe they even complain about irrelevant things, such as: Susie wears the same dress every day; John the bookkeeper doesn't write legibly, and so on, and so on. Anything—just so they can be unhappy. And they succeed very well, too. They are decidedly unhappy people—on the job and generally elsewhere too. NMA possesses them entirely.

And this is true regardless of the type of work involved. If you want to be happy and satisfied, you can be: you will control your mental attitude and reverse your talisman from NMA to PMA; you will look for ways and means to create happiness.

If you can bring happiness and enthusiasm into your work situation, you'll be making a contribution that few others could equal. You will make your work fun and your job satisfaction will be measured in smiles—and in productivity, too.

A definite goal made her enthusiastic. In one of our classes, we were talking about this principle of bringing enthusiasm into one's job, when a young lady in the rear of the classroom raised her hand. She got to her feet and said:

'I've come here with my husband. What you say may be all right for a man in business, but it's no good for a housewife. You men have new and interesting challenges every day. But it's not like that with housework. The trouble with housework is... it's just too darned daily.'

This seemed like a real challenge to us: there are a lot of people who have jobs that are 'just too darned daily'. If we could find some way to help this young lady, perhaps we could help others who thought their work was routine. We asked her what made her housework seem so 'daily', and it turned out that she had no sooner finished making the beds when they were dirtied again, washing the dishes when they were soiled again, cleaning the floors when they were muddied again. 'You just get these things done so they can get undone,' she said.

'It does seem frustrating,' the instructor agreed. 'Are there any women who do enjoy housework?'

'Well, yes, I guess there are,' she said.

'What do they find in housework to interest them and keep them enthusiastic?'

After a moment's thought the young woman replied, 'Maybe it's their attitude. They don't seem to think their work is confining; they seem to see something beyoud the routine.'

This was the crux of the problem. One of the secrets of job satisfaction is being able to 'see beyoud the routine'. It is knowing that your work is *leading somewhere.* This is true whether you are a housewife or a file clerk, a gasoline pump operator or the president of a large corporation. You'll find satisfaction in routine chores only when you see them as stepping stones. Each chore is a stone, leading in a direction that you choose.

Use the step-stone theory. The answer, then, for this young housewife, was to find some goal which she really wanted to achieve, and to find a way to make her routine daily housework lead to the attainment of that goal. She volunteered the information that she had always wanted to take her family on a trip around the world.

'All right,' the instructor said. 'Well settle on that Now, set yourself a time limit. When do you want to go?'

'When the baby is twelve years old,' she said. 'That will be six years from now.'

'Now, let's see. This will take a little doing. You will need money, for one thing. Your husband will have to be able to take off for a year. You will have to plan an itinerary. You will want to study up on the countries you will be visiting. Do you suppose you can find a way to let bed-making, dishwashing, floor-scrubbing, and meal-planning be stepping stones toward your goal?'

A few months later the lady in this story came to see us. It was apparent the minute she walked into the room that here was a woman who had succeeded proudly.

'It's amazing,' she told us, 'How well this stepping-stone

idea has worked! I haven't found a single chore that doesn't fit in. I use my cleaning time as a thinking and planning time. Shopping time is a wonderful time to expand our horizons: I deliberately buy foods from other countries: foods that we will be eating on our trip. And I use the meal time as a teaching time. If we are having Chinese egg noodles, I read all I can find about China and its people, and then at dinner I tell the family all about them.

'Not one of my duties is dull or uninteresting to me anymore. And I know they never will be again, thanks to the *step-stone theory!*'

So, no matter how humdrum or tiresome your job may be, if at the end of it you see a goal that you desire, that job can bring satisfaction to you. This is a situation which confronts many persons in all walks of life. One young man may want to be a doctor, but he has to work his way through school. The job he takes will be decided by many factors, such as hours, location, rate of pay, and so on. Aptitude will have little to do with it. A very intelligent, ambitious, young man may end up behind a soda fountain, washing cars, or digging ditches. Certainly the job offers him no challenge or stimulation. It is merely a means to an end. Yet because he knows he is going where he wants to go, to him whatever strains the job may impose on him are worth the end result.

Sometimes, however, the price to be paid on a given job is too high in relation to the goal which it will purchase. And if such a job should happen to be yours, change your job. For if you are unhappy at your job, the poisons of this dissatisfaction spread into every phase of living.

If, however, the job is worth the price but you are still unhappy, develop inspirational dissatisfaction. Dissatisfaction can be positive or negative, good or bad, depending upon the circumstances. Remember: A positive mental attitude is the right mental attitude in a given situation.

Develop inspirational dissatisfaction! Charles Becker, former president of Franklin Life Insurance Company, says: 'I would urge that you be dissatisfied. Not dissatisfied in the sense of disgruntlement, but dissatisfied in the sense of that 'divine discontent' which throughout the history of the world has produced all real progress and reform. I hope you will never be satisfied. I hope you will constantly feel the urge to improve and perfect not only yourself, but the world around you.'

Inspirational dissatisfaction can motivate persons from sinner to saint, failure to success, poverty to riches, defeat to victory, and misery to happiness.

What do you do: when you make a mistake? when things go wrong? when misunderstandings develop with others? when you meet defeat? when everything seems black? when it appears that there is no way to turn? when it looks as if a satisfactory solution to your problem is impossible?

Do you: Do nothing and allow disaster to overtake you? Do you fold up? Become frightened? Run away?

Or, do you develop inspirational dissatisfaction? Do you turn disadvantages into advantages? Do you determine what you want? Do you apply faith, clear thinking, and positive action, knowing that desirable results can and will be achieved?

Napoleon Hill says *every adversity has the seed of an equivalent benefit.* Isn't it true that in the past what seemed to be a great difficulty or an unfortunate experience has inspired you to success and happiness that might not otherwise have been achieved?

Inspirational dissatisfaction can motivate you to succeed. Albert Einstein was dissatisfied because Newton's laws didn't answer all his questions. So he kept inquiring into nature and higher mathematics until he came up with the theory of relativity. . . And from that theory the world has developed the method of breaking the atom, learned the secret of transmuting energy into matter and vice versa, and dared and succeeded to conquer space—and all sorts of amazing things we very likely would not have accomplished if Einstein had not developed inspirational dissatisfaction.

Now, of course, we are not all Einsteins, and what results from our inspirational dissatisfaction may not change the world. But it can change our world and we can move forward in the direction we want to go. Let us tell you what happened to Clarence Lantzer when he became dissatisfied with his job.

Was it worth it? Now Clarence Lantzer had been a streetcar conductor in Canton, Ohio, for years. And one day he woke up in the morning and decided that he didn't like his job. It was too much the same. He was sick and tired of it. The more Clarence thought about the matter, the more dissatisfied he became. And he seemed to be unable to quit thinking about it. His dissatisfaction grew almost to an obsession. Clarence was mightily dissatisfied.

But when you have worked for a company as long as Clarence had worked for his streetcar company, you don't just quit because you decide that you are unhappy. At least; not if you are interested in whether or not your bread will be buttered.

Besides, Clarence had taken the PMA Science of Success course, and he had learned that one could be happy on any job if one wanted to. The thing to do was to adopt the right attitude.

So Clarence decided to take a sensible view of the situation and see what he could do about it. 'How can I be happier on the job?' he asked himself.

And he came up with a very good answer indeed. He

decided that he would be happier if he made others happy.

Now there were many people whom he could make happy, for he met many folks on his streetcar every day. He had always been able to make friends readily, so he thought: 'I'll use this trait to make each day a little brighter for every person who boards my car.'

Clarence's plan was wonderful—the customers thought. They enjoyed his little courtesies and cheerful greetings immensely. And they were happier, and so was Clarence, as the result of his cheerfulness and consideration.

But his supervisor took the opposite attitude. So, the supervisor called Clarence in and warned him to stop all this unwonted affability.

But Clarence paid no attention to the warning. He was having a good time making others happy. And as far as he and the customers were concerned, he was making a terrific success of his job.

Clarence was fired!

So Clarence had a problem—and that was good. At least, according to the PMA Science of Success course, it was good. Clarence decided that perhaps he had better visit Napoleon Hill (who was living in Canton at the time) and see how and why this problem was so good. He called Mr. Hill and arranged for an appointment the next afternoon.

'I've read *Think and Grow Rich*, Mr. Hill, and I've studied the PMA Science of Success, but somewhere I must have gotten off on the wrong track.' And he told Napoleon Hill what had happened to him. 'Now what do I do?' he concluded.

Napoleon Hill smiled. 'Let's look at your problem,' he said. 'You were dissatisfied with your work as it was. You did exactly right. You tried to use your best asset, your friendly and affable disposition, to do a better job and get and give more satisfaction on the job. The problem arises from the fact that your superior didn't have the imagination to see the value of what you were doing. But that's wonderful! Why? Because now you are in a position to use your fine personality for even greater goals.'

And Napoleon Hill showed Clarence Lantzer that he could use his fine abilities and friendly disposition to much better advantage as a salesman than as a streetcar conductor. So Clarence applied for and got a job as an agent for the New York Life Insurance Company.

The first prospect Clarence called on was the president of the streetcar company. Clarence turned his personality loose on this gentleman, and came out of the office with an application for a $100,000 policy!

The last time Hill saw Lantzer, he had become one of New York Life's biggest producers.

Are you a square peg in a round hole? The characteristics, abilities, and capacities that make you happy and successful in one environment may create an opposite reaction in another. You have a tendency to do well what you want to do.

You are called a 'square peg in a round hole' when you work or engage in activities that do not come naturally, and that are inwardly repellent. In such an unhappy situation you can change your position and place yourself in an environment that is pleasing to you.

It may not be feasible to change your position. You can then make adjustments in your environment to coincide with your characteristics, abilities, and capacities so that you will be happy. When you do this, you 'square the hole'. This solution will help change your attitude from negative to positive.

If you develop and maintain a burning desire to do so, you can even neutralize and change your tendencies and habits by establishing new ones. You can 'round the peg' if you are sufficiently motivated. But before you achieve success in changing your tendencies and habits, be prepared to face mental and moral conflicts. You can win if you are willing to pay the price. You may find it difficult to pay each necessary installment particularly the first few. But when you have paid in full, the newly established traits will predominate. The old tendencies and habits will become dormant. You will be happy because you will be doing what now comes naturally.

To guarantee success it is desirable that you try zealously to maintain physical, mental, and moral health during the period of such an internal struggle.

In the next chapter, 'Your Magnificent Obsession,' you will see how to neutralize your mental conflicts.

PILOT NO. 14
Thoughts to Steer By

1. Satisfaction is a mental attitude.
2. Your own mental attitude is the one thing you possess over which you alone have complete control.
3. Memorize: I feel healthy! I feel happy! I feel terrific!
4. When you set a goal—aim higher!
5. Know the rules and understand how to apply them.
6. Set your target and keep trying until you hit it.
7. See beyoud the routine. Use the step-stone theory.
8. *Develop inspirational dissatisfaction.*
9. What do you do if you are a square peg in a round hole?

DEFEAT MAY BE A STEPPING STONE OR A STUMBLING BLOCK DEPENDING ON WHETHER YOUR ATTITUDE IS POSITIVE OR NEGATIVE

15

YOUR MAGNIFICENT OBSESSION

With the idea that we are about to give you, you can have riches far beyond your fondest hope.

This idea will bring you a wealth of happiness. For your personality will expand. And you will receive affection and love, both of a quality and a quantity you have never before dreamed possible.

This principle was expressed dramatically on many occasions by the author, Lloyd C. Douglas. When Douglas retired from the ministry he moved into a more extended form of inspirational teaching: the writing of novels. His ministry had reached hundreds; his books reached thousands; his movies, millions. And to each he preached the same basic message. But it was never so clearly expressed as in the novel *The Magnificent Obsession.* The principle is so obvious here that those who need it most may not see it at all. It is simply this:

Develop an obsession—a Magnificent Obsession—to help others.

Share yourself without expecting a reward, payment, or commendation. And above all else—keep your good turn a secret.

And, if you do this, you will set in motion the powers of a universal law. For, try as you will to avoid payment for your good deed—blessings and rewards will be showered upon you.

No matter who you are, you can have a Magnificent

Obsession. Every living person can help others by sharing a part of himself.

You don't have to be rich or powerful to develop a Magnificent Obsession. Regardless of who you are, or what you have been, you can create inside yourself a burning desire to be helpful to others.

Take, for example, the sinner with a magnificent obsession.

You'll never know his name. That's a secret. When he was asked to help the Boys Clubs of America—an organization the sole purpose of which is the building of character in children—with a small donation, he refused. In fact, he was more than rude to the man who had called to interview him on this occasion.

'Get out!' he said. 'I'm sick and tired of people asking me for money!'

As the representative was walking toward the door to leave, he stopped, turned around, and looked kindly at the man sitting behind his desk. 'You may not wish to share with the needy. But I do. I'll share with you a part of what I have—a prayer: May God bless you.' And then he turned swiftly and left.

You see, with a flash of inspiration the Boys Club representative had remembered: '. . . silver and gold have I none, but such as I have give I unto you.' And a few days later an interesting thing happened.

The man who had said, 'Get out!' knocked on the door of the Club representative's office and asked, 'May I come in?' He brought with him a part of what he had to share: a check for half a million dollars. As he laid the check on the desk, he said: 'I am giving this on one condition: that you never let anyone know that I did it.'

'Why not?' he was asked.

'I don't want my name to represent to boys and girls that

I am good. I'm not a saint. For I have been a sinner.'

And that is why you'll never know his name. Just he, the Boys Club representative, and the Greatest Giver of All know the name of the sinner whose money was donated for the purpose of helping boys and girls avoid doing the wrong things he had done.

Like the Boys Club representative, you may not have money, but you can share by giving a part of what you have. And like him, you can be a part of a great cause. And you, too, when you give, can give generously.

Your most preciously valued possessions and your greatest powers are often necessarily invisible and intangible. No one can take them. You and you alone can share them.

The more you share, the more you will have.

Now if you doubt this, you can prove it to yourself by giving: a smile to everyone you meet; a kind word; a pleasant response; appreciation with warmth from the heart; cheer; encouragement; hope; honor, credit, and applause; good thoughts; evidence of love for your fellow-men; happiness; a prayer for the godless and the godly; and time for a worthy cause with eagerness.

If you do experiment by giving any one of the above, you will also prove to yourself what we have found is one of the most difficult principles to teach those who need it most: how to cause desirable actions within yourself. Until you do learn, you will fail to realize that what is left with you when you share it with others will multiply and grow; and what you withhold from others will diminish and decrease. Therefore, *share that which is good and desirable and withhold that which is bad and undesirable.*

Be a part of a great cause. We know of a mother who lost her only child: a beautiful, happy, teenage girl who brought laughter and inspiration to all who were fortunate enough to know her. In attempting to neutralize the grief of her loss, this mother developed a most magnificent obsession and became a part of a great cause. Today she is among the many thousands of American women who are making this world a better world to live in. Because of the wonderful work she is doing and the beauty of her Magnificent Obsession, we wrote and asked her if she would be land enough to share with us the inspiration which helped her develop her Magnificent Obsession. Her response was:

"The searing agony of losing our beloved daughter is never far away in my mind. Conceived in love and nurtured with love, she held our entire future and all our hopes in every sense of the words. The Almighty took our only child from us at the age of fourteen-and-a-half. it Is impossible to describe our loss. The bright promise of the future went dull, for the light of our lives had been snuffed out. Everything that we had lived to the full became empty. All that was sweet turned bitter.

'My husband and I reacted as does everyone. Our very existence was encompassed by the eternally unanswered question: WHY? My husband retired, we sold our home, and seeking an escape, did extensive traveling. Only when we came face to face with the harsh reality that we couldn't run away from our sadness and our memories did we return. Slowly, ever so slowly, we recognized that our loss was not exclusive. We had sought solace and found none, for our motives were self-centered. It took months for my mind to begin to accept the fact that all the joys of children and good health and security are blessings the Almighty loans to each of us. These infinite mercies which we finite persons presume to take for granted should each be cherished for their true meaning and great and irreplaceable value.

'How could I earn the right to keep my other blessings? How could I show my appreciation and thanks to Heaven for allowing me my husband's love, for living in this great nation of ours, for my friends and my five unimpaired senses, for all the good things that surrounded me? Now my efforts to find myself began to move in the right direction.

'Although bereft of my dearest possession, the Almighty had given me, in recompense, an empathy with people and a clearer understanding of the problems besetting each of us. Proportionately, my own understanding in relation to adjusting to my loss grew apace, as my service in helping others increased.

'I sought to find the niche in social work that would ultimately give me the opportunity to leave my small heritage for humanity in lieu of my beloved daughter and found the answer in City of Hope.

'Now, as surely as time passes, my peace of mind, call it a Magnificent Obsession if you will, gains in stature. It is my earnest wish that all who suffer loss of a loved one can find comfort and serenity in service to others.'

Today the City of Hope, national medical and research center, renders *entirely free patient care*. Its services are dispensed on the highest humanitarian level in the belief that 'Man is his brother's keeper'. This wonderful mother found peace of mind in a truly Magnificent Obsession.

The entire nation—in fact the entire world—can be affected by the Magnificent Obsession of just one man who wants to share a part of what he has. Orison Swett Marden was a man who shared a part of what he had and developed a Magnificent Obsession that changed the attitude of people from negative to positive.

The seeds of thought in a book grew into a Magnificent Obsession. At the age of seven Orison Swett Marden became an orphan. He was 'bound out' for his room and board. At an early age he read *Self-Help*, by the Scottish author Samuel Smiles who, like Marden, had become an orphan as a young boy and had found the secrets of true success. The seeds of thought in *Self-Help* created a burning desire in Marden which grew into his magnificent obsession and made his world a better world in which to live.

During the boom that preceded the panic of 1893, Marden owned and operated four hotels. Since their operation was entrusted to others, he was devoting much of his time to writing a book. Actually, he was fulfilling a desire to write a book that would motivate American youth as *Self-Help* had motivated him. He was working diligently on his inspirational manuscript when an ironical twist of fate struck him and tested his mettle.

Marden entitled his work *Pushing to the Front*. And he took as his motto: 'Let Every Occasion Be a Great Occasion for You Cannot Tell When Fate May Be Taking Your Measure for a Larger Place!'

And at that very instant Fate was taking his measure for a larger place. The misfortune that struck him would have ruined many a man. What happened?

The panic of 1893 struck. Two of the Marden hotels burned to the ground. His manuscript, nearly completed, was destroyed. His tangible wealth went down the drain, wiped out.

But Marden had a Positive Mental Attitude. He looked about him to see what had happened to the nation and himself. His first conclusion was that the panic was brought on by fear: fear of the value of the American dollar; fear caused by the failure of a few large corporations; fear of stock values; and fear of industrial unrest.

Those fears caused the stock market to crash. Five hundred and sixty-seven banks and loan and trust companies, as well as a hundred and fifty-six railway companies, failed. Strikes were prevalent. Unemployment affected milions of persons. Because of drouth and heat, farmers experienced crop failures.

Marden looked about him at the shambles in material things and human lives. He saw the great need for someone or something to inspire the nation and its people. Offers came to him to manage other hotels. He turned them down. A desire had caught hold of him, a Magnificent Obsession. And he combined it with PMA. He set to work on a new book. His new motto, a self-motivator: *Every occasion is a great occasion!*

'If ever there was a time when America needed the help of a positive mental attitude, it is now,' he told friends.

He worked over a livery stable and lived on one dollar and a half each week. He worked almost unceasingly, day and night. He completed the first edition of *Pushing to the Front* in 1893.

The book received immediate acceptance. It was used extensively in the public schools as a textbook and as a supplementary reader. Business houses circulated it among their employees. Distinguished educators, statesmen and members of the clergy, merchants, and sales managers commended it as a most powerful motivator to a positive mental attitude. And, in time, it was printed in twenty-five different languages. Millions of copies were sold.

Marden, like the authors of *Success Through a Positive Mental Attitude*, believed that *character is the cornerstone in building and maintaining success.* He believed the highest and best achievements are noble manhood and womanhood, and that the achievement of true integrity and well-rounded character is in itself success. He taught the secrets of financial and business success. But he also entered a perpetual protest against dollar chasing and over-reaching greed. He taught *there is something infinitely better than making a living: It is making a noble life.*

Marden showed how some men may make millions and still be utter failures. Those who sacrifice their families, reputation, health—everything—for dollars are failures in life, regardless of how much money they may accumulate. He also taught that one may succeed without becoming a president or a millionaire.

Perhaps one of the greatest achievements of Marden's Magnificent Obsession was the awakening of men and women to the realization that they could experience success if they would only employ the virtues, they would like their children to have.

Perhaps fully as rewarding to Marden, *Pushing to the Front* was instrumental in changing the attitude of an entire nation from negative to positive. And that influence was felt throughout the world.

Marden demonstrated that a burning desire can generate the drive to action that is imperative for great achievement.

As you have seen, it took courage and sacrifice for Orison Swett Marden to bring his Magnificent Obsession into reality.

A Magnificent Obsession does take courage. You may need to stand alone in combating and repelling the ridicule and ignorance of the experts. Like great discoverers, creators, inventors, philosophers, and geniuses, you may be termed 'crazy,' 'nuts,' or a 'crackpot.' The experts may say what you are trying to do can't be done. With time your burning desire and constant effort will bring your Magnificent Obsession into reality. When they say, 'It can't be done', find a way to do it!

A Magnificent Obsession will conquer in spite of the obstacles that stand in its way! Many years ago, a student at the University of Chicago and his friends went to hear a lecture by Sir Arthur Conan Doyle on spiritualism. They went for a lark. They meant to scoff. One of these students, J. B. Rhine, was impressed by the seriousness of the speaker. He began to listen.

Certain ideas impressed him. He couldn't dismiss them from his mind. Sir Arthur Conan Doyle referred to men of great repute who were searching into the realm of psychic phenomena. J. B. Rhine decided to investigate and to engage in some research.

In referring to the incident some time ago, Dr. Rhine, Director of The Parapsychology Laboratory at Duke University in North Carolina, said: 'There were things said there that I should have known as a college student. During and after the lecture I began to recognize some of them. My education had omitted many of the things that were important, such as ways of seeking the unknown. I began to see some of the faults of the educational system of the day.'

He became interested in the freedom of all to secure new knowledge. He began to resent a system whereby seeking the truth in any form, or on any issue, became a taboo. He began to develop a burning desire to learn the truth scientifically regarding man's psychic powers. His burning desire turned into a Magnificent Obsession.

Rhine had planned to devote his life to college teaching. He was warned that he would lose his reputation and that his earning power as a teacher would be impaired. His friends and college professors ridiculed him and endeavored to discourage him.

Some began to shun him. 'I must find out for myself,' he told a scientist friend.

The friend responded: 'When you do find out, keep it to yourself! No one is going to believe!'

He did keep his discoveries to himself until he was able to develop confirmed scientific proof. Today he is honored and respected throughout the world.

Over the past forty-five years his battles have been figuratively *knuckle fighting* every inch of the ground in combating taboos, ignorance, antagonism, and ridicule.

One of the greatest obstacles with which Dr. Rhine has been constantly plagued over the years has been the lack of the necessary money for expanding his research. At one time, for example, his only EEG machine was assembled from the remains of one found in a junk pile.

It had been discarded by a hospital.

Have you ever thought that you can develop a Magnificent Obsession by becoming a part of a great cause and by sharing a part of what you have? If you have, you already realize that there are many college and university professors today whose Magnificent Obsessions are to seek the truth in various fields so that all mankind may be benefited by their discoveries. Because such persons spend all their time in searching for these truths, they are almost always handicapped by the lack of money to buy necessary equipment, provide for their own livelihood and the livings of others engaged in working on the project, etc.

You can become a part of such a cause and thus fulfill a magnificent obsession of your own. You can find such a dedicated person in almost any college or university.

Money and a Magnificent Obsession! You might ask: How can we mention money in the same breath with a Magnificent Obsession? If you did we would respond: 'Isn't money good?'

Is money good? Is money good? Many negative-minded persons say, 'Money is the root of all evil'. But *the Bible* says: Love of money is the root of all evil. And there is a big difference between the two even though one little word makes the difference.

It has been amazing to the authors to observe negative-minded persons react unfavorably to *Think and Grow Rich* and its contents. For these negative-minded persons might earn in a single year more than they now earn in a lifetime by changing their attitude from negative to positive. To do this it would be necessary to clear the cobwebs from their thinking regarding money.

In our society money is the medium of exchange. Money is power. Like all power, money can be used for good or for evil. *Think and Grow Rich* has motivated many thousands of its readers to acquire great wealth through PMA. They have been inspired in *Think and Grow Rich* by the biographies of such men as: Henry Ford, William Wrigley, Henry L. Doherty, John D. Rockefeller, Thomas Alva Edison, Edward A. Filene, Julius Rosenwald, Edward J. Bok, and Andrew Carnegie.

Now the men whose names you have just read established Foundations which even to this day have in the aggregate in excess of one billion dollars: money set aside exclusively for charitable, religious, and educational purposes. Today expenditures and grants from these Foundations total in excess of $200 million in a single year.

Is money good? We know it is.

The Magnificent Obsessions of these men will live in perpetuity.

And the story of the life of Andrew Carnegie will convince the reader that Carnegie shared with others a part of what he had: money, philosophy, and *something more*, In fact, *Success Through a Positive Mental Attitude* would not have been written if it were not for Andrew Carnegie. That is why this book is dedicated to him, and to you.

Let's talk about him and you. Let's learn from his philosophy. Let's see how we can apply it in our lives.

A simple philosophy grew into a Magnificent Obsession! A poor Scottish immigrant boy became the richest man in America. His inspiring story and motivating philosophy are found in the *Autobiography of Andrew Carnegie.*

As a boy and throughout his life Carnegie was motivated by a simple fundamental philosophy: *Anything in life worth having is worth working for!* This simple philosophy grew into a Magnificent Obsession.

And before he died at the age of eighty-three, Carnegie had worked diligently for many years to share his great wealth intelligently with those then living and with future generations.

While he lived, Carnegie was successful in giving approximately a half billion dollars through direct grants, Foundations, and trusts. His contribution of millions of dollars for the establishment of libraries is a well-known example of the application of his standard:

Anything in life worth having is worth working for!

And the books in these libraries have been, and will continue to be, of benefit only to those persons who work to get the knowledge, understanding, and wisdom they contain by reading and studying them.

In the year 1908, Napoleon Hill, at the age of eighteen, while working his way through college as a reporter for a magazine, interviewed the great steelmaker, philosopher, and philanthropist. The first interview lasted three hours. And then the great man invited the youngster to his home.

For three days Carnegie indoctrinated Napoleon Hill with his philosophy. And be finally inspired the young reporter to devote at least twenty years of his life to study, research, and find the simple, underlying principles of success. Andrew Carnegie told Napoleon Hill that his greatest wealth consisted not in money but in what he termed—the philosophy of American achievement. He commissioned Napoleon Hill as his agent to share it with the world.

And in this book, he is sharing it with you.

While he lived, Andrew Carnegie helped Napoleon Hill by

giving him letters of introduction to the great men and women of his day. He advised him. He shared his thoughts with him. He helped him in every way, with but one exception—money. For he said, *'Anything in life worth having is worth working for.'*

Now he knew that this self-motivator, when applied, would attract happiness and physical, mental, and spiritual health as well as wealth. Everyone can learn and apply Andrew Carnegie's principles.

It is customary for a man to share a part of his tangible wealth with his loved ones as he goes through life, or he may do so in his will. This world would be a better world to live in if each person would leave, as an inheritance to posterity, the philosophy and know-how that brought him happiness, physical, mental and spiritual health and wealth—as did Andrew Carnegie.

The writings of Napoleon Hill make available to you the principles whereby Carnegie acquired his great wealth. They are just as applicable to you as they were to him.

Another wealthy man who had a Magnificent Obsession and shared a part of what he had was Michael L. Benedum. His close friend, United States Senator Jennings Randolph, told us Benedum started on a salary of twenty-five dollars a week and became one of the richest men in America. He was worth over one hundred million dollars. And yet, the turning point in his career followed a very minor incident.

As a young man of twenty-five, Benedum courteously gave his seat on a train to an elderly stranger. To Benedum it was the obvious thing to do. And the elderly stranger turned out to be John Worthington, General Superintendent of the South Perm Oil Company. In the conversation that followed, Worthington offered Mike Benedum a job. Benedum accepted and eventuall became 'the discoverer of more oil than any other single individual who ever lived.'

Some people say you can judge a man by the philosophy by which he lives. Mike Benedum's philosophy about money went something like this: 'I'm just a trustee for it and will be held accountable for the good I can accomplish with it, both in the community as a whole and in behalf of opportunities for people coming up—even as I was given an opportunity, back when.'

Like so many others with a Magnificent Obsession, Benedum lived to a ripe old age. On his eighty-fifth birthday, he said: 'I have been asked how I keep going at my age. My formula is to keep busy so that the years go by unnoticed. To despise nothing except selfishness, meanness, and corruption. To fear nothing except cowardice, disloyalty, and indifference. To covet nothing that is my neighbor's except his kindness of heart and his gentleness of spirit. To think many, many times of my friends and, if possible, seldom of my enemies. As I see it, age is not a question of years. It is a state of mind. You are as young as your faith, and today I think I have more faith in my fellow man, in my country, and in my God than I have ever had.'

You live longer with a Magnificent Obsession. Of course, it's the old story: the man who has something to live for lives longer. We realized this when we became well acquainted with men like the Honorable Herbert Hoover and General Robert E. Wood, who were doing so much for American youth when they shared their time and money with the Boys Clubs of America. And they were long-lived because of their Magnificent Obsessions. They devoted their thinking and time to projects that benefited others and, because their lives were the good lives of men with Magnificent Obsessions, they experienced the pleasure and therapeutic value of the esteem and love of their fellow men.

Of course, you may not have the material wealth of an Andrew Carnegie or a Michael L. Benedum but that does not deprive you of building your own Magnificent Obsession. At least, it didn't Irving Rudolph.

They're all in jail but my brother and me! Irving devoted his life to helping boys in blighted neighborhoods. This work was in gratitude for having been saved by a new Boys Club in the rough neighborhood in which he was raised.

How did Irving Rudolph get started in Boys Club work?

He lived in a poor neighborhood —North Avenue and Halsted Street in Chicago. He traveled with a tough crowd. There was plenty of trouble. Plenty of things for boys to get into that they shouldn't. And not much to occupy their time to keep them out of trouble. One day a Boys Club was started in an abandoned church in the neighborhood.

'My brother and I were the only two fellows in our gang who visited the Club,' Irving explained. 'They're all in jail but my brother and me. If it hadn't been for the Lincoln Unit Boys Club, we'd be there, too.'

Irving was grateful for what the Boys Club did for him and his brother. And he devoted his life to helping boys in blighted neighborhoods. Through his enthusiasm and zeal, large donations were received to support the Chicago Boys Clubs. Through him, men and women of influence were attracted to this cause.

'I feel that my work is only a token payment of my gratitude to a Higher Power for bringing me and my brother under this influence,' Irving explained. Then he added, 'Just visit a Boys Club. See for yourself the good work that is being done. You will then feel a part of what I feel for the kids who have the need I had.'

Now there are thousands of men and women who are

fulfilling their Magnificent Obsessions in sacrificing time and money to help the Boy Scouts of America. Your life has benefited from their Magnificent Obsessions if...

IF...

If you do your best to try never to violate your honor by lying or cheating and always try to fulfill the responsibility with which you are entrusted...

If you keep clean in thought and body—if you exemplify clean habits, clean speech, clean sport—if you associate with a clean crowd...

If you stand up for the rights of others against the undesirable influence and coaxing of friends and threats of enemies—if defeat inspires you to try to succeed —if you have the courage to face danger in spite of fear...

If you work faithfully and make the best of your opportunities—if you don't wantonly destroy property—if you save money so that you can pay your own way in this world and yet be generous to those in need and give financial help and time to worthy causes—if you do a good turn each day without expecting compensation...

If you are a friend to all and a brother to every living man, woman, and child regardless of race, color, or creed ...

If you are prepared to learn to know dangers, to avoid negligence and to know the remedies necessary to help injured persons and save human lives, to share the duties and responsibilities in your home and place of business...

If you are polite to all, especially to the weak, helpless, and unfortunate...

If you will not kill or hurt any living creature needlessly, but strive to protect all living animals... If you smile when you can, do your work promptly and cheerfully—and if you never shirk or grumble at responsibilities or hardships.. .

If you are loyal to all to whom loyalty is due, to the members of your family, the firm for which you work and your country...

If you respect duly constituted authorities and obey that which does not violate your moral code...

If you do your best to do your duty to God and your country, to help other people at all times, to keep yourself physically strong, mentally awake, and morally straight...

Then you live and act in response to the imprint in your subconscious mind of the Oath and Law of the Boy Scouts of America. What kind of a person would you be if you lived up to these standards?

America is great because its people live by a great philosophy. It can be symbolized in the phrase *The Great American Heart.*

Henry J. Kaiser was another with a Magnificent Obsession. He did so much to make his world a better world to live in. A quotation that hung on the wall of a blacksmith shop in England inspired him as it may also inspire you. It is:

> 'What! Giving again?' I ask in dismay.
> 'And must I keep giving and giving away?'
> 'Oh no,' said the angel looking me through,
> 'Just keep giving till the Master stops giving to you!'

In reading up to this point you started *Where the Road to Achievement Began.* You were awakened by *Five Mental Bombshells for Attacking Success.* And you have been given the *Key to The Citadel of Wealth.* Now: *Get Ready to Succeed!* That is the purpose of the following chapters.

PILOT NO. 15
Thoughts to Steer By

1. To develop a Magnificent Obsession: Share yourself with others without expecting a reward, payment or commendation. *Keep your good turns a secret.*
2. Regardless of who you are, or what you have been, you can create inside yourself a burning desire to be helpful to others. You can develop your own Magnificent Obsession if you have PMA.
3. When you share with others a part of what you have, that which remains will multiply and grow. The more you share, the more you will have. Therefore, share that which is good and desirable, and withhold that which is bad and undesirable.
4. You can develop your own Magnificent Obsession by becoming a part of a good cause, as did the mother who lost her only child.
5. Character is the cornerstone in building and maintaining success. But how can you improve your own character? *Success Through a Positive Mental Attitude* will help you find the right answers.
6. There is something infinitely better than making a living: it is making a noble life. Do you believe this? If you do, what will you do about it?
7. A burning desire can generate the drive to action that is imperative to great achievement. To develop a burning desire to achieve a specific goal, daily keep the goal before you. And strive to achieve it.
8. It takes courage and sacrifice to develop and maintain a Magnificent Obsession. You may need to stand alone against the ridicule and ignorance of others, as did Dr.

Joseph Banks Rhine.

9. Some people say money is the root of all evil. But *The Bible* says: Love of money is the root of all evil. The good or evil of money is contingent on a little difference. That little difference is whether your attitude is positive or negative.
10. Men like Andrew Carnegie, Henry Ford, Michael Benedum used the power of their money to establish charitable, educational, and religious Foundations. The good that has been done by the Magnificent Obsessions of such men will live in perpetuity!
11. *Anything in life worth having is worth working for.*
12. When you are asked to give money or time to a worthy cause, repeat to yourself:

'What! Giving again?' I ask in dismay.
'And must I keep giving and giving away?'
'Oh no,' said the angel looking me through,
'Just keep giving till the Master stops giving to you!'

THAT WHICH YOU SHARE
WITH OTHERS WILL MULTIPLY
AND THAT WHICH YOU
WITHHOLD WILL DIMINISH!

PART IV

GET READY TO SUCCEED!

16

HOW TO RAISE YOUR ENERGY LEVEL

How is your energy level today? Did you wake up eager to face the tasks ahead? Did you push your chair back from the breakfast table with the feeling that you were rarin' to go? And did you plunge into your work with enthusiasm?

You didn't? Perhaps for some time now you just haven't had the vim and vigor you think you should have. Perhaps you feel tired before the day begins, and drag through your work without joy.

If so, let's do something about it!

Vernon Wolfe, track coach, is an expert who can show us what to do. He is one of the outstanding coaches in the country. Under his tutelage, several high school students have broken national prep school records.

How does he train these stars? Wolfe has a double prescription. He teaches them to condition both their *minds* and their *bodies* simultaneously.

'If you *believe* you can do it,' says Vernon Wolfe, 'most of the time you *can*. It's mind over matter.'

You have two types of energy. One is physical, the other is mental and spiritual. The latter is by far the more important, for from your subconscious mind you can draw vast power and strength in time of need.

Think, for example, of the great feats of strength and endurance you've read about people performing while under the stress of intense emotion. There is an automobile accident and a husband is pinned under the overturned car. In her moment of fear and determination, his tiny and frail wife manages to raise the car enough to free him! Or the insane person, his mind dominated by his subconscious running wild, can break, lift, bend, and smash with a force he never could hope for during periods of normality.

In a series of articles for *Sports Illustrated*, Dr. Roger Bannister told how he first broke the four-minute mile on May 6, 1954, by training both his mind and his muscles to accomplish this long- sought dream of the athletic world. For months, he conditioned his subconscious into the belief that the record, which some people claimed was unattainable, could be achieved. Others thought of the four-minute mark as a barrier. Bannister thought of it as a gateway which, if he once passed through, would I open the way to many new records for himself and other milers.

And of course, he was right. Roger Bannister led the way. In a period of little more than four years after he first set a four-minute mile, the feat was performed 46 times by himself and other runners! And in one race, at Dublin, Ireland, on August 6,1958, five runners ran the mile in less than four minutes!

The man who taught Roger Bannister the secret was Dr. Thomas Kirk Cureton, director of the physical fitness laboratory at the University of Illinois. Dr. Cureton has developed revolutionary ideas concerning the body's energy level. They apply, he says, to both athletes and non-athletes. They can make a runner run faster and the average man live longer.

'There is no reason why,' Dr. Cureton says, 'any man can't be as fit at 50 as he was at 20—providing he knows how to train his body.'

Dr. Cureton's system is based on two principles: (1) Train the whole body. (2) Push yourself to the limit of endurance, extending the limit with each workout.

'The art of record-breaking,' he says, 'is the ability to take more out of yourself than you've got. You punish yourself more and more and rest between spells.'

Dr. Cureton became acquainted with Roger Bannister while running physical fitness tests on European athletic stars. He noticed that Bannister's body was wonderfully developed in some ways. For example, his heart was 25 per cent larger than normal in relation to his body size.

But, in other ways, Bannister wasn't as well developed as the average man. Bannister took Cureton's advice to develop his whole body. He learned to condition his mind by taking up mountain climbing. This taught him how to overcome obstacles.

Equally important, he learned to break big goals down into little ones. Roger Bannister reasoned that a man ran a single quarter-mile faster than he ran the four quarters of a full mile. So he trained himself to think of the four quarters in the mile separately. In his training, he would dash a quarter mile, then jog a lap around the track to rest. Then he would dash another quarter mile. Each time, he aimed to run the quarter in 58 seconds or less. Fifty-eight times four equals 232 seconds, or three minutes and 52 seconds. He ran to the point of collapse. Then he would rest. Each time, the point of collapse was pushed back a little. When he finally ran his great race, it was in three minutes, 59.6 seconds!

Dr. Cureton taught Roger Bannister that 'the more the body endures, the more it will endure.' Beliefs about 'overtraining' and 'staleness', he says, are myths.

But he emphasizes that rest is as important as exercise

activity. The body needs to rebuild in even larger quantities what has been tom down in exercise. That's how strength, vitality, energy are developed. The body and mind both recharge themselves during periods of rest and relaxation. If you don't give them a chance to do so, severe damage—and even death—can result.

Is it time to recharge your battery? There's no glory in being the richest man in the graveyard. You don't want to be the best scientist, doctor, executive, salesman, or employee lying—prematurely—under the most ornate headstone. A loved mother, wife, father, son, or daughter can bring happiness. Why then, bring grief, instead? Why be confined to a mental sanitarium or he embalmed six feet under a blanket of beautiful green grass—simply because a needless drain damaged a battery that wasn't recharged?

The small child doesn't know when he is excessively tired. But he surely shows it in his behavior and actions. The adolescent may realize he is over-fatigued, but refuse to admit it—even to himself. Then sexual, family, scholastic, and social problems may seem unsolvable and unbearable. They may motivate him to temporary or permanent destructive acts—acts that injure himself and others.

When your energy level is low, your health and your desirable characteristics may be subdued by the negative. You, like a storage battery, are dead when your energy level is zero. What is the solution? Recharge your battery? How? Relax, play, rest, and sleep!

How to tell when your battery needs recharging. Here is a checklist to help you determine your present energy level. You can use it whenever you feel that your energy level is slipping. If you are a well-balanced person, your battery may need recharging when you act and feel:

Unduly sleepy or tired
Tactless, unfriendly, suspicious
Querulous, insulting, hostile
Irritable, sarcastic, mean
Nervous, excitable, hysterical
Worrisome, fearful, jealous
Rash, ruthless, excessively selfish
Excessively emotional, depressed, or frustrated

PMA demands a good energy level—and vice versa! When you are fatigued, your usually positive, desirable feelings, emotions, thoughts, and actions have a tendency to turn negative. When you are rested and in good health, the direction is changed back to positive. Fatigue often brings out the worst within you. When your battery is charged and your energy and activity level is up to standard, you are at your best! That is when you think and act with PMA!

If your feelings and actions indicate that your better qualities are being subdued by those which are undesirable and negative, it's time to recharge your battery!

Yes, to maintain your level of both physical and mental energy you need to exercise both your body and mind. But there is a third factor. Your body and mind both need to be fed properly. You help to maintain your physical body by taking in quantities of wholesome, nutritious foods. You maintain your mental and spiritual vigor by absorbing mental and spiritual vitamins from inspirational and religious books.

Vitamins—necessary for a healthy mind and body! George Scarseth, Ph.D., former Director of Research for the American Farm Research Association in Lafayette, Indiana, told about a village on the seacoast of Africa. The village is more advanced than a community of similar tribes in the interior. Why? Because

its inhabitants are physically stronger and more mentally alert— they have more bodily energy— than the ulterior tribesmen. The difference between the tribesmen on the coast and those living inland stems from a difference in diet. The village tribesmen in the ulterior do not have a sufficient amount of protein whereas those on the coast obtain quantities from the fish they eat.

In his book, *Climate Makes the Man*, Clarence Mills wrote that the United States Government found some inhabitants of the Isthmus of Panama excessively sluggish in their mental and physical activity. A scientific study disclosed that both the plant and animal life, on which they depended for food, lacked the B vitamins. When thiamine was added to their diet, the same people became more energetic and active.

If you suspect that your diet is deficient in certain vitamins and elements so that your energy level is depressed, you should do something about it. A good cookbook can help you, and there are government pamphlets available at low cost. If the condition persists, have a physical checkup.

Like your body, your subconscious mind will accept and absorb mental and spiritual vitamins without effort. But, unlike your physical body, the subconscious will digest and retain unlimited quantities. Unlike your stomach, it never becomes stuffed! It will take and hold as much as you feed it—and still hold more!

Where will you find these mental and spiritual vitamins? In books such as those recommended in Chapter 22, 'The Amazing Power of a Bibliography!'

In effect, the subconscious mind is like a battery. From it, you can obtain tremendous surges of mental and spiritual energy which often transmute themselves into physical vitality. These jolts of energy will go to waste if we permit them to be short-circuited by needless negative emotions. But used constructively, this energy can multiply itself many times, just as a powerhouse generator produces vast amounts of useful power.

The late William C. Lengel, who was a prominent editor in-chief in the book publishing business, illustrated this point beautifully in an article for *Success Unlimited* magazine. Lengel described how energy is wasted through needless 'worry, hate, fear, suspicion, anger and rage'.

'All these waste elements,' he said, 'could just as easily be transformed into power-producing units.'

To illustrate his point, Mr. Lengel drew a picture of an electrical power plant: "...the open mouths of the furnaces, the red flames roaring inside, the water in the steam gauges bobbing at proper temperature level, the steam driving the pistons turning the great generators, the copper commutators—golden surfaces—revolving so fast they seem motionless, green and blue sparks flashing from under the brushes, thick cables hooked up to the switchboard, carrying the electric current throughout a city for thousands of useful purposes.

'Then the other side of the picture,' Lengel continued. 'Same plant, same boilers, engines, generators. The only difference being that the switchboard was dark and the heavy cables, instead of being hooked up to the switchboard were stuck down into a barrel of water while the workmen ran tests on the plant. All of the power is, in effect, wasted. Not an elevator able to run, not a machine able to operate, not a single bulb able to light.'

And Lengel concluded that in the same way 'a failure uses up as much energy in his work at failing as a successful person uses in winning success'.

Tommy Bolt, the golf champion, used to waste his energy that way. If he sliced a ball or missed the green, he would let go with a fit of temper. Frequently, he'd become so angry that he'd wrap a golf club around the nearest tree.

When he read the famous prayer of St. Francis of Assisi, it changed him into a man who directed his energy into the most fruitful channels. The prayer Tommy new peace of mind and ever since then he carried in his pocket a card imprinted with a portion the prayer. It reads:

> God grant me the serenity to accept the things I cannot change, the courage to change the things I can, and the wisdom to know the difference.

Man is the only member of the animal kingdom who, through the functioning of his conscious mind, can voluntarily control his emotions from within, rather than be forced to do so by external influences. He alone can deliberately change habits of emotional response. The more civilized, cultured, and refined you are, the easier you can control your emotions and feelings—if you choose to do so.

Fear, for example, is good under certain circumstances. If it were not for fear of water, many children would drown. However, it is entirely possible that you are wasting your mental and spiritual energy in this or other misdirected emotions. If so, you can throw a switch to direct the energy into useful channels. How? *By keeping your mind on the things you do want and off the things you don't want.* Your emotions are immediately subject to action. Therefore, get into action. Substitute a positive feeling for the negative one. For example, if you are fearful and want to be courageous, act courageous!

If you want to be energetic, act energetic. But make sure, of course, that your energy is expended to a good and useful purpose.

Dawn Fraser of Australia gives us a wonderful case in point. Born on the 'wrong side of the tracks' in Bal-main, a waterside suburb of Sydney, Dawn had an anemic body. But she had a king-size determination to become a great swimming champion. She became the world's fastest woman swimmer. She was good. But sometimes she wasn't quite good enough to satisfy herself.

While flying home from the Cardiff Empire Games, she read a book. It was *Think and Grow Rich*.' I found Napoleon Hill's formulas for success most inspiring,' she says. 'I began thinking about our defeat by the English girls in the medley relay when, in the freestyle leg, I swam 60.6 seconds. That was six-tenths of a second faster than my own world record, but still not good enough to give us the 12-yard start we needed.

'I wondered whether I had given everything in me on that final lap.'

Dawn Fraser began thinking about the dream she'd had for so long—to become the first woman to swim 100 meters in less than 60 seconds. 'The Magic Minute', she called it.

'If I could have made that final leg in the magic minute, we might have won,' she thought.

'From that moment the old hope of cracking the minute became a burning desire with me. Call it a controlled obsession if you like. I made it my major ambition and formed a plan of positive action with the magic minute as my goal. As Mr. Hill advises, I decided to go the extra mile—mentally as well as physically.'

In addition to training her body, Miss Fraser now conditions her mind as well. Although she has yet to achieve her 'Magic Minute' as of this writing, she has cracked record after record. Athletic coaches throughout Australia have been attracted to study Napoleon Hill's teachings, according to Thomas H. Wyngard, an Australian newspaperman.

'Top coaches, in their search for methods that will give their champions just that little bit extra over and above their regular scientifically devised training program, are finding new inspiration in the doctrines of the great American expert,' Wyngard says.

'They are adapting Napoleon Hill's technique of mental approach to what is, essentially, a physical problem. Some have taken the PMA Science of Success course so they may apply the principles correctly.'

Is it time for you to recharge your battery? Have you now begun to apply the principles presented in *Success Through a Positive Mental Attitude*? Are you ready to become a champion? If so, you will want to learn how you can enjoy good health and live longer—the subject of our next chapter.

PILOT NO. 16
Thoughts to Steer By

1. How is your energy level at this moment?
2. What is your most important source of physical, mental, and spiritual energy?
3. How can you apply the principles Dr. Thomas Kirk Cureton taught to Roger Bannister so that you31 have extra energy to achieve your own goals?
4. Do you push to the limit of your endurance-then rest and try again?
5. Is it time to recharge your battery?
6. How can you avoid or neutralize fatigue?
7. Are most of your meals based on well-balanced diets?
8. Do you take spiritual and mental vitamins daily by reading inspirational material or listening to inspirational tapes or records?
9. Is your energy being directed toward useful channels? Or is it being short-circuited and wasted?
10. 'A failure uses up as much energy in his work at failing as a successful person uses in winning success.'
11. 'God grant me the serenity to accept the things I cannot change, the courage to change the things I can, and the wisdom to know the difference.'
12. When is the emotion of fear justified? Unjustified?
13. To be energetic, *act* energetically!

INCREASE YOUR ENERGY
LEVEL THROUGH PMA!

17

YOU CAN ENJOY GOOD HEALTH AND LIVE LONGER

Positive Mental Attitude plays an important role in your health and your day-to-day energies and enthusiasms for your life and your work. 'Every day in every way, through the grace of God, I am getting better and better,' is no pie-in- the-sky jargon for the man who recites the sentence several times each day upon awakening and again before going to bed.

In one sense, he is putting PMA forces to work for him. He is using the forces which attract the better things of life to him. He is using the forces which the authors of *Success Through a Positive Mental Attitude* want you to use.

How PMA aids you. PMA will help you develop mental and physical health and a longer life. And NMA will just as surely undermine mental and physical health and shorten your life. It all depends upon which side of the talisman you turn up. Positive Mental Attitude properly employed has saved the lives of many persons because someone close to them had a strong Positive Mental Attitude. The following incident proves the point.

The baby was only two days old when the doctor said, 'The child won't live.'

'The child will live!' responded the father. The father had a Positive Mental Attitude—he had faith—he believed in the miracle of prayer. He prayed. He also *believed* in action. And he got into action! He placed the child under the care of a pediatrician who also had a Positive Mental Attitude—a doctor who knew from experience that for every physical weakness Nature provides a compensating factor. The child did live!

I CAN'T GO ON!
DEATH SEPARATES PAIR—FOR INSTANT

The above headline appeared in the *Chicago Daily News*. The article mentioned that a building engineer—a sixty-two- year-old man—came home and went to bed with chest pains and shortness of breath. His wife, who was ten years younger, became alarmed and began hopefully to rub her husband's arms to increase circulation. But he died.

'I can't stand to go on any more,' the widow told her mother, who was beside her.

And then the widow died. She died that very same day!

The baby that lived and the widow who died demonstrate the powerful forces of positive and negative mental attitudes. Knowing that accentuating the positive will attract good things to you and accepting the negative will bring the bad, isn't it common sense to develop positive thoughts and attitudes?

If you have not already done so, now is the time to develop a PMA philosophy. Prepare for any possible emergency. Always have something to live for. And remember, when you have something to live for, the subconscious mind forces upon your conscious mind strong motivating factors to keep you alive in times of emergency. We need look no further than Rafael Correa to prove our point.

An eventful night. He was only twenty years of age. His family was not wealthy, yet it was particularly well esteemed. Therefore, six doctors and a young intern had struggled all night in that small operating room at San Juan, Puerto Rico, trying to save Rafael's life. Now, after twelve hours of unceasing watchfulness and attention, they were tired. And they were sleepy. Try as they would, they were finally unable to hear his heart beat. They couldn't find his pulse.

The head surgeon took a knife and cut the blood vessels in Rafael's wrist. The fluid was yellow. The surgeon hadn't used an anesthetic—for the boy's body was so weak that pain didn't seem possible. The doctors thought he could not hear what they were saying. And they spoke as if he were dead. One said, 'Not even a miracle can save him now!'

The chief surgeon took off his surgical coat and prepared to leave the room. The young intern asked, 'May I have the body?' 'Yes,' was the response. The doctors left the room.

It has been written: *So we do not lose heart... Because we look not to the things that are seen but to the things that are unseen; for the things that are seen are transient, but the things that are unseen are eternal.*

They could see the physical body, but Rafael was a mind with a body. What was happening to the mind of Rafael Correa which was not visible?

In that twilight state between life and death, Rafael was not able consciously to move his body. But because of the positive mental attitude he had developed in his subconscious mind by reading inspirational books, his mind was communicating with a Higher Power. He felt that God was with him.

He began to speak to God as a friend—like a man talking with another. 'You know me—You are inside me—You are my blood—You are my life—You are my everything. There is but one mind—one principle—one substance in the universe, and I am one with all else.'

'If I die, I don't lose anything. I just change form. But I am only twenty years old. Dear God, I'm not afraid to die—but I'm willing to live! If You choose to give me life, someday, somehow, I'll be able and willing through Your mercy to lead a better life and to help others.'

As the intern approached Rafael, he looked at Rafael's face and observed the twitching of his eyelids and a teardrop falling from the comer of his left eye. 'Doctor, doctor, come quickly! I think he's alive!' he called excitedly.

It took more than a year for him to regain his strength, But Rafael Correa did live!

Some years later Rafael flew from San Juan to Chicago to ask the authors to hold a three-evening PMA seminar at San Juan. It was then that Rafael told us his story of that eventful night in his life.

We were inspired by his story and particularly also by the fact that since he had been granted his life, he was trying to make good on his promise to help others. We flew to San Juan to conduct the seminar.

While we were in San Juan, Rafael introduced us to the chief surgeon who had been with him all that night, and the doctor confirmed Rafael's story. During the course of the conversation, we asked Rafael, 'What was the name of the book that influenced you in your hour of need?' Rafael replied:

'I had read many inspirational books, but I believe the thoughts that went through my mind that night were primarily from *Science and Health, With Key to the Scriptures* by Mary Baker Eddy.'

As proved by Rafael, inspirational books are tremendously instrumental in changing lives. And there is no book with more inspiration and motivation than *The Bible*. *The Bible* has changed the lives of more persons than any other book. It has helped countless thousands to develop physical, mental, and moral health. Reading *The Bible* has developed a greater understanding of Its truths in many persons and caused them to draw closer to their own church. This is because *The Bible* has motivated them to positive action.

An inspirational book like the one you are now reading can also motivate you. It can be the catalyst which starts you on the road to desirable, positive action and success.

Use a book as a catalyst. The dictionary defines a catalyst in physical chemistry as a substance that causes or accelerates a chemical reaction. The dictionary further states that an anticatalyst, or negative catalyst, retards a reaction.

The authors recommend that you use good inspirational books as positive catalysts to accelerate your progress toward achievement of true success in life. And they hasten to warn that you choose such catalysts with care. In Chapter 22 of this book, entitled '*The Amazing Power of a Bibliography*,' you will find listed many books which the authors guarantee can act as positive catalysts in your life—if you are ready.

Martin J. Kohe in his book Your Greatest Power tells of a British regiment that used the 91st Psalm as a catalyst to aid them not just to achieve a material goal, but for the very preservation of life itself.

Kohe wrote: 'F. L. Rawson, noted engineer and one of England's greatest scientists, in his book, Life Understood, gives an account of a British regiment under control of Colonel Whitlesey, which served in the World War for more than four years without losing a man. This unparalleled record was made possible by means of active cooperation of officers and men in memorizing and repeating regularly the words of the 91st

Psalm, which has been called the Psalm of Protection.'

Protection of your life can also be accomplished by protecting your health. And, let there be no misunderstanding about it! Your health is one of your most valuable assets. Many a man today would be more than willing to trade his wealth for good health.

'I'd rather have my health than his money!' It is said that a healthy, ambitious eighteen-year-old clerk in a produce firm in Cleveland, Ohio, developed a major definite aim of becoming the world's richest man. At the age of fifty-seven he retired on doctor's orders. Like many American businessmen, he had if—stomach ulcers and shot nerves! In addition, he was a hated man. 'I'd rather have my health than his money,' many said. John K. Winkler tells the story in *John D., a Portrait in Oils.*

Can money buy physical and mental health, a longer life—and the esteem of your fellowmen? When John D. Rockefeller retired from active business, his major definite aims were to develop a healthy body, maintain a healthy mind, live a long life and later, to win the esteem of his fellowmen. Could money buy these? It did! Here's how Rockefeller did it and what it can mean to you: Rockefeller:

- Attended the Baptist Church services every Sunday and took notes to learn the principles that he might apply daily.
- Slept eight hours every night and took short naps every day. And through rest he avoided harmful fatigue.
- Took a bath or shower every day. He was neat and clean in his appearance.
- Moved to Florida to a climate conducive to his good health and longevity.
- Lived a well-balanced life. For fresh air and sunshine

were absorbed while he daily engaged in his favorite outdoor sport—golf. And indoor games, reading, and other wholesome activities were enjoyed with regularity.

- Ate slowly, in moderation, and chewed everything well. The saliva in his mouth was permitted to mix with the masticated foods and liquids. And they were well digested before they were swallowed. They were swallowed at body temperature. Foods too hot or too cold for the mouth were not dumped into his stomach to bum or freeze its lining.
- Digested mental and spiritual vitamins. For grace was said at each meal. And at dinner, it was his custom to have his secretary, a guest, or a member of his family read *The Bible*, a sermon, an inspirational poem, a motivating article from a newspaper, magazine or book.
- Employed Dr. Hamilton Fisk Biggar full time. Dr. Biggar was paid to keep John D. well, happy, and alive. He did this through motivating his patient to develop a cheerful, happy attitude. And Rockefeller lived to be ninety-seven.
- Didn't want the hatred of his fellowmen to be inherited by the members of his family. Therefore, he began intelligently to share a part of his possessions with the needy.
- At first Rockefeller's motive was primarily a selfish one. He wanted a good reputation. Then something happened! By acting generous, he became generous. And by bringing happiness and health to many through his charitable and philanthropic contributions, he found them for himself.
- And the Foundations he established will benefit mankind for generations to come. His life and money

> were instruments for good. This world is a better and healthier world to live in because of John D. Rockefeller!

You shouldn't have to amass a fortune before you come to realize that PMA will attract perfect health. But there are some other ingredients which should be used along with PMA and one of them is health education. Don't be ignorant about your health.

The price of ignorance is sin, sickness and death! What do you know about *Hygiene*? *Hygiene* is defined as 'a system of principles or rules designed for the promotion of health'.

Social Hygiene often refers specifically to venereal contagion. Ignorance of physical, mental, and social hygiene can lead to sin, sickness, and death.

If you are timid in discussing such matters, read *Venture of Faith* by Mary Alice and Harold Blake Walker. Today, because of PMA, the family, schools, churches, press, the medical profession, federal and state governments, and youth organizations endeavor to lift the dark cloud of ignorance regarding physical, mental, and social hygiene through education. Prevention is taught as well as cure.

But a cure for alcoholism is not so easy to come by as education in hygiene. Alcoholism ranks as the fourth largest health problem in the nation. It follows mental and moral disease and is one of the greatest contributors to those two diseases. The economic cost of alcoholism is 25 billion dollars per year. The greater portion of this is loss of time to industry, followed by hospital costs and physical damages— caused mainly by automobile accidents. But the money loss is negligible compared to the loss of physical, mental, and moral health, and the loss of life attributable to alcoholism.

An alcoholic has a mental illness which lies dormant until

his first drink. If he doesn't start the habit, liquor doesn't have the power of attraction for him. If he drinks, the affinity is strong, and he will drink to excess. If he drinks to excess, the attraction may become irresistible, or seem so. And when he tries to resist and doesn't succeed, he may believe he cannot be cured.

What happens to excessive drinkers? Alcohol is known to alter the brain waves as recorded by the scientific instrument known as an electroencephalograph. It has a most potent influence on nerve cell metabolism which results in slow rhythms and eventual suppression of voltage and brings about a change in the level of consciousness.

A human body is alive only as long as its subconscious mind functions. It can be kept alive for a long time without the functioning of the conscious mind. There are degrees of consciousness.

Sanity is that healthy state of mind when the activities of the conscious and the subconscious are in proper balance. And while they work together, each has its specific duties; each has inhibiting factors. While sometimes it is healthful and wholesome for a person to do the things he wants to do but which are forbidden. Judgments and actions should be the result of the conscious and subconscious working in balance.

The intellect and other powers of the conscious mind act as a governor regulating the subconscious when a person is in a conscious state of activity. As the activity of this governor slows down, the machine begins to run wild, and the individual may act in an illogical manner. His uncontrolled activities may range from a simple foolish act to a state of mind commonly known as insanity.

As the inhibiting barriers are lowered, due to the effect of alcohol on the brain cells, the restraining controls of the conscious mind become less effective. When the emotions, passions, and other activities of the subconscious mind have too free a rein, without proper regulation by the balance wheel of the intellect, the individual in this semi-conscious state of mind will commit foolish and undesirable acts due to alcoholic influence.

Alcoholism is indeed a dread disease. If allowed to control a person's life, it can render that person physically, mentally, and morally ill and send him to a living hell. Once alcohol has gained control in a person's life, it does not readily relinquish its hold.

But there is a cure!

There's always a cure! What's the cure? Stop drinking! For the alcoholic, this is more easily said than done. The important thing is that *it can be done.* He can do it!

When you develop a positive mental attitude, you don't give up trying because you have previously failed or because you know of cases where others have failed. You can be motivated and receive hope from successful experiences. A baby learning to walk isn't criticized for falling after taking the first three steps. It is given credit for the progress it makes in response to its conscious effort.

The alcoholic may find help in a number of places. Complete cures for alcoholism have been affected by environmental influences in the religious therapy of established churches; rescue missions like the Pacific Garden Mission in Chicago; revival meetings of evangelists like Oral Roberts; Alcoholics Anonymous; medical and psychiatric help including hypnosis; private hospitals such as the Keeley Institute at Dwight, Illinois; or an inspirational book like I Dare You!

However, each individual must win his own internal victory. But, generally, it is necessary for him to come under the environmental influence of someone who will help him through suggestion until he takes control of his own power. Or, if you will, until he has a positive mental attitude developed beyoud the point of relapsing into a negative mental attitude. PMA can do wonders for the alcoholic if only he will put it to work for him. And PMA will work wonders for you, too, in attracting health and longevity.

Uncertainty about your health can undermine your PMA: by causing you to worry about every little ache or pain. The longer you remain uncertain, the more your attitude changes direction from positive to negative. And if the symptoms you have noticed really do denote a condition that requires attention, the longer you remain uncertain and do nothing, the greater are the opportunities for that condition to develop. Don't be uncertain about your health. Get into action!

Take the guesswork out of your health! He was a young, dynamic, successful automobile sales manager. His whole future was ahead of him, yet he was mighty low! In fact, he expected to die! He even selected and purchased his cemetery lot and made all arrangements for his burial. He got his house in order. But here's what actually happened.

At times he became short of breath. His heart beat rapidly. His throat choked up. Eventually he went to his family doctor, who was a very successful physician and surgeon. The doctor advised him to takc a resl, lo take life easy, to retire from the work he loved, the thrilling game of selling automobiles.

The sales manager stayed home for a while and rested his body, but because of fears, his mind was not at ease. He still became short of breath. His heart would beat rapidly. His throat would choke up. It was summer-time, and his doctor advised him to vacation in Colorado.

He was carried into the Pullman compartment. Colorado,

with its healthful climate, inspirational mountains, did not prevent the manifestation of his fears. He would frequently experience shortness of breath, rapid beating of the heart, and the same choked-up feeling. Within a week he returned home. He believed death was coming.

'Take the guesswork out of it!' This salesman was told (as you might be told) by one of the authors. 'You have everything to gain and nothing to lose by going to a clinic such as Mayo Brothers at Rochester, Minnesota. *Do It Now!'* At his request he was driven to Rochester by a relative. He was actually afraid that he might die en route.

When the sales manager went through the clinic, he was told what was wrong with him. The doctor said, 'Your difficulty is that you breathe in too much oxygen.' He laughed and said, 'That's silly!' The doctor responded, 'Jump up and down fifty times as if you were jumping rope.' He became short of breath; his heart beat rapidly; and his throat choked up.

'What can I do about it?' the young man asked. The doctor responded, 'When you feel this condition coming on, you can: (1) breathe into a paper bag, or (2) just hold your breath for a little while,' and the doctor handed the patient a paper bag. The patient followed instructions. His heart stopped beating rapidly, breathing became normal, and his throat didn't bother him. He left the clinic a happy man.

Whenever the symptoms of his illness occurred, he would just hold his breath for a short time, and his body would function normally. After a few months he lost his fears, and his symptoms disappeared. This happened more than 30 years ago. He hasn't required medical attention since.

Of course, not all cures are so easily affected. There are times when you may have to use all your resources before aid is found. However, it is wise to continue the search with persistence and a positive mental attitude. Such determination and optimism usually pay off. It did for another sales manager. Let us tell you about him.

There is always a cure —find it. This particular sales manager registered in a small-town hotel and fell and broke a leg as he entered the room assigned to him. The hotel manager took our sales manager to the nearest hospital where an attending physician set his leg. A few days later it was considered safe for him to be moved, and he returned to his home.

He convalesced for several weeks under the attention of his family physician. But while he seemed to improve, the fracture did not heal. After many weeks, the doctor told him that he would get progressively worse: he would become a cripple. This sales manager was very much disturbed because his work required that he be on his feet.

He discussed the matter with one of the authors who said, 'Don't believe it! There is always a cure—find it! Take the guesswork out of it. *Do It Now!*' He was told the story of the automobile sales manager as it has been told to you, and it was suggested that he make arrangements to go to Mayo Brothers Clinic.

He also left the clinic a happy man. Why? He was told, 'Your system needs calcium. We could load you with it, but the calcium would wear off. Just drink a quart of milk a day.' He did. In time the injured leg became as strong as the sound one.

A positive mental attitude applied to health takes into consideration the possibility of accidents. In fact, *Safety first* is a PMA symbol. From it you receive the suggestion to become alert and enforce your desire to live—to save life and property.

Be sure you're not driving to your own funeral. A newspaper article carried a headline reading: 'Late for a Funeral, Six Die in 105 MPH Blowout' The lead read:

Six funerals were precipitated on Sunday by the crash of an automobile whose driver was stepping on the gas in fear he and his relatives would be late for one funeral.

Drive carefully if you want to be physically and mentally healthy, and if you want to live longer. As a pedestrian, be alerted to the hazards and obey traffic laws. And when you ride with another person at the wheel of the automobile, remember you are at the mercy of his physical and mental weaknesses, if any, as well as the mechanical condition of his car. Have the courage to refuse to ride with an intoxicated driver, or in an automobile in which the brakes don't operate properly—even if you own the car. 'The life you save may be your own!'

Safety first saves lives with PMA. Although it cost one million dollars a floor for each of its forty-one stories, the Prudential Building in Chicago was the most inexpensive office building of its kind ever constructed. Why?

It didn't cost a single life! There were no serious accidents. Safety factors were installed because of PMA.

In comparison, negative mental attitudes comprising ignorance and carelessness, caused in tragic accidents:

One death for every one hundred feet of height of the Empire State Building!

One hundred and ten deaths in the construction of Hoover Dam!

One life for every one hundred and ten feet in the construction of the San Francisco-Oakland Bay Bridge! Eighty deaths in the construction of the Colorado River Aqueduct!

One thousand two hundred and nineteen deaths in the construction of the Panama Canal! (There were four thousand seven hundred sixty-six additional fatalities during the construction of this project from other causes.)

Ninety-seven deaths in the building of Grand Coulee Dam and the Columbia River Basin Project!

Of course, no one actually knows when tragedy will strike. But it always is better to be prepared. You will be prepared if you have a positive mental attitude. Aunt Kitty was.

When tragedy strikes! Aunt Kitty lost her only son when he was nine years old. Like many good housewives and mothers, she had no business training. But Aunt Kitty did have a strong religious faith. She knew that in spite of her great loss, it was her job to go on living and contributing her share to make this world a better world to live in. But how could she maintain physical and mental health so that she could go on?

Aunt Kitty decided that in order to ease her pain and fill the great void in her life she would have to: keep very busy and do whatever her abilities would permit to make other people happy, since she could no longer do this for her son.

So she got a job as a waitress in a busy restaurant. Her hours were long. Her work made it mandatory to talk with people and to act cheerful. Faith in her religion and a sincere interest in other people, combined with work and time, neutralized her pain and saved her physical and mental health.

Actually, your health may be affected by many internal influences. And some of these influences may be mental figments of the imagination.

High school girl gets pains before examinations! Because of the inter-relationship between the mind and body, the subconscious mind may create apparent bodily disorders induced by emotional disturbances to bring about a specific desired result. A true-life experience will prove the point.

A high school girl experienced severe backaches the morning

of any day on which she was to take a German or history examination. She didn't like either subject. She wasn't properly prepared. Her pains were so severe that she believed she couldn't get up from bed. She was not pretending. She suffered.

A peculiar characteristic of the pain was that about 3:30 in the afternoon, when school was over for the day, the pain would subside. On the same evening when her boyfriend came to call, the pain would marvelously disappear!

This girl, you probably are thinking, could do with a little psychiatry. She could. She and many others like her have been helped through religion and psychiatry. The two are not as far apart as many may think. Why?

Religion and psychiatry. Rules and regulations for physical and mental health and a longer life were woven into religion long before words similar to physiology, psychology, and psychiatry became part of any language. This is especially true regarding the application of techniques affecting the subconscious mind.

It is easy to see why psychiatric clinics and counseling services are becoming an integral part of church organizations regardless of their religious denominations.

The minister to millions helps the sick! The Rev. Norman Vincent Peale and Smiley Blanton, M.D., established The American Foundation of Religion and Psychiatry, which is now known as the Institutes of Religion and Health. It is a nonprofit, nonsectarian clinic in New York City. Anyone with an emotional problem is eligible for help regardless of race, religion, or ability to pay. Today there is a full and part time professional staff of thirty-five composed of psychiatrists, ministers, psychologists, and psychiatric social workers.

If you would like information on how to establish a counseling service in your church, write the Institutes.

What lies ahead? Mental and physical health are two great rewards of a positive mental attitude. It is true: a positive mental attitude takes effort, patience, and practice to gain and maintain. But a definite purpose, clean and clear thinking, creative vision, courageous action, persistence and true perception, all applied with enthusiasm and faith will go far to help you achieve and maintain a positive mental attitude.

And what lies ahead as you approach your definite goals?

Happiness lies ahead.

If you are happy now, you will wish to maintain and increase this wonderful happiness which you already have. If you are not happy now, you will want to learn how you can be happy. Let's turn to Chapter 18, entitled 'How To Be Happy' to find additional PMA success principles to speed us in our pursuit of happiness.

PILOT NO. 17
Thoughts to Steer By

1. You can have more perfect health. A positive mental attitude affects your health. It attracts good health to you. A negative mental attitude attracts ill health.
2. Thinking good thoughts, positive and cheerful thoughts, will improve the way you feel. What affects your mind also affects your body.
3. A positive mental attitude toward the ones you love may be the means of saving their lives. Remember the father who saved the life of his infant son by going into action with a positive mental attitude.
4. Learn to practice PMA instead of giving in to NMA as the engineer's wife did. Her NMA allowed death to claim her.
5. Develop within you a positive mental attitude so powerful that it seeps down from your conscious into your subconscious mind. If you do, you will find that in times of need and emergency, it will automatically flash back to your conscious mind. Even in the greatest emergency of life: death.
6. Make a study of *The Bible* and other inspirational books. They will both inspire and teach you how to motivate yourself to positive desirable action and thus help you achieve the goals you desire.
7. Learn to use the 17 success principles and to apply them to your life. Have you memorized them?
8. All the wealth in the world cannot, by itself, buy good health. But you can achieve good health by striving for it and observing simple rules of hygiene and good health habits. Remember, John D. Rockefeller had to retire at the age of 57 because of ill health, but through a positive

mental attitude and wholesome living, he reached the ripe old age of 97.

9. PMA recognizes the importance of education in physical, mental, and social hygiene, and that ignorance of these subjects can mean sin, sickness, and death. Keep abreast of current developments affecting your mental, moral, and physical health.
10. Never abandon hope—*for there is a potential cure for every ailment.* Develop PMA and take the guesswork out of your health by seeking aid at the right time.
11. PMA repels accidents and tragedies by keeping the person with PMA alert to dangers at all times. Should tragedy strike, however, PMA can guide you in meeting reverses calmly and deliberately.
12. A sound mind and sound body are attainable if you will put PMA to work for you. Remember—you can enjoy good health and live longer with PMA.

I FEEL HEALTHY!
I FEEL HAPPY!
I FEEL TERRIFIC!

18

CAN YOU ATTRACT HAPPINESS?

Can you attract happiness?

Abraham Lincoln once made the remark, 'It has been my observation that people are just about as happy as they make up their minds to be.'

There is very little difference in people, but that little difference makes a big difference. The little difference is *attitude*. The big difference is whether it is *positive* or *negative*.

Persons who want to be happy will adopt a positive mental attitude and be influenced by the PMA side of their talisman. Thus, happiness will be attracted to them. And those who turn on NMA make a business of being unhappy. They don't attract—they repel happiness.

'I want to be happy…' A popular song starts off with words that contain a great deal of truth: 'I want to be happy, but I won't be happy, 'til I make you happy, too!'

One of the surest ways to find happiness for yourself is to devote your energies toward making someone else happy. Happiness is an elusive, transitory thing. And if you set out to search for it, you will find it evasive. But if you try to bring happiness to someone else, then it comes to you.

Writer Claire Jones, wife of a professor in the religion department at Oklahoma City University, tells of a happiness they experienced during their early married life. 'We lived in a small town the first two years we were married,' she recalls, 'and our neighbors were a very old couple, the wife nearly blind and confined to a wheelchair. The old man, not very well himself, kept house and cared for her.

'My husband and I were decorating our Christmas tree a few days before Christmas, when we decided on impulse to fix a tree for the old people. We bought a small one, decorated it with tinsel and lights, wrapped a few small gifts, and took it over the night before Christmas.

'The old lady cried as she gazed dimly at the sparkling lights. Her husband said over and over, 'But it's been years since we had a tree.' They mentioned that tree nearly every time we visited them during the next year.

'The next Christmas they were both gone from the little house. It was a small thing we had done for them. But we were happy that we'd done it.'

Now the happiness they experienced as a result of their kindness was a very deep, warm feeling the memory of which will remain with them. It was a very special kind of happiness that comes to those who do kind deeds.

But the kind of happiness which is most common and most constant comes closer to being a state of contentment: a state of being neither happy nor unhappy.

You are a happy person during a period when you predominantly experience that positive state of mind in which you are happy combined with that neutral state of mind in which you are not unhappy.

And you can be happy, content, or unhappy. For the choice is yours. The determining factor is whether you are under the influence of a positive or negative mental attitude. And that factor you can control.

Handicaps are no barrier to happiness. Surely if ever there was a person who might have been expected to complain of unhappiness Helen Keller was that person. Born deaf, mute, and blind, deprived of knowledge of normal communication with the persons who surrounded her, she had only her sense of touch to help her to reach out to others and to experience the happiness of loving and being loved.

But reach out she did, and through the aid of a devoted and brilliant teacher who in love reached out to Helen Keller, that deaf, mute, and blind little girl became a brilliant, joyful, happy woman. Miss Keller once wrote:

> Anyone who out of the goodness of his heart speaks a helpful word, gives a cheering smile, or smooths over a rough place in another7s path knows that the delight he feels is so intimate a part of himself that he lives by it The joy of surmounting obstacles which once seemed unremovable, and pushing the frontier of accomplishment further—what joy is there like unto it?
>
> If those who seek happiness would stop one little minute and think, they would see that the delights they already experience are as countless as the grasses at their feet, or the dewdrops sparkling upon the morning flowers.

Helen Keller counted her blessings and was profoundly grateful for them. Then she shared the wonder of these blessings with others, and caused them to feel delight Because she shared that which is good and desirable, she attracted unto herself more of that which is good and desirable. For the more you share, the more you will have. And if you share happiness with others, happiness will grow richer within you.

But if you share misery and unhappiness, you will attract misery and unhappiness to yourself. And we all know of persons who are eternally having troubles—not problems, or opportunities in disguise. Theirs are spelled t-r-o-u-b-l-e. No matter what happens to them, it just isn't good. And this is because they are always sharing their troubles with others.

Now there are many lonely people in this world who long for love and friendship but never seem to get it Some repel that which they seek with NMA. Others curl up in their little comers and never venture out. They secretly hope that something good will come to them, but they do not share any of the good which they enjoy. They do not realize that when you withhold from others that which you have which is good and desirable, your own portion of the good and desirable diminishes.

Others, however, have the courage to do something about their loneliness, and they find their answer in sharing the good and beautiful with others. There was one such little boy who was a very lonely, unhappy little boy indeed. When he was born his backbone was arched into a grotesque hump and his left leg was crooked. Looking at the infant, the doctor assured the boy's father: 'But he'll get along all right.'

The family was poor. And the baby's mother died before he was a year old. As he grew up, other children shunned him because of his misshapen body and his inability to participate successfully in many of their activities. Charles Steinmetz was his name. And he was a lonely, unhappy little fellow.

But the Great Giver of All Good had not overlooked this little fellow. To compensate for his misshapen body, Charles had been endowed with an extraordinarily keen mind. Using the greatest asset available to him, Charles ignored his physical disabilities about which he felt he could do nothing, and worked to excel with his mind. At five, he could conjugate Latin verbs. At seven he learned Greek and a smattering of Hebrew. At eight, he had a good understanding of algebra and geometry.

When he went on to college, he excelled in all his studies.

In fact, he was graduated with honors. He had carefully saved his pennies so he could rent a dress suit for the occasion. But with the inconsiderate cruelty that is so often characteristic of persons under the influence of NMA, the school authorities posted a notice on the bulletin board excusing Charles from the ceremonies.

At long last it occurred to Charles that instead of trying to force respect for himself from people by making them take notice of his mental capacities, he would cultivate their friendship; he would use his abilities not to attract notice and to satisfy his own ego, but for the furtherance of the good of mankind. To start his new way of life, he boarded a ship and came to America.

Having reached this country, Charles Steinmetz began to look for a job. Several times he was rebuffed because of his appearance, but he finally landed a job with General Electric as a draftsman at $12 a week. In addition to his regular duties he spent long hours in electrical research, and he endeavored to cultivate the friendship of his fellow employees by trying to share with them that which he had that was good and desirable.

After some time, the chairman of the board of General Electric Company recognized the rare genius of this man, and said to Charles: 'Here is our entire plant. Do anything you want with it. Dream all day, if you wish. Well pay you for dreaming.'

Charles worked hard, long and earnestly. During his lifetime he patented more than 200 electrical inventions and wrote many books and papers on problems of electrical theory and engineering. He knew the satisfaction of a job well done. And he also knew the satisfaction of making contributions which went far to make this world a better place to live in. He accumulated wealth and acquired a lovely home which he shared with a young couple he knew. Thus, Steinmetz experienced the happiness of a full and useful life.

Happiness begins at home. The greater part of the life of each of us is spent in our homes, with our families. And unfortunately, that dwelling which should be a haven of love, happiness, and security too often turns into an antagonistic place where the members do not enjoy happy and harmonious relationships. Problems in the home can arise for many reasons.

In one of our PMA Science of Success classes a very gifted, aggressive young man of about twenty-four was asked, 'Have you a problem?'

'Yes!' he replied, 'My mother. In fact, I have decided to leave home this weekend.'

When the student was asked to discuss his problem, it became evident that the relationship between him and his mother was not harmonious. It was apparent to the instructor that her aggressive, dominant personality was similar to his.

The class was informed that the personality of an individual can be compared to the powers of a magnet. When two like powers are in line and push or pull in the same direction, they are drawn to each other by attraction. When the powers are opposed to each other, they resist and repel one another.

When they are placed side by side and both confront the same outside forces, the individuals like the magnets remain separate entities. Yet their strength to attract and repel these forces is increased even though between themselves they are opposed.

The instructor continued by saying, 'It appears that your behavior and that of your mother are so similar that you can determine how she reacts to you by the way you react to her. You can probably evaluate her feelings by analyzing your own. Therefore, you can solve your problem easily!

'*When two forceful personalities are opposed and it is desirable that they live together in harmony, at least one must use the power of PMA.*

'Here's your specific assignment for this week: When your mother asks you to do something, *do it cheerfully.* When she expresses an opinion, agree with her in a pleasant, sincere manner, or don't say anything. When you are tempted to find fault with her, find something good to say. You will have a most pleasant experience. She will probably follow your example.'

'It won't work!' responded the student. 'She is just too hard to get along with!'

'You're absolutely right,' responded the instructor. 'It won't work unless—you try to work it with a positive mental attitude.'

A week later the young man was asked how he was coming along with his problem. His response was: 'I am happy to say that there hasn't been one unpleasant word between us all week. You might be interested in knowing that I have decided to stay at home.'

When parents don't understand their children. There is a tendency for a person to assume that everyone always likes what he likes and always thinks the way he thinks. For people have a tendency to judge the reactions of others by their own reactions.

Now, like the young man who had a problem with his mother, such a conclusion would at times be correct. But many parents often have problems with their children because they fail to realize that the personality of the child is different from theirs. It is a mistake for parents not to realize that time changes both the child and them. For they don't adjust their mental attitudes to compensate for the changes within the child and themselves.

'I don't understand her!' the father said. A lawyer and his wife had five wonderful children. The parents were unhappy because their oldest daughter, who was a freshman at high school, didn't respond to her parents the way they expected. The daughter was unhappy, too.

'She's a good girl, but I don't understand her,' she does not work in the house; yet shell toil for hours at the piano. In the summer I got her a job at the department store, but she didn't want to work. She just wants to play the piano all day!'

It was our recommendation that the parents and daughter be given an Activity Vector Analysis by one of the authors. In Chapter 10 entitled: 'How to Motivate Others,' you have read about Activity Vector Analysis. These results were very revealing. We found that the girl possessed ambitions, energies, and traits so far beyoud either of the parents that it would be difficult for them to comprehend her reactions to them until they understood that each person is different.

The parents thought that while it was nice to know how to play a piano, it was good for a girl to work at home and work in a store in the summer. A passion to be a pianist was just a waste of time. 'She will get married some day and will have to keep house. She should be more practical,' the parents reasoned.

The daughter's capacities and the tendencies that motivated her were explained to the parents. Reasons were given why it was hard for them to understand her. An explanation was also given to the daughter as to why her parents thought one way and she another. When the three endeavored to understand what brought about their problem and how they could adjust to it with a positive mental attitude, they were able to live together in greater harmony.

To have a happy home, be understanding. To be happy, be understanding of other people. Realize that another person's energy level and capacities may not be the same as yours. He may not think like you. Try to understand that what he likes may not be what you like. When you realize this, you will find it easier to develop a PMA in yourself and to do that which will create desirable reactions in others.

Opposite poles of a magnet attract each other and do persons with opposite personality traits. And where there is a community of interest, two individuals may experience a happy association together although each has opposite characteristics in many respects. One may be ambitious, aggressive, confident, and optimistic and possess tremendous drive, energy, and stick-to-itiveness. The other may have a tendency to be satisfied, fearful, timid, shy, tactful, and humble and may lack confidence in himself. Often such persons are attracted to each other, and when associated together complement, strengthen, and inspire each other.

And they blend their personalities and thus the extremes of each become neutralized. What would grow into rigidity on the part of one and frustration on the part of the other is thus avoided.

Would you be happy and inspired if you were married to a person whose personality was exactly like yours? Be truthful with yourself. The answer would probably be 'no'.

Children, too, can be taught to be understanding and to be appreciative of all that their parents do for them. Much unhappiness is caused in homes because the children do not appreciate and understand their parents. But whose fault is it? The child's or the parents' or both?

Some time ago we had an appointment with the president of a large and successful organization. His name has appeared in a favorable light in every large newspaper in the country for the good work he did while holding public office. Yet on the day we saw him, he was most unhappy. 'No one likes me! Even my children hate me! Why is this?' he asked.

Actually, this man is a person of good intent. He gave

his children everything that money would buy. He deliberately kept them from the needs that forced him as a child to gain the strength he developed as a man. He tried to protect them from those things in life that to him were not beautiful. He eliminated the necessity for them to struggle as he had had to struggle. He never asked or expected appreciation from his sons and daughters when they were children and he never got it. Yet he assumed that they understood him without endeavoring to find out.

Things would have been different had he taught his children to be appreciative and to gain strength by at least partially fighting their own battles. He experienced happiness in making them happy without teaching them to be happy by making others happy. Therefore, they made him unhappy. Perhaps if he had confided in them when they were growing up and told of the struggles he had endured for their benefit, they might have been more understanding.

But there is no need for this man, or anyone in a like situation, to remain unhappy. He can turn up the PMA side of his talisman and try earnestly to make himself known to and understood by his dear ones.

And he can take the time to show that he loves them by sharing *himself* instead of just giving them those material things with which his wealth can supply them. If he shares himself as liberally as he shared his money with them, he will experience the rich reward of having them return love and understanding to him.

Of course, this man had meant well. He had the right intent toward his children and toward others. But he had not been sensitive to their reactions. He had simply assumed that they would understand. And he had not taken the time to help them to do so.

Now this man could help himself by reading inspirational books. We recommended several including: *How to Win Friends and Influence People.* And we told him that his children were people.

Attract and repel through verbal communications. Regardless of who you are—you are a wonderful person! Yet certain individuals may not think so. If you feel that they react unfavorably with unwarranted antagonism to the many things you say and do, you can do something about it. They are just as human as you are.

You have the power to attract and repel! You can use this power wisely to attract the right friends and repel those who have an undesirable or injurious influence on you. With a negative mental attitude—you are apt automatically to repel the good things in life and attract the undesirable including the wrong kind of friends.

Undesirable reactions on the part of others may be due to what you say and how you say it; or because of your true inner feelings and attitudes. The voice, like music, is often a reflection of the mood, attitude, and hidden thoughts of the mind. It may be just as difficult for you to realize that the fault lies with you as it is for you to take the initiative and correct yourself when you realize the fault does at times lie with you—*but you can do it!*

You can learn from a good salesman. For he is forced to train himself to be sensitive to the reactions of prospective customers—and do something about it.

The customer is always right attitude of successful merchants is a most difficult attitude for some individuals to adopt; yet—it gets results!

If you would endeavor to make your relatives happy with the same positive mental attitude that a salesman uses to sell his merchandise to prospective customers, your home and social life would become a more happy and successful one—that is if you have a problem of personality conflict at home.

If your feelings are frequently hurt because of what people say, or how they say it, it is quite likely that you yourself are frequently guilty of offending others by what you say or how you say it. Try to determine the true reasons for your reactions of hurt feelings and then avoid causing the same reactions in others.

If gossip offends you, you can assume that you shouldn't gossip or you will offend others.

If you find someone's tone of voice and attitude towards you objectionable, avoid offending others by speaking or acting in the same manner.

If you are not happy when someone yells at you in an angry voice, assume that it is repellent to another if you yell at him—even though he is your five-year-old son, or a very close relative.

If you feel offended because another person misunderstands your intent, show your confidence—give other persons the benefit of the doubt.

If you do not find arguments, sarcasm, humor with a personal sting, or criticism of your ideas, friends or relatives pleasant, it is logical to assume that others will not find them pleasing either.

And if you like to be complimented—if you like to be remembered—if it makes you happy to know that someone thinks of you: you can safely assume that others will be happy if you compliment them, or remember them, or drop them a note to let them know you are thinking of them.

A letter can bring happiness. *Absence makes the heart grow fonder*—if letters are exchanged. For many a marriage has taken place because love grew stronger through absence.

Poetry, imagination, romance, idealism, ecstasy develop warmth and understanding through the exchange of letters. Each individual can express thoughts that might never be expressed if the written word is not used as the medium. Letters of endearment need not, and should not, stop with marriage. Samuel Clemens (Mark Twain) wrote loving notes to his wife daily even when they were at home. They lived a life of real happiness together.

You are what you think. To write—you must think. When you write a letter, you crystallize your thinking on paper. Your imagination is developed by recollecting the past, analyzing the present and perceiving the future. The more often you write, the more you take pleasure in writing. By asking questions, you, as the writer, direct the mind of the recipient into desired channels. You can make it easy for him to respond to you. Thus, when he does, he becomes the writer and you receive additional joy as the recipient.

The receiver of the letter you write is forced to think in terms of you. If your letter is well-thought-out, both his reason and his emotions can be directed along desired paths. Inspiring thoughts will be imprinted indelibly in his memory when they are being recorded in his subconscious mind as he reads.

Can you attract happiness? Yes, of course you can attract happiness. How? You can attract happiness with PMA.

A positive mental attitude will attract to you all the health, wealth, and happiness you desire. And a positive mental attitude consists of such plus characteristics as: faith, hope, charity, optimism, cheer, generosity, tolerance, tact, kindliness, honesty, good-finding, initiative, truthfulness, straightforwardness, and good common sense.

Contentment. As a nationally syndicated columnist, Napoleon Hill once wrote an article entitled 'Contentment'.

You may find it helpful. Here is what it said:

> The richest man in all the world lives in Happy Valley.
>
> He is rich in values that endure, in things he cannot lose—things that provide him with contentment, sound health, peace of mind and harmony within his soul.
>
> Here is an inventory of his riches and how he acquired them:
>
> 'I found happiness by helping others to find it.
>
> 'I found sound health by living temperately and eating only the food my body requires to maintain itself.
>
> 'I hate no man, envy no man, but love and respect all mankind.
>
> 'I am engaged in a labor of love with which I mix play generously; therefore, I seldom grow tired.
>
> 'I pray daily, not for more riches, but for more wisdom with which to recognize, embrace, and enjoy the great abundance of riches I already possess.
>
> 'I speak no name save only to honor it, and I slander no man for any cause whatsoever.
>
> 'I ask no favors of anyone except the privilege of sharing my blessings with all who desire them.
>
> 'I am on good terms with my conscience; therefore, it guides me accurately in everything I do.
>
> 'I have more material wealth than I need because I am free from greed and covet only those things I can use constructively while I live. My wealth comes from those whom I have benefited by sharing my blessings.
>
> 'The estate of Happy Valley which I own is not taxable. It exists mainly in my own mind, in intangible riches that cannot be assessed for taxation or appropriated except by those who adopt my way of life. I created this

estate over a lifetime of effort by observing nature's laws and forming habits to conform with them.'

There are no copyrights on the Happy Valley man's success creed. If you will adopt it, the creed can bring you wisdom, peace, and contentment.

In his book, *The Power of Faith*, Rabbi Louis Bienstock said this on the subject of happiness:

'Man was born together—all of one piece. It is the kind of world he has fashioned that has torn him apart. A world of folly! A world of falsehood! A world of fear! With the power of faith, let him put himself together again—faith in himself, faith in his fellowmen, faith in his destiny, faith in his God. Then and only then will the world be truly together. Then and only then will man find happiness and peace.'

Remember, *if the man is right his world will be right*, He can attract happiness just as he can attract wealth, unhappiness, or poverty. Is your world right? Or are guilt feelings keeping you from winning the success you want? If so, you will want to read our next chapter to insure happiness in your life.

PILOT NO. 18
Thoughts to Steer By

1. Abraham Lincoln once said: 'It has been my observation that people are just about as happy as they make up their minds to be.' Will you make up your mind to be happy? If not, will you make up your mind not to be unhappy?
2. There is very little difference in people, but that little difference makes a big difference. The little difference is *attitude*. The big difference is whether it is *positive* or *negative*.
3. One of the surest ways to find happiness for yourself is to devote your energies toward making someone else happy.
4. If you search for happiness, you will find it elusive. But if you try to bring happiness to someone else, it will return to you many times over.
5. If you share happiness, and all that is good and desirable, you will attract happiness, and the good and desirable.
6. If you share misery and unhappiness, you will attract misery and unhappiness to yourself.
7. Happiness begins at home. Members of your family are people. Motivate them to be happy just like a good salesman motivates his prospects to buy.
8. When two forceful personalities are opposed and it is desirable that they live together in harmony, at least one must use the power of PMA.
9. Be sensitive to your own reactions and to the reactions of others.
10. Would you like to live contentedly in Happy Valley?

TO BE HAPPY MAKE
OTHERS HAPPY!

19

GET RID OF THAT GUILT FEELING

You have a guilt feeling. That's good!

But get rid of that feeling of guilt.

A sense of guilt is good. And every living person regardless of how good or bad he may be will sometimes experience a feeling of guilt. This feeling is the result of a 'still, small voice' speaking to you. And your conscience is that 'still, small voice'.

Now think for a moment: What would happen if one did not feel a sense of guilt after doing wrong? For the person who does not have a feeling of guilt for doing a specific wrong act is often unable to distinguish between right and wrong—or hasn't been trained to know the difference between right and wrong as regards that act. Or he may not be sane.

For many feelings of guilt are inherited. And others are acquired. We know a mental conflict often will develop when inherited emotions and passions are bridled by the society in which one lives; and people in one environment may have an entirely different code of ethics that is opposed to the code of those in another. Yet in each instance where the individual has been taught a specific, ethical standard and violates it, he develops a feeling of guilt.

In some instances, however, the violation of a moral standard of society is good because *the standard itself may be bad.*

And we reiterate: a feeling of guilt is good: It even motivates persons of the highest moral standards to worthwhile thought and action.

For there was a righteous man who hated and unrelentingly persecuted people of a religious minority. But he developed a feeling of guilt. And the world knows he righted his wrong when his feelings of guilt motivated him to desirable action. For he became a great evangelist. And his thoughts, words, and actions have changed the history of the world during the past two thousand years. Saul of Tarsus was his name.

And then there was a man whose feeling of guilt for what he believed to be the misdeeds of his life made him so remorseful that he, too, was motivated to desirable action. In prison he spent his days writing a book. And his book is a classic reference for teaching nobility of character and beauty of life. John Bunyan was his name.

And then there was also the sinner we discussed in Chapter Fifteen who donated a half million dollars to the Chicago Boys Clubs and who also donated a million dollars to his church. Now he did this to atone in part for his guilt. For he provided money to prevent boys and girls from falling into the traps and snares of life that he had experienced.

Even a benefactor to mankind like Dr. Albert Schweitzer was motivated by the sense of guilt. For he felt guilty that he had fallen short of his responsibilities to his fellowmen. And because he could, but was not, doing something worthwhile, his sense of guilt prompted him to start his great mission.

Now do you see that a feeling of guilt with PMA is good? But then there is a feeling of guilt with NMA. And that is bad.

For not every guilt feeling brings about beneficial remits. Now when the individual has a guilt feeling and does not get rid of that guilt feeling with PMA, the results are often most harmful.

And the great psychologist Sigmund Freud says: "The further our work proceeds and the deeper our knowledge of the mental life of neurotics penetrates, the more clearly two new factors force themselves upon our notice which demand the closest attention as sources of resistance... They can both be included under the one description of "need to be ill" or "need to suffer"... the first of these two factors is the *sense of guilt or consciousness of guilt.*'

And Sigmund Freud is right. For feelings of guilt have motivated men to destroy their lives, mutilate their bodies, or injure themselves in other ways to atone for their wrongdoing. Now today, fortunately, such methods are seldom practiced. And they are not permitted in civilized countries. Yet their counterpart can be found. For the conscious mind may not feel guilty but the subconscious mind does.

And the subconscious mind never forgets.

And it uses its powers as effectively as the conscious mind. For it fulfills the need of the individual who doesn't rid himself of the feeling of guilt with PMA. It makes him ill. It makes him suffer.

A guilt feeling can teach you consideration for others. Consideration for others is a quality each of us has to learn to develop. The new-born baby cares little for the comfort and convenience of anyone else. He wants what he wants when he wants it. So right at that point in his development he begins to learn, little by little, that there are others alive, too, and that, to some extent at least, he will have to allow them some consideration. But selfishness is a common human trait, and it lessens in each of us only through development. When we get old enough to understand that such feelings are not good, we feel a twinge of guilt when we indulge in selfishness. This is good, for it causes us to think twice when the occasion arises and we can choose between pleasing ourselves or pleasing others concerned.

Thomas Gunn's six-year-old grandson was visiting him at his home in Cleveland, Ohio. The youngster would run to the comer every evening to meet his grandfather when he returned from work. This made the grandfather very happy. When the youngster met him, he would give his grandson a small bag of candy.

One day the boy ran to the corner and greeted his grandfather in excitement and anticipation with: 'Where's my candy?' The elderly gentleman tried to conceal his emotion. 'Did you meet me every evening,' he hesitated before continuing, 'just for a bag of candy?' The boy was handed the small bag that his grandfather had taken out of his pocket. Nothing more was said as they walked to the house. The child was hurt. He was unhappy. He didn't eat the candy. It didn't seem desirable any more. He had injured someone whom he loved.

That night as the six-year-old and his grandfather knelt down and said their prayers aloud together, the youngster added one all his own: 'Please, God, let grandfather know I love him.'

The boy's unhappiness and remorse because of what he had done were good. Why? Because they forced him to take action to get rid of that guilt feeling and make amends for what he had done.

To get rid of that guilt feeling, make amends. Feelings of guilt can arise from many varied causes. But a sense of guilt brings with it a feeling of indebtedness... indebtedness that must be reduced and eliminated.

And this is very well illustrated by the story of the young doctor in Lloyd C. Douglas' novel *The Magnificent Obsession.* For you will recall that in that story the young man who is the hero felt that he owed the world a debt because his life had been saved at the cost of the life of a great brain surgeon who had been a real blessing to the world.

But it was this feeling of debt which caused the young man to become a brain specialist equal in ability to the man whose life he felt he had taken. And from the diary of the man who had gone on, the young man learned a philosophy of life which caused him to develop a Magnificent Obsession. Thus, because of his guilt feeling, he too became a worthwhile person.

Now every story is somebody's story. And every day in your daily newspaper you read somebody's story: someone like Jim Vaus whose life was saved in more ways than one because he responded to an irrevocable decision to get rid of his feeling of guilt. For he got into action.

To get rid of that guilt feeling, get into action! Sometimes people get caught in a web of wrongdoing, and they seem to be unable to free themselves from it. For they give up trying. And then they become more and more entangled, until finally it takes an almost earthshaking experience to set them free. Such was the case with Jim Vaus.

Jim Vaus is a man who literally owes his life to his decision to say 'I will' and yet this decision came quite late in life. For a good many years, Jim had been running head on into the Commandments. He seemed to be trying to violate them all, one by one. The first time he broke the injunction, 'Thou shalt not steal,' he was still in college. One day he stole $92.74; he went to the airport, bought a ticket, and headed for Florida. A little later he stole again, this time in an armed robbery. He was caught and put in jail. Shortly thereafter he was granted amnesty so that he could join the Army; yet even in the Army he got into trouble. The court martial read, '... for diverting government property to private use...'

And so, it went. Jim Vaus' career kept sliding downhill. The more often he did wrong, the more guilt he felt. Guilt leads to guilt, as well as lies and deception to hide it.

Now Jim didn't consciously feel more guilty—because his conscious sense of guilt had become deadened. But not so with his subconscious mind. For that's where the guilt feeling accumulated without Jim's realizing it.

And, as in the instances you often read of in your newspaper, it took an earthshaking experience to awaken him.

Now Vaus was eventually released from the Army; he married and moved to California where he set up an electronics consultant business. One day a man known simply as Andy came to Jim and outlined a big idea for beating the races with an electronic device. Within weeks Jim was deeply involved with the underworld. And he was driving a nine-thousand-dollar car. He had a fine home in the suburbs, and more business than he could handle.

One day Jim had an argument with his wife. She wanted to know where all the money was coming from, and he wouldn't say. So, she started to cry. Jim couldn't stand to see his wife cry. For he loved her. Jim's conscience bothered him. Because he wanted to humor her, he suggested a ride out to the beach. On the way, they got caught in a traffic jam: hundreds of cars were pouring into a parking lot.

'Oh look, Jim,' said Alice. 'It's Billy Graham! Let's go. It might be interesting.'

And still trying to humor her, Jim went along. But shortly after he sat down, he became emotionally disturbed: It seemed to him that Graham was talking directly to him. For Jim's conscience bothered him so badly that it seemed he had been singled out. Graham's text was:

'What does it profit a man if he gains the whole world and loses his soul?'

Then Graham was saying:

'There's a man here who has heard all this before, who is

hardening his heart. With pride he stiffens his neck, and he is determined to leave without making a decision. But this will be his last chance.'

His last chance? To Jim the thought was startling. Perhaps he had a premonition. Or perhaps he was ready. What did the preacher mean?

Graham was giving a call to come forward. He wanted people to take a physical step that symbolized a decision. What was happening, Jim wondered. Why did he feel like crying? Suddenly he found himself speaking. 'Let's go, Alice.' Dutifully Alice walked to the aisle, and turned as if to go out of the tent. Jim, who was following her, caught her arm and turned her around.

'No, dear,' he said. 'This way... '

Years later, after Jim had changed his life completely, he was giving a speech in Los Angeles. And then he told of his experiences with the underworld. He told about the day of his decision; on which day he had been instructed to fly to St. Louis on a wire-tapping assignment. 'I never reached St. Louis,' he said. 'I found the courage to reach my knees instead.'

And in his speech Jim told of his blessings and how he had thanked God for them, asked for forgiveness, had tried to neutralize his wrongdoing, and stressed the application of the Golden Rule.

After the lecture, a lady came up to him and said, 'Mr. Vaus, I think you might like to know something. I was working in the Mayor's office at the time you were supposed to go to St. Louis. On that day a teletype was received from the FBI. It said, Mr. Vaus, that you were going to be met in St. Louis by a rival gang. And shot dead.'

A recommended formula for getting rid of guilt. Your own 'last chance' may not be as dramatic as this. But there is a wonderful lesson in the story of Jim Vaus, nonetheless. How was Jim able to get rid of his guilt feelings? He did it by following a clear-cut pattern. It is the pattern all of us can follow.

> ...First of all, you listen as you hear advice, a lecture, an inspirational sermon that could change your life.
>
> ...Then you count your blessings, and thank God for them. Feel sincerely sorry and ask for forgiveness. When you realize your blessings, it isn't difficult to become sincerely sorry for the wrongs you have done. And truly to repent Then you will have the courage to ask for forgiveness from God.
>
> ...You must take the first step forward. This is important because it is a symbol through a physical gesture that you make in the direction of a changed life. When Jim walked down the aisle, he was making a public announcement that he had become sorry for his past and was now ready to change his life.
>
> ...Also, you must make amends by taking the second step forward: begin immediately to right every wrong.
>
> ...And then the most important step of all: apply the Golden Rule. This should be easy. For now, when you are tempted to do wrong, that 'still, small voice' will whisper to you. And when it does, stop and listen. Count your blessings. Picture yourself in the other fellow's place. And then make your decision to do what you would want done if you actually were in his position.

So this is the formula for getting rid of your guilt feelings. If you are having trouble with temptation, and if subsequent guilt is keeping you from using your energy in a constructive direction, learn the pattern for freedom from guilt Relate it to your own life. Apply it. And step away toward success.

Success Through a Positive Mental Attitude urges you to use the powers of your conscious and subconscious mind to:

- Seek the truth.
- Motivate you to take constructive action.
- Cause you to strive to achieve the highest ideals you can conceive, consistent with good physical and mental health.
- Live intelligently in your society.
- Help you abstain from that which will cause unnecessary injury.
- Start you from where you are and get you to where you want to be regardless of what you are or what you have been.

Anything which deters you from noble achievements in life should be cast aside. And this places upon you the burden to know or find out what is right or wrong, and to know what is good or evil under a given circumstance and at a given time.

You are acquainted with the Ten Commandments, the Golden Rule, and other standards of good in the society in which you live. And it is for you to determine the standards which will guide you to your desired goals.

'It is one thing to know the goal, and quite another thing to work toward it,' writes Bishop Fulton J. Sheen in *Life Is Worth Living*. Choose your goals! Work toward them! Direct your thoughts, control your emotions, get into action and you ordain your destiny. You can find the answer if you keep seeking it. How? One important aid is to 'catch character.'

Catch. 'Character is something that is caught, not taught,' was a thought-provoking quotation of Arthur Burger, former

Executive Director of the Boys Clubs of Boston. It appeared in a *Reader's Digest* article entitled '400,000 Boys Are Members of the Club'.

Catch has two distinct meanings: (1) 'affected by exposure to environment' (often subconscious reaction); and (2) 'seize and hold' (conscious action).

One effective way to catch character is to place yourself or your children in an environment that will develop desirable thoughts, motives, and habits. If your selected environment it is not sufficiently effective after a reasonable time, make substitutions and changes.

But character can also be taught. And if parents would devote more time to teaching character, both by precept and example, their children would catch and learn this admirable quality so necessary for success.

What makes a delinquent? E. E. Bauermeister, former Supervisor of Education at the California Institution for Men at Chino, California, says: 'Our youngsters need the guidance in choosing right from wrong which they should receive at home... when we start talking about juvenile delinquency, we should rename it and put the responsibility where it belongs. We have a case of parent delinquency in America today. Parents are not assuming the obligations and responsibilities that are theirs.

'Everyone has been born with a potential of good character...'

J. Edgar Hoover made this statement: 'You can read volumes upon volumes as to the cause of crime, but crime is literally caused by the lack of one thing, a feeling of moral responsibility on the part of people.'

And the reason the people lack a feeling of moral responsibility is because they lack a guilt feeling. Thus, they do not develop their own characters, for their conscience is dulled and doesn't guide them. And from their faulty unmoral and amoral characters their children can neither catch nor learn character.

When one virtue is in conflict with another. Sometimes it is not so easy to decide whether one should say *yes* or no. For the question to be resolved may involve a conflict between virtues. And every person at some time is faced with such a conflict and must make a decision. He must choose: between what he wishes to do and what he ought to do; or between what he wants and what society expects of him.

And such a choice must necessarily be made between virtues, such as: love, duty, and loyalty. As examples: (a) love and duty to a parent in conflict with the love and duty to a husband or wife; (b) loyalty to an individual in conflict with loyalty to another individual; or (c) loyalty to an individual in conflict with loyalty to an organization or society.

Let's illustrate with the story of the salesmen who worked with George Johnson. For they were faced with a conflict between loyalty to an individual and loyalty to another Individual and the organization he represented.

George Johnson trained, encouraged, inspired, and financed a salesman whom we will call John Black.

George had complete confidence in John. He liked him. He gave him a break. He let him service his best customers—long established accounts. In the company contract it was agreed that in the event of termination the salesman would in no way molest the company's business or interfere with its sales organization. Mr. Johnson gave Black the book *Think and Grow Rich*. It motivated John to action—the wrong action! John didn't read what was unwritten. His only interest was the acquisition of money. He believed the end justified any means. Because of his negative standards he responded aggressively with a negative mental attitude.

'George Johnson is just like a father to me. Yes, I think of him as a father,' the salesman said, but at the same time he secretly planned to transfer the company's customers and sales force to a competing concern for—money.

John was welcomed in the homes of his fellow salesmen. For they were unaware of his thoughts or plans. When he called at their homes he relied upon the honesty and decency of the individuals to live up to a promise and not to betray his secret. He would ask, 'How would you like to double your earnings? How would you like to have greater security?' The response would be: 'Sounds good! What's it all about?'

Black would answer, 'I don't want anyone to upset the apple cart; therefore, I'll tell you only *if you promise me on your honor not to tell anyone.* Do you make a solemn promise?'

When the answer was *yes*, he endeavored to entice them over to the competing organization. He tried to neutralize their pangs of conscience by referring to real or imaginary dissatisfactions.

The other salesmen were 'on the spot'. On the one hand, they had given John their solemn promise not to tell what he was doing. On the other hand, they knew what he was doing would be harmful to their employer. And they owed a greater loyalty to George Johnson and the organization he represented.

The salesmen had the courage to try to clear the cobwebs of John's thinking and to show him that what he was contemplating was not right. When he didn't respond but persisted in his own way, they knew what to do: They gave George Johnson the facts. They chose adherence to courage, honesty, and loyalty. They knew how to decide between right and wrong when one virtue was in conflict with another.

There are many such conflicts. In your life you will be faced with the necessity to make decisions in instances where virtues are in conflict with other virtues. And what will your decision be? Perhaps the following will aid you:

Do that which your conscience tells you will not develop a guilt feeling. It's the right thing to do. To assist you in coming to the right decision under such circumstances, complete the *Success Quotient Analysis* in the following chapter.

PILOT NO. 19
Thoughts to Steer By

1. You have a guilt feeling. That's good! But get rid of that guilt feeling!
2. To get rid of that guilt feeling, make amends.
3. A recommended formula to help you get rid of guilt is:
   (a) Listen to advice, a lecture, sermon, etc., and relate and assimilate the principles.
   (b) Count your blessings and thank God for them.
   (c) Then become truly sorry for your wrongdoings. True sorrow necessarily incorporates a sincere decision to stop the wrongdoing.
   (d) Take the first step forward: Acknowledge your guilt and your intention to make amends.
   (e) Make amends insofar as you are able.
   (f) Memorize, understand and try to apply the Golden Rule in your dealings with others.
4. Anything which deters you from noble achievements in life should be cast aside.
5. Character can be *caught* and *taught.*
6. What do you do when two virtues are in conflict with one another?
7. The burden is upon you to find what is right or wrong, and to know what is good or evil under a given circumstance and at a given time. One of the best ways to learn is to expose yourself with regularity to a religious environment, and to seek Divine Guidance daily.

YOU HAVE A GUILT FEELING—THAT'S GOOD.
BUT GET RID OF THAT GUILT FEELING!

PART V

ACTION PLEASE!

NEGLIGENCE

Remember that you and you alone can eliminate your real limitations when you learn and employ the art of motivation with PMA. These limitations are:

1. A negative mental attitude and your neglect to change to a positive mental attitude
2. Ignorance, through your neglect, to learn how to use the powers of your mind
3. Your neglect to engage in thinking, study and planning time to set and achieve desirable goals
4. Your neglect to take the necessary action when you know what to do and how to do it
5. Your neglect to learn how to recognize, relate, assimilate and apply universal principles that, when applied, can help you achieve any objective you may have that doesn't violate the laws of God or the rights of your fellow men
6. That which you set up in your own mind, or accept, as insurmountable

Also remember: Negligence is one of the quickest and easiest habits to neutralize and overcome if you want to neutralize and overcome it.

20

NOW IT'S TIME TO TEST YOUR OWN SUCCESS QUOTIENT

You have read all but the last three chapters of *Success Through a Positive Mental Attitude*. And now would be a good time to take a look at your own mental attitude. And you can do this for yourself.

But before you do, we want you to know our attitude is:

The burden of teaching is upon the person who wants to teach.

And with whom does the burden of learning lie? Perhaps J. Milbum Smith has the answer. Now J. Milburn Smith rose from *assistant to the office boy to president* of the Continental Casualty Company of Chicago. He told us:

The burden of learning is on the person who wants to learn, not on the person who wants to teach.

And he also said:

'A 'have-not' is a person who believes that an idea is not good for him unless he himself originates it.

And I say:

'Copy from success! Everything I have done I have borrowed from another person or business.' And he continued:

'Be respectful and listen to those who have experience.

'For the experienced man had something I wanted. And that's why I associated with older and successful men. For I took what they had: the good, their knowledge and experience, but not their weaknesses. And then I added this to what I had. Thus, I profited even by their mistakes as well as my own.

To learn, one must *pay the price*. And I was willing to pay it for I was not taught. I learned. Knowledge? You must seek it out!'

Copy from success, says J. Milburn Smith.

And you can begin by asking yourself some questions: Am I willing to pay the price? Am I willing to take the good, the knowledge and the experience, but not the weaknesses of the men I have read about in this book?

And if your answer is yes, then we have a suggestion that we know will help you. But let's first remind you that as you have read the pages of this book, you have frequently been called upon to answer questions about yourself. And although these may have appeared to have been simple questions, in reality: is there anything harder than to evaluate one's self correctly? 'Know thyself' is probably the most difficult admonition ever given to man.

And to assist you to *know thyself* the authors have prepared a personal analysis questionnaire which has helped many men and women to do this more satisfactorily. You have already taken many tests intelligence, aptitude, personality, vocabulary, and all the rest.

But this one is different. We call it your *Success Quotient Analysis*. And it is based on the 17 success principles which have been responsible for the worthwhile achievements of the world's outstanding leaders in all fields. It has many purposes:

> To direct your thoughts in desired channels.
>
> To crystallize your own thinking.
>
> To indicate your present position on the road to success. To encourage you to decide exactly where you

want to be.

To measure your chances of reaching your desired destination.

To indicate your present ambitions and other characteristics. To motivate you to desirable action with PMA.

Our suggestion. And now our suggestion is that you immediately try to answer the following Success Quotient Analysis: thoughtfully and truthfully, to the best of your ability. Try not to fool yourself. For this test will be valid only if you answer every question with the truth as you now see it.

Success Quotient Analysis

1. Definiteness of purpose	*Yes*	*No*
(a) Have you decided upon a definite major goal in life?	___	___
(b) Have you set a time limit for reaching that goal?	___	___
(c) Do you have specific plans for achieving your goal in life?	___	___
(d) Have you determined what definite benefits your goal in life will bring you?	___	___

2. Positive mental attitude	*Yes*	*No*
(a) Do you know what is meant by a positive mental attitude?	___	___
(b) Do you control your mental attitude?	___	___

	Yes	No
(c) Do you know the only thing over which anyone has complete power of control?	___	___
(d) Do you know how to detect a negative mental attitude in yourself and others?	___	___
(e) Do you know how to make PMA a habit?	___	___

3. Going the 'Extra Mile'	*Yes*	*No*
(a) Do you know when an employee is entitled to more pay?	___	___
(b) Do you know of anyone who has achieved success in any calling without doing more than he was paid to do?	___	___
(c) Do you believe anyone has a right to expect an increase in salary unless he is doing more than he is paid for?	___	___
(d) If you were your own employer, would you be satisfied with the sort of service you are now rendering as an employee?	___	___

4. Accurate thinking	*Yes*	*No*
(a) Do you make it your duty constantly to learn more about your occupation?	___	___
(b) Is it your habit to express 'opinions' on subjects with which you are not familiar?	___	___

		Yes	No
	(c) Do you know how to find the facts when you need knowledge?	___	___
5.	Self-discipline	*Yes*	*No*
	(a) Do you hold your tongue when angry?	___	___
	(b) Is it your habit to speak before you think?	___	___
	(c) Do you lose your patience easily?	___	___
	(d) Are you generally even- tempered?	___	___
	(e) Is it your habit to allow your emotions to overpower your reason?	___	___
6.	The master mind	*Yes*	*No*
	(a) Are you influencing other people to help you attain your goal in life?	___	___
	(b) Do you believe that a person can succeed in life without the aid of others?	___	___
	(c) Do you believe a man can easily succeed in his occupation if he is opposed by his wife or other members of his family?	___	___
	(d) Are there advantages when an employer and an employee work together in harmony?	___	___
	(e) Are you proud when a group to which you belong is praised?	___	___
7.	Applied faith	*Yes*	*No*
	(a) Do you have faith in Infinite Intelligence?	___	___

(b) Are you a person of integrity? ___ ___

(c) Do you have confidence in your ability to do what you decide to do? ___ ___

(d) Are you reasonable free from these seven basic fears (1) fear of poverty? (2) fear of criticism? (3) fear of ill health? (4) fear of loss of love? (5) fear of loss of liberty? (6) fear of old age? (7) fear of death? ___ ___

8. Pleasing Personality *Yes* *No*

(a) Are your habits offensive towards others? ___ ___

(b) Is it your habit to apply the Golden Rule? ___ ___

(c) Are you liked by those with whom you work? ___ ___

(d) Do you bore others? ___ ___

9. Personal Initiative *Yes* *No*

(a) Do you plan your work? ___ ___

(b) Must your work be planned for you? ___ ___

(c) Do you possess outstanding qualities not possessed by anyone in your line of work? ___ ___

(d) Is it your habit to procrastinate? ___ ___

(e) Is it your habit to try to create better plans for doing your work more efficiently? ___ ___

10. Enthusiasm *Yes* *Yes*

(a) Are you an enthusiastic person? ___ ___

(b) Do you direct your enthusiasm toward carrying out your plans? ___ ___

(c) Does your enthusiasm overpower your judgment? ___ ___

11. Controlled attention *Yes* *No*

(a) Is it your habit to concentrate your thoughts on what you are doing? ___ ___

(b) Are you easily influenced to change your plans or your decisions? ___ ___

(c) Are you inclined to abandon your aims and plans when you meet opposition? ___ ___

(d) Do you keep working regardless of unavoidable distractions? ___ ___

12. Teamwork *Yes* *No*

(a) Do you get along harmoniously with others? ___ ___

(b) Do you grant favors as freely as you ask them? ___ ___

(c) Do you have frequent disagreements with others? ___ ___

(d) Are there great advantages in friendly cooperation among co-workers? ___ ___

(e) Are you aware of the damage one can cause by not cooperating with coworkers? ___ ___

13. Learning from defeat *Yes* *No*

(a) Does defeat cause you to stop trying? ___ ___

	Yes	No
(b) If you fail in a given effort, do you keep trying?	___	___
(c) Is temporary defeat the same as failure?	___	___
(d) Have you learned any lessons from defeat?	___	___
(e) Do you know how defeat can be converted into an asset that will lead to success?	___	___

14. Creative vision	*Yes*	*No*
(a) Do you use your imagination constructively?	___	___
(b) Do you make your own decisions?	___	___
(c) Is the man who only follows instructions always worth more than the man who also creates new ideas?	___	___
(d) Are you inventive?	___	___
(e) Do you create practical ideas in connection with your work?	___	___
(f) When desirable, do you seek sound advice?	___	___

15. Budgeting time and money	*Yes*	*No*
(a) Do you save a fixed percentage of your income?	___	___
(b) Do you spend money without regard to your future source of income?	___	___
(c) Do you get sufficient sleep each night?	___	___

		Yes	No
	(d) Is it your habit to employ spare time studying self-improvement books?	___	___
16.	Maintenance of sound health	*Yes*	*No*
	(a) Do you know five essential factors of sound health?	___	___
	(b) Do you know where sound health begins?	___	___
	(c) Are you aware of the relation of relaxation to sound health?	___	___
	(d) Do you know the four important factors necessary for the proper balancing of sound health?	___	___
	(e) Do you know the meaning of 'hypochondria' and 'psychosomatic illnesses?	___	___
17.	Using cosmic habit force as it pertains to your personal habits	*Yes*	*No*
	(a) Do you have habits which you feel you cannot control?	___	___
	(b) Have you recently eliminated undesirable habits?	___	___
	(c) Have you recently developed any new, desirable habits?	___	___

Here's how to rate your answers. All the following questions should have been answered NO: 3c - 3d - 4b - 5b -5c -5e-6b-6c - 8a - 8d - 9b - 9d - 10c - lib - 11c -12c - 13a - 13c - 14c - 15b - 17a. All other questions should have been answered YES. Your score would have been 300 if all the questions had been answered 'No' or 'Yes' as shown above. This is a perfect score and very few people have ever made such a score. Now let's see what your score was.

Number of 'No' answers instead of 'Yes': __ x 4 = __

If you answered 'No' to any of the meaning questions that should have been answered 'Yes,' deduct four points for each one:

Add the subtotals together, and subtract from 300. This will be your score.

Illustration:

Number of 'Yes' answers instead of 'No': 3 × 4 =	12
Number of 'No' answers instead of 'Yes': 2 × 4 =	8
Total Number of Wrong Answers	20
Perfect score	300
Minus Total Number of Wrong Answers	-20
Your Score	280

Find your rating below

300 points —— Perfect (Very Rare)

275 to 299 points —— Good (Above Average)

200 to 274 points —— Fair (Average)

100 to 199 points —— Poor (Below Average)

Below 100 points —— Unsatisfactory

You have now taken an important step to success and happiness.

You have tried to answer the questions in this Success Quotient Analysis searchingly and honestly. If not, you will. Now the important thing to remember is that these results are not final and unchangeable. If you scored high, it means you will be able to assimilate and practice the principles in this book rather quickly.

If your score was not so high don't despair! Apply PMA! You *can* achieve great success in life!

When you need help from a psychologist to find out what business or profession you may be fitted for, he will frequently ask you to take a battery of tests.

The picture that emerges from these tests may show you what your particular tendencies are. However, the psychologist does not regard the result of these tests as final. He always arranges for a personal interview to find out that which a test will not answer.

He uses the results of the tests and the interview to counsel you and to evaluate your progress.

In the same way *you* can use the first score on the questionnaire as a means of measuring your own ever-growing success quotient.

Read *Success Through a Positive Mental Attitude* from cover to cover once more. And again. And again. Read it aloud with your husband, wife, or a close friend, discussing it point by point. Read it until every principle becomes a part of your life, motivating your every action.

Then, when you have earnestly applied these principles for three months, take the S.Q. test again. Not only will many wrong answers become right ones, but answers you gave correctly the first time will be more emphatic and confident.

Your Success Quotient can serve you as more than a yardstick, however. It can serve to underline those areas where you need to work hardest for self-improvement. It will also reveal your areas of special strength.

For your future is ahead of you. You have the power to direct your thoughts and control your emotions. Just awaken the sleeping giant within you.

How?

You will find your answer in the next chapter.

PILOT NO. 20
Thoughts to Steer By

1. Review the Success Quotient Analysis frequently until you can truthfully state to yourself: 'I can now make the right answer to each question.' Each of the questions will direct your mind in a specific channel whereby you can easily determine what you can and should do.
2. There is a value in solving problems or developing desirable habits by asking yourself the proper questions. Write them down, and then, in your thinking time, strive to find the proper solutions to obtain the results you desire.

> SOW AN ACT AND YOU REAP A HABIT. SOW A HABIT AND YOU REAP A CHARACTER. SOW A CHARACTER AND YOU REAP A DESTINY.

21

AWAKEN THE SLEEPING GIANT WITHIN YOU

You are the most important living person.

'Stop and think about yourself: In all the history of the world there was never anyone else exactly like *you*, and in all the infinity of time to come, there will never be another.'

You are the product of *your*: heredity, environment, physical body, conscious and subconscious mind, experience, and particular position and direction in time and space... and *something more*, including powers known and unknown.

You have the power to affect, use, control or harmonize with all of them. And you can direct your thoughts, control your emotions and ordain your destiny with PMA.

For *you* are a *mind* with a *body*.

And your mind consists of dual, invisible gigantic powers: the conscious and subconscious. One is a giant that never sleeps. It is called the subconscious mind. The other is a giant which when asleep is powerless. When awakened, his potential power is unlimited. This giant is known as the conscious mind. When the two work in harmony, they can affect, use, control or harmonize with all known and unknown powers.

What wouldst thou have? 'What wouldst thou have? I am ready to obey thee as thy slave—I and the other slaves of the lamp,' said the genie.

Awaken the sleeping giant within you! It is more powerful than all the genie of Aladdin's lamp! The genie are fictional. Your sleeping giant is real!

What wouldst thou have? Love? Good health? Success? Friends? Money? A home? A car? Recognition? Peace of mind? Courage? Happiness? Or, would you make your world a better world in which to live? The sleeping giant within you has the power to bring your wishes into reality.

What wouldst thou have? Name it and it's yours. *Awaken the sleeping giant within you!* How?

Think. *Think with a positive mental attitude.*

Now the sleeping giant, like the genie, must be summoned with magic. But you possess this magic. The magic is your talisman, with the symbols PMA on one side and NMA on the other. The characteristics of PMA are the plus characteristics symbolized by such words as faith, hope, honesty, and love.

You are launched on a great journey. We have called the resumes at the end of the chapters 'pilots'. That is because you are going somewhere. You are not standing still. You are on your way through rough and often unfamiliar waters. To reach the end of your journey successfully, you will need many of the skills of the navigator. As the compass of a ship is affected by disturbing magnetic influences, requiring the pilot to make certain allowances in order to keep the vessel on its right course, so you must take account of the powerful influences affecting you as you navigate through life.

A compass is corrected to give true readings regardless of variation and deviation. The same applies to life where the variations are environmental influences. And the deviations are the negative attitudes within your own conscious and subconscious mind. You must correct these deviations as they occur in your plotting.

Ahead of you may be disappointments, adversities, and dangers. These are the rocks and hidden shoals past which you must sail on your course. And this you can do when your compass is compensated for variation. For if you are aware of the coral reefs and tides, you can capitalize on each.

You can select the environmental influence of the light of a lighthouse or sound of a buoy to steer a course that will bring you towards your destination without serious mishap.

Now when plotting a course, you must rely upon the accuracy of your compass. Compensating the compass is not an exact science. A necessary safeguard is unceasing watchfulness on the navigator's part. It is possible, however, to correct a compass very effectively.

Just as a magnetic needle is in direct line with the north and south magnetic poles, so when your compass is compensated, you will automatically react in line with your objective, your highest ideal. *And the highest ideal of man is the will of God.*

This book will now go with you on your journey to success. *Success Through a Positive Mental Attitude* will bring you success, wealth, physical, mental and spiritual health, and happiness when—you react favorably to it. Remember what Andrew Carnegie said:

'Anything in life worth having is worth working for.' Awaken the sleeping giant! In the next chapter entitled 'The Amazing Power of a Bibliography' you will discover the art of reading an inspirational book in a manner that will help you to awaken the sleeping giant within you.

PILOT NO. 21
Thoughts to Steer By

1. What wouldst thou have? Love? Good health? Success? Friends? Money? A home? A car? Recognition? Peace of mind? Courage? Happiness? Or would you make your world a better world in which to live?
2. Name it and it can be yours—if you learn and employ the principles found in this book that are applicable to you.
3. Think. Think with a positive mental attitude. And follow through with desirable action.
4. Compensate your compass to avoid dangers and thus arrive safely at your chosen destination.
5. The highest ideal of man is the will of God.
6. Awaken the sleeping giant within you!

AWAKEN THE SLEEPING
GIANT WITHIN YOU!

22

THE AMAZING POWER OF A BIBLIOGRAPHY

This chapter is a bibliography. And this bibliography has amazing potential power. For within it may lie the hidden button which pushed can be used to unleash the power within you—the untapped, unused vast resources that you alone possess. And we hope it will start a chain reaction that will help you in achieving true success. For if you want to motivate yourself and others: Say it with a book.

Say it with a book. In *Success Through a Positive Mental Attitude* the authors have used a technique that has proved exceedingly effective in their writings, lectures, and counseling service. We recommend self-help books which experience has proved cause a desirable and positive reaction in the reader.

Now in the twentieth century, America has been particularly fortunate in developing a group of authors who have the unique talent to write in a manner that sows seeds of thought which motivate those who are searching for self-improvement to find it. The reader reacts with desirable *action*.

While some of the books we recommend are out of print, the universal truths contained in them are just as true today as the day they were written. And such books can be obtained from used bookstores or rented from your library.

Again, we urge you to read, study, understand, and apply

the principles in inspirational, self-help action books, magazines and newspaper articles. Read everything you can find about those who had successful careers in your own field to determine what principles you can use to succeed. Also read success stories about people in other kinds of work and find the common denominator, the principle involved.

Share with others a part of what you possess that is good and desirable: an inspirational, self-help action book, article, editorial or poem.

Now, that's what Nate Lieberman has done. For many years he was a manufacturer's representative. He had a Magnificent Obsession. Over a period of years, he shared thousands of inspirational books with his friends. And it was Nate Lieberman who made Emerson and Mr. Stone close friends with a gift of Emerson's Essays. And likewise, he introduced him to the authors of *Suggestion and Autosuggestion*, *The Law of Psychic Phenomena and Invention* and *The Unconscious*, and many more.

Now this sharing of ideas and ideals is a marvelous thing—you give them away and still keep them for yourself, too.

Brownie Wise knew this. Brownie needed to support herself and her son, who was ill. Her meager salary wasn't enough to pay for her son's medical care. Therefore, she obtained a parttime sales job for Tupperware Home Parties, Inc., to augment her income.

She needed money. With it, her son could have the best medical attention. They could move to a climate that would help restore his health. Brownie Wise prayed for help. She found it.

She read an inspirational book, *Think and Grow Rich*. She read it once and then read it again. In fact. Brownie read the book six times. Then she recognized the principles she was looking for and something happened. She made it happen! She saw how she could apply these principles to her own situation and these ideas were put into action. It wasn't long before her earnings from Tupperware exceeded $18,000 a year. And within a few years, her income rose to over $75,000 annually. In due course she became vice-president and general manager of the company. Brownie Wise enjoyed the distinction of being recognized as one of the outstanding woman sales managers in the United States. She continued her successful career and eventually became president of Viviane Woodard Cosmetics Corporation.

This outstanding business woman's success began with a book and continued with a book. Much of her achievement is due to the successful motivation of her representatives. She shared what she had learned from reading *Think and Grow Rich*. Brownie Wise bought copies of the book for her sales representatives. They were urged to read *Think and Grow Rich* as many times as she had, and to apply the principles in their own lives.

And the story of Lee S. Mytinger and William S. Casselberry, Ph.D., is another example of the value of inspirational, self-help action books in the achievement of success. These men helped nature bring good health to men, women, and children through the sale of Nutrilite, a food supplement which contains vitamins and minerals. Their sales grossed many millions of dollars annually.

Mytinger and Casselberry read *Think and Grow Rich*. They assimilated what they read and got into action. Part of their success was due to their ability to motivate their distributors with mental and spiritual vitamins. They did this with the same book that had inspired them. Each new employee received an inspirational lecture course teaching him the fundamentals of success. They distributed thousands of self-help books because they knew what amazing effects these books have on sales representatives' productivity and success.

W. Clement Stone uses inspirational literature extensively in his organization. His company buys thousands of books for distribution to employees, stockholders, and representatives. The success and growth of his companies have been phenomenal—not by accident.

How to read a book. There is an art to reading a self-help book. When you read, concentrate. Read as if the author were a close personal friend and were writing to you—and you alone.

Now you recall that Abraham Lincoln, when he read, took time for reflection in order that he might relate and assimilate the principles into his own experience. It would be wise to follow his good example.

Determine what you are looking for before you read a self-help book. If you know what you are looking for you are more apt to find it than if you don't have a specific purpose. If you really want to recognize, relate, assimilate and apply success principles that are contained between the covers of an inspirational book, you must work at it. A self-help book is not to be skimmed through the same way that you might read a detective novel. Mortimer J. Adler in How to Read a Book urges the reader to follow a definite pattern. Here's an ideal one:

Step A. *Read for general content.* This is the first reading. It should be a fast reading, to grasp the sweeping flow of thought that the book contains. But take the time to underline the important words and phrases. Write notes in the margins and write down briefly the ideas that flash into your mind as you read. Now this obviously may only be done with a book that you own. But the notations and markings make your book more valuable to you.

Step B. *Read for particular emphasis.* A second reading is for the purpose of assimilating specific details. You should pay particular attention to see that you understand and really grasp any new ideas the book presents.

Step C. *Read for the future.* This third reading is more of a memory feat than it is a reading task. Literally memorize passages that have particular meaning to you. Find ways they can relate to problems you are currently facing. Test new ideas; try them; discard the useless and imprint the useful indelibly on your habit patterns.

Step D. *Read—later—to refresh your memory, and to rekindle your inspiration.* There is a famous story about the salesman who is standing up in front of a sales manager saying: 'Gimme that old sales talk again, I'm getting kinda discouraged.' All of us may become discouraged. We should re-read the best of our books at such times to rekindle the fires that got us going in the first place.

We shall list some inspirational, self-help action books (a few are instructional) that can motivate you to desirable action. Each contains hidden treasures that you can discover for yourself.

But before you go over the list and thus complete your first reading of *Success Through a Positive Mental Attitude*, let us once more remind you: *Share with others a part of what you have that is good and desirable, and awaken the sleeping giant within you.* Then this book, *Success Through a Positive Mental Attitude*, will not be an ending. It will be the beginning of a new era in your life.

Make the ending what you choose.

The Bible

(a) Let us walk honestly, as in the day; not in rioting and drunkenness, not in chambering and wantonness, not in strife and envying. But put ye on the Lord Jesus Christ, and make not provision for the flesh, to fulfill the lusts thereof (Romans 13:13-14)

(b) As a man thinketh in his heart, so is he. (Proverbs 23.7)

(c) If thou canst believe, all things are possible to him that believeth. (Mark 9:23)

(d) Lord, I believe; help Thou mine unbelief. (Mark 9:24)

(e) According to your faith be it unto you. (Matthew 9:29)

(f) Faith without works is dead. (James 9:20)

(g) What things so ever ye desire, when ye pray, believe that ye receive them, and ye shall have them. (Mark 11:24)

(h) If God be for us, who can be against us? (Romans 8:31)

(i) Ask and it shall be given you; seek and ye shall find; knock and it shall be opened unto you. (Matthew 7:7)

(j) Naked, and ye clothed me; I was sick and ye visited me; I was in prison, and ye came unto me. (Matthew 25:31-35)

(k) Go ye into all the world. (Mark 16:15)

(l) For the good that I would I do not: but the evil which I would not, that I do. (Romans 7:19)

(m) For what I would, that I do not; but what I hate that I do. (Romans 7:15)

(n) Silver and gold have I none; but such as I have I give thee. (Acts 3:6)

(o) The love of money is the root of all evil. (I Timothy 6:10)

(p) Thou shalt not steal. (Exodus 20:15)

Books for Further Reading

1.	Adler, Mortimer J.	*How to Read a Book* published by Simon & Schuster
2.	Alger, Horatio	*Robert Coverdale's Struggle* published by Hurst & Company
3.	Baudoin, Charles	*Suggestion and Autosuggestion* published by The Macmillan Company
4.	Beaty, John Y.	*Luther Burbank, Plant Magician,* published by Julian Messner, Inc.
5.	Bettger, Frank	*How I Raised Myself from Failure to Success in Selling* published by Prentice-Hall, Inc.
6.	Bienstock, Louis	*The Power of Faith* published by Prentice-Hall, Inc.
7.	Brande, Dorothea	*Wake Up and Live* published by Simon & Schuster
8.	Brazier, Mary A.B.	*The Electrical Activity of the Nervous System*—A textbook for students, published by Macmillan Company
9.	Bristol, Claude M.	*The Magic of Believing* published by Prentice-Hall
10.	Bristol, Claude M. & Sherman, Harold	*TNT, Power within You* published by Prentice-Hall
11.	Burbank & Hall	*Training of the Human Plant* published by The Century Company
12.	Campbell, Walter S.	*Writing: Advice and Devices* published by Doubleday
13.	Carnegie, Andrew	*Autobiography of Andrew Carnegie,* published by Houghton Mifflin Company
14.	Carnegie, Dale	*How to Win Friends and Influence People,* published by Simon & Schuster

15.	Clarke, Edwin Leavitt	*The Art of Straight Thinking* published by Appleton-Century- Crofts, Inc.
16.	Clason, George S.	*The Richest Man in Babylon* published by Hawthorn Books, Inc.
17.	Collier, Robert	*Secret of the Ages* published by Robert Collier
18.	Colson, Charles	*Born Again* published by Chosen Books
19.	Copi, Irving	*Introduction to Logic* published by The Macmillan Company
20.	Coue, Emile	*Self-Mastery Through Conscious Autosuggestion* published by American Library Service
21.	Dakin & Dewey	*Cycles* published by Henry Holt & Company
22.	Danforth, William H.	*I Dare You* published by the 'I Dare You' Committee, Checkerboard Square, St. Louis, Missouri
23.	Dewey, Edward R. & Mandino, Og	*Cycles: The Mysterious Forces That Trigger Events* published by Hawthorn Books, Inc
24.	Dey, Frederic Van Rensselaer	*The Magic Story* published by DeVorss & Company
25.	Douglas, Lloyd C.	*Magnificent Obsession* published by Houghton Mifflin Company
26.	Dumas, Alexander	*The Question of Money*
27.	Durant, Will	*The Story of Philosophy* published by Simon & Schuster
28.	Eddy, Mary Baker	*Science and Health, With Key to the Scriptures*, published by Charles H. Gabriel
29.	Einstein, Albert	*Essays in Science* published by Philosophical Library

30.	Elliot, Paul L. & Wilcox, William S.	*Physics, A Modern Approach* published by The Macmillan Company
31.	Franklin, Benjamin	*Autobiography of Benjamin Franklin*
32.	Freud, Sigmund	*An Outline of Psychoanalysis* published by W. W. Norton & Company
33.	Gordon, Arthur	*Norman Vincent Peale: Minister to Millions*, published by Prentice-Hall, Inc.
34.	Hayakawa, S. I.	*Language in Thought & Action,* published by Harcourt, Brace & Company
35	Hill, Napoleon	*The Law of Success* published by Hawthorn Books, Inc. *Think and Grow Rich* published by Hawthorn Books, Inc. *How to Raise Your Own Salary* published by Combined Registry Company *Science of Success Course* published by Combined Registry Company
36	Hudson, Thomas Jay	*The Divine Pedigree of Man* published by Hudson-Cohan Publishing Company, Inc. *The Law of Psychic Phenomena*, published by A.C. McClurg & Company
37	Hunter, Edward	*Brainwashing* published by Farrar, Straus & Cudhay
38	James, Williams	*Principles of Psychology* published by Henry Holt & Company
39	Jones, Francis A	*The Life Story of Thomas A. Edison* published by Grosset and Dunlap
40	Jones, Jim	*If You Can Count to Four* published by Whitehorn Publishing Company Inc
41	Kobe, Martin J	*Your Greatest Power* published by Combined Registry Company

42	Maltz, Maxwell	*Psycho-Cybernetics* published by Prentice-Hall, Inc
43	Mandino, Og	*The Greatest Salesman in the World* published by Fredrick Fell Publishers, Inc. *The Greatest Secret in the World* published by Fredrick Fell Publishers, Inc.
44	Marden, Orison Swett	*Pushing to the Front* published by the Success Company
45	Mills, Clarence, M.D.	*Climate Makes the Man* published by Harper & Brothers
46	Moutmasson, Joseph-Marie	*Invention and the Unconscious* published by Harcourt, Brace & Company
47	Moor, Robert E. and Schultz, Maxwell I.	*Turn on the Green Lights in Your Life* published by Hawthorn Books, Inc.
48	Newman, Ralph	*Abraham Lincoln: His Story in His Own Words*, published by Doubleday & Company
49	Osborn, Alex F.	*Applied Imagination* published by Charles Scribner's Sons *Your Creative Power* published by Charles Scribner's Sons
50	Overstreet, Harry and Bonaro	*What We Must Know About Communism* published by W. W. Norton & Company
51	Packard, Vance	*The Hidden Persuaders* published by David McKay Company, Inc.
52	Peal, Norman Vincent	*The Power of Positive Thinking* published by Prentice-Hall, Inc.
53	Rhine, Joseph B.	*New World of The Mind* published by William Sloan & Associates *The Reach of The Mind* published by William Sloan & Associates
54	Rhine, Joseph B. and J.C. Pratt	*Parapsychology* published by C.C. Thomas

55	Rickover, Rear Admiral H.G.	*Education and Freedom* published by E.P. Dutton & Company
56	Scheinfeld, Arnam	*The New You and Heredity* published by J.P. Lippincott
57	Sheen, Msgr. Fulton J.	*Life Is Worth Living* published by McGraw-Hill Co.
58	Smiles, Samuel	*Self-Help* published by Belford, Clarke & Company
59	Stone, W. Clement	*The Success System that Never Fails* published by Prentice-Hall, Inc.
60	Sweetland, Ben	*I Can* published by Cadillac Publishing *I Will* published by Prentice-Hall Inc.
61	Walker, Harold Blake	*Power to Manage Yourself* published by Harper & Brothers
62	Walker, Mary Alice and Walker, Harold Blake	*Venture of Faith* published by Harper & Brothers
63	Winkler, John K.	*John D. A portrait in Oils* published by Vanguard Press
64	Witty, Dr. Paul Andrew	*The Gifted Child* published by D.G. Heath & Company

PILOT NO. 22
Thoughts to Steer By

1. Like Brownie Wise, Mytinger and Casselberry, W. Clement Stone and many other managers of successful sales organizations, you can motivate yourself and others to desirable action with inspirational self-help books—books that can be evaluated by actual results achieved by the reader.
2. Brownie Wise found it necessary to read *Think and Grow Rich* six times before she recognized the principles that she could apply. Then something happened. She made it happen. Develop your mind power by studying *Success Through a Positive Mental Attitude* as often as is necessary to understand how to achieve any desirable goal that doesn't violate the laws of God or the rights of your fellow men.
3. When you read an inspirational, self-help action book:
    a. Concentrate.
    b. Read as if the author were a close personal friend and were writing to you —and you alone.
    c. Know what you are looking for.
    d. Get into action—try the principles that are recommended.
4. Evaluate the book *Success Through a Positive Mental Attitude* by what you actually think and do to make yourself a better person, and to make your world a better world for you and others to live in.
5. You are a better person and your world will be a better world in which to live because you have read *Success Through a Positive Mental Attitude*. Isn't that true?

SUCCEED THOUGH PMA—
YOU CAN IF YOU REALLY
WANT TO! DO YOU?